Lecture Notes in Computer Science 3956

Commenced Publication in 1973
Founding and Former Series Editors:
Gerhard Goos, Juris Hartmanis, and Jan van Leeuwen

Editorial Board

Gilles Barthe   Benjamin Grégoire
Marieke Huisman   Jean-Louis Lanet (Eds.)

Construction and Analysis of Safe, Secure, and Interoperable Smart Devices

Second International Workshop, CASSIS 2005
Nice, France, March 8-11, 2005
Revised Selected Papers

 Springer

Volume Editors

Gilles Barthe
Benjamin Grégoire
Marieke Huisman
INRIA Sophia Antipolis
Projet EVEREST
2004 route des Lucioles, B.P. 93, 06902 Sophia Antipolis Cedex, France
E-mail: {Gilles.Barthe,Benjamin.Gregoire,Marieke.Huisman}@sophia.inria.fr

Jean-Louis Lanet
Gemplus La Vigie
Avenue du Jujubier, Z.I. Athelia IV, 13705 La Ciotat Cedex, France
E-mail: jean-louis.lanet@gemplus.com

Library of Congress Control Number: 2006924174

CR Subject Classification (1998): D.2, C.3, D.1, D.3, D.4, F.3, E.3

LNCS Sublibrary: SL 4 – Security and Cryptology

ISSN   0302-9743
ISBN-10   3-540-33689-3 Springer Berlin Heidelberg New York
ISBN-13   978-3-540-33689-1 Springer Berlin Heidelberg New York

Springer is a part of Springer Science+Business Media

springer.com

© Springer-Verlag Berlin Heidelberg 2006
Printed in Germany

Typesetting: Camera-ready by author, data conversion by Scientific Publishing Services, Chennai, India
Printed on acid-free paper   SPIN: 11741060   06/3142   5 4 3 2 1 0

Preface

This volume contains a selection of refereed papers from participants of the second "Construction and Analysis of Safe, Secure and Interoperable Smart Devices" (Cassis) workshop, held March 8-11, 2005 in Nice, France:

http://www-sop.inria.fr/everest/events/cassis05

The workshop was organized by INRIA (Institut National de Recherche en Informatique et en Automatique), France. It was attended by over 70 participants, who were invited for their contributions to relevant areas of computer science.

The aim of the CASSIS workshop is to bring together experts from the smart devices industry and academic researchers, in order to stimulate research on formal methods and security, and to encourage the smart device industry to adopt innovative solutions drawn from academic research. In order to address the different issues raised by the evolution of smart devices, the workshop consisted of seven thematic sessions:

Session 1: Research trends in smart devices
The session was organized by Jean-Jacques Vandewalle from Gemplus. It provided perspectives on possible evolutions of smart devices. The keynote speaker was Gilles Privat from France Telecom R&D.

Session 2: Web services
The session was organized by Cédric Fournet and Andy Gordon from Microsoft Research Cambridge. It focused on security issues for web services, including trust and identity management, and formal and automatic verification of web services deployments. The session was followed by a panel discussion on security of web services, chaired by Andy Gordon. The keynote speaker was Cédric Fournet.

Session 3: Virtual machine technology
This session was organized by Benjamin Grégoire. It covered new developments in Java technology for developing generic, adaptable and maintainable platforms for smart devices. The keynote speaker was Sophia Drossopoulou from Imperial College London.

Session 4: Security
This session was organized by Gilles Barthe and Marieke Huisman. It studied security issues from a wider perspective and addressed issues such as electronic voting, Internet threat analysis, privacy and language-based security. The keynote speaker was Dan Wallach from Rice University, Texas.

Session 5: Validation and formal methods
This session was organized by Thomas Jensen from IRISA Rennes. It focused on verification techniques for Java-like applications, including run-time verification, program analyses, and interactive verification. The keynote speaker

was Klaus Havelund from Kestrel Technology at NASA Ames Research Center.

Session 6: Proof-Carrying Code

The session was organized by Adriana Compagnoni. It presented Proof-Carrying Code architectures and their application to advanced security policies concerning resource control and information flow. The keynote speaker was George Necula from the University of California at Berkeley.

Session 7: Embedded devices

The final session was organized by Traian Muntean, from Marseilles University, and Jean-Louis Lanet, now at Gemplus. The session focused on technology issues that arise from the evolution of embedded devices into networked mobile devices. The keynote speaker was Rajesh Gupta from the University of California at Irvine.

The organizers would like to thank the session organizers, speakers and participants for helping to make CASSIS 2005 a stimulating and enjoyable event. The organizers would also like to acknowledge financial support from ERCIM, Gemplus International S.A, and Oberthur Card Systems. A special thanks goes to the support teams at INRIA Sophia Antipolis, and in particular to Nathalie Bellesso and Monique Simonetti for their help in organizational matters.

December 2005

Gilles Barthe
Benjamin Grégoire
Marieke Huisman
Jean-Louis Lanet

Organization

Organizing Committee

Gilles Barthe   INRIA Sophia-Antipolis, France
Benjamin Grégoire   INRIA Sophia-Antipolis, France
Marieke Huisman   INRIA Sophia-Antipolis, France
Jean-Louis Lanet   INRIA DirDRI Sophia-Antipolis, France

Referees

Frederic Besson   Thomas Jensen   German Puebla
Christophe Bidan   Florian Kammueller   Tamara Rezk
Lilian Burdy   Gerwin Klein   Bernard Serpette
Pierre Cregut   Peter Gorm Larsen   Robert De Simone
Guillaume Dufay   Bruno Legeard   Mario Sudholt
Sandro Etalle   Francesco Logozzo   Pierre Vanel
Andy Gordon   Fabio Martinelli   Jerome Vouillon
Valerie Issarny   Mariela Pavlova
Romain Janvier   Olivier Potoniee

Table of Contents

The Architecture of a Privacy-Aware Access Control Decision Component

Claudio A. Ardagna, Marco Cremonini, Ernesto Damiani,
Sabrina De Capitani di Vimercati, and Pierangela Samarati

Dipartimento di Tecnologie dell'Informazione,
Università degli Studi di Milano,
Crema 26013, Italy
{ardagna, cremonini, damiani, decapita, samarati}@dti.unimi.it

Abstract. Today many interactions are carried out online through Web sites and e-services and often private and/or sensitive information is required by service providers. A growing concern related to this widespread diffusion of on-line applications that collect personal information is that users' privacy is often poorly managed and sometimes abused. For instance, it is well known how personal information is often disclosed to third parties without the consent of legitimate data owners or that there are professional services specialized on gathering and correlating data from heterogeneous repositories, which permit to build user profiles and possibly to disclose sensitive information not voluntarily released by their owners. For these reasons, it has gained great importance to design systems able to fully preserve information privacy by managing in a trustworthy and responsible way all *identity and profile information.*

In this paper, we investigate some problems concerning identity management for e-services and present the architecture of the Access Control Decision Function, a software component in charge of managing access request in a privacy-aware fashion. The content of this paper is a result of our ongoing activity in the framework of the PRIME project (*Privacy and Identity Management for Europe*) [18], funded by the European Commission, whose objective is the development of privacy-aware solutions for enforcing security.

1 Introduction

From the growing offering of e-services provided by a number of organizations, users have not only gained benefits in terms of variety and richness of accessible services. The drawback of such an increase in service provision is that a corresponding growing amount of personal information is communicated by users of e-services to the corresponding providers. Personal identifiable information (PII) are required by e-service providers for many legitimate reasons (e.g., to offer personalized services). Also, requiring personal information permits to mitigate abuses of e-services and to avoid, for example, the access by means of automatic software instead of physical users. Finally, personal information of

G. Barthe et al. (Eds.): CASSIS 2005, LNCS 3956, pp. 1–15, 2006.

e-service users is needed for marketing purposes, such as promoting new services or producing access statistics for advertisers.

However, despite all these reasons for collecting personal information are certainly legitimate, many concerns exist about the privacy of e-service users. Such concerns are motivated by observing that the number and type of personal information collected by service providers permit to easily profile user's habits and preferences in a very detailed and precise way. In addition, it is well known how personal information is often disclosed to third parties without the consent of legitimate data owners or that there are professional services specialized on gathering and correlating data from heterogeneous repositories, which permit to build user profiles and possibly to disclose sensitive information not voluntarily released by their owners.

As a consequence, users concerned about their private information are increasingly refusing to benefit from such a widespread offering of e-services because they prefer not to have their personal data under the control of anyone at anytime.

A key aspect to address these concerns is the notion of *privacy-aware access control*, which encompasses and combine the notions of *privacy* and of *access control* in an homogeneous framework. Traditional access control systems are based on regulations (policies) that establish who can, or cannot, execute certain actions on some resources and the way they compute access decisions is based on the requester's credentials carrying her identity and other personal information (e.g., affiliation, membership, and so on) [10].

Other requirements that traditional access control systems usually do not take into account are related to *data usage*, which is the possibility to specify how data accessed by an authorized party must be handled. This represents a novel feature for access control that is no simply concerned with authorizing the access to data and resources but also with defining and enforcing the way data and resources are subsequently managed. Also, in modern systems, the definition of an access control model is complicated by the need to formally represent complex policies, where access decisions depend on the application of different rules coming from laws practices, organizational regulations, and so on.

Privacy awareness and features to manage requesters credentials accordingly are not taken into account by access control systems in use today. Requiring privacy awareness means that credentials and personal information of users that request e-services cannot be freely available and manageable by service providers. Privacy poses constraints on which data can be required for a certain service and on the way personal information once collected by a service provider can be handled, released to third parties, or recorded.

Despite recent advancements in access control models have permitted to use generic attributes/properties of both requesters and resources, access control systems are not yet designed for enforcing privacy policies.

Therefore, by considering privacy issues, there is the need to improve authorization policies and models and to develop new solutions for access control, authorization specification, and enforcement. The development of such solutions will require to investigate open research problems as well as to implement an access control architecture addressing privacy concerns from its foundations.

In this paper, we describe an approach aimed at providing users with a privacy-aware access control system that enforces privacy requirements. In particular, we present the architecture of the *Access Control Decision Function* (ACDF), an autonomous software component for controlling access to data in the framework of e-services. The ACDF component is based on a flexible model and XML-based language [2]. Our work has been carried out in the context of the Privacy and Identity Management for Europe (PRIME) project, an European project whose goal is the development of privacy-aware solutions for enforcing security.

The remainder of this paper is organized as follows. Section 2 summarizes the main contributions in the field of privacy-aware access control and describes the way our approach differs from the previous ones. Section 3 describes the new requirements for a privacy-aware access control and gives an overview of the PRIME project. Section 4 summarizes our proposal for a privacy-aware access control policy. Section 5 presents the architecture of the Access Control Decision Function, explaining its interactions with external components and the overall work flow. Finally, Section 6 draws our conclusions and sketches future work.

2   Related Work

A number of projects and research papers about privacy have been presented in the last few years, although not many of them have addressed the issue of privacy-aware access control. More in detail, two lines of research are closely related to the topic of this paper: *i)* the definition and development of access control and privacy languages, and *ii)* the definition of infrastructures to protect and preserve privacy of either services or clients.

For what concerns the first research topic, some languages have been defined starting from languages for access control as *XACML* (eXtensible Access Control Markup Language) [22] to data handling languages (i.e., languages regulating how personal information could be managed once collected) as for instance *P3P* (Platform for Privacy Preferences Project) [5, 8] and *EPAL* (Enterprise Privacy Authorization Language) [4, 5].

XACML [22] is an XML-based language used to define access control policies. The main differences between XACML and the language developed for our ACDF component are that XACML does not consider data handling constraints, it does not explicitly support neither privacy features nor variables in the definition of policies (a feature that permits to greatly enhance policy expressiveness), and it is not integrated with the ontological approach that our ACDF solution exploits in the more general context of the PRIME Project. In addition to the language, XACML defines both an architecture for the evaluation of policies and a communication protocol for messages interchange. The most important difference between the XACML's system design and architecture and our proposal is that XACML assumes to have all the information about a requester available at the time of policy evaluation and access control decision. In our ACDF component, instead, a negotiation phase between a requester and a provider is carried out in order to establish the number and type of credentials that, on the one hand, are sufficient for the service provision and, on the other hand, minimize the disclosure of personal information.

P3P [5, 8] is a project widely acknowledged that addresses the need of a user to assess that the privacy practices adopted by a server provider comply with her privacy requirements. Supporting data handling policies in Web-based transactions is the goal of P3P, which permits the definition of server privacy practices in a standard format, allowing users to automatically understand and match these practices against their privacy preferences. Thus, users need not read the privacy policies at every site they interact with but they are always aware of the server practices in data handling. Some drawbacks of P3P are the lacking of a formal and unambiguous language to define user privacy preferences, of a technical mechanism to verify that Web sites respect users policies and of a process to negotiate the privacy practices between the interacting parties. In addition, P3P scope is restricted to Web sites only.

EPAL [4, 5] is an XML-based markup language that formalizes enterprise-internal privacy policies. It approaches the problem on the server side and addresses the need of a company to specify access control policies, with reference to attributes/properties of the requestor, to protect private information of its users. EPAL is designed to enable organizations to translate their privacy policies into IT control statements and to enforce policies that may be declared and communicated in P3P. XACML, however, includes most (if not all) of the expressive power of EPAL.

Considering projects that aim at developing an architecture to preserve security and privacy, several have been proposed. International Security, Trust, and Privacy Alliance (ISTPA) [13] is an open, policy-configurable model consisting of several privacy services and capabilities, intended to be used as a template for designing solutions and covering security, trust, and privacy requirements. The goal of the framework is to set the basis for developing products and services that support current and evolving privacy regulations and business policies.

Reasoning on the Web with Rules and Semantics (REWERSE) [6, 19] is an european network of excellence on the semantic web whose objective is to enrich the Web with so-called intelligent capabilities for data and service retrieval, composition, and processing. REWERSE's research activities will be devoted to several objectives such as *policy specification, composition, and conformance* aiming at user-friendly high-level specifications for complex Web systems.

Enterprise Privacy Architecture (EPA) [17] is an IBM project that wants to improve enterprises e-business trust. EPA represents a new approach to privacy that tries to help organizations to understand how privacy impacts business processes. EPA defines privacy parties, rules, and data for new and existing business processes and provides privacy management controls based on consumer preferences, privacy best practices, and business requirements.

Finally, TRUSTe [21] is an organization dedicated to preserving customer privacy and assisting e-commerce with customer privacy concerns. It certifies and monitors Web site privacy practices.

3   Requirements for a Privacy-Aware Access Control

In general, an environment well-suited for users needing a private and secure way for using e-services should support at least the following basic requirements.

- *Privacy.* A digital identity solution should be respectful of the users rights to privacy and should not disclose personal information without explicit consent.
- *Minimal disclosure.* Service providers must require the least set of credentials needed for service provision, and users should be able to provide credentials selectively, according to the type of on-line services they wish to access.
- *Anonymity support.* As a special but notable case of minimal disclosure, many services do not need to know the real identity of a user. Pseudonyms, multiple digital identities, and even anonymous accesses must be adopted when possible.
- *Legislation support.* Privacy-related legislation is becoming a powerful driver toward the adoption of digital identities. The exchange of identity data should not then violate government legislation such as the Health Insurance Portability and Accountability Act (HIPPA) or Gramm-Leach-Bliley Act (GLB).

With respect to these privacy-based requirements, the usual way of designing access control systems is not satisfactory. In particular, selective disclosure of credentials is normally not implemented, because users' attributes, for example inserted into X.509 identity certificates [14] or collected as attribute certificates [11], are defined according to functional needs, making it easier to collect all credentials in a row instead of iteratively asking for the ones strictly necessary for a given service only. With XACML the same requirement holds and credentials are collected entirely before policy evaluation. Pseudonymity, multiple identities, and anonymity are also usually not supported.

These new requirements regarding an improved management of digital identities are among the motivations of the PRIME project [18], a large-scale research effort aimed at developing an identity management system able to protect users personal information and to provide a framework that can be smoothly integrated with current architectures and on-line services.

More specifically, providing the users with the control of their personal data and permitting anonymous interactions are some of the main goals of the PRIME project. Next, users should also be able to use different pseudonyms during interactions with other parties, a feature that reduces the risk of profiling by making different transactions performed by the same user unlinkable one with the others. Another goal of the PRIME project is to define privacy rules governing the system usage. The rules should establish how to use the system and, in particular, allow the definition of policies to define trust relationships, privacy preferences, and authorization rules.

Following the definition of an enhanced authorization model based on privacy awareness, policies must be effectively enforced at the receiving end. The enforcement of privacy policies is a more complicate task than the enforcing of traditional access control policies because they have several additional features such as obligations, policy composition and negotiation. The privacy-enhancing technical components developed within the PRIME project will be integrated to produce a privacy-enhancing digital identity management system [1, 3, 15].

4   A Privacy-Aware Access Control Model and Language

To define a privacy-enhanced access control system based on the concept of digital identity, we first need to identify the main characteristics that the corresponding access control model should possess.

- *Policy formats.* Parties need to specify protection requirements on the data they make available using a format both human and machine readable, easy to inspect and interchange.
- *Access control rules.* Access control rules should be able to make use of partial identities associated with users. Also, it is important to be able to specify access control rules about subjects accessing the information and about resources to be accessed in terms of rich ontology-based metadata (e.g., Semantic Web-style ones) increasingly available in advanced e-service applications [9].
- *User-driven constraints.* In addition to traditional server-side access control rules, users should be able to specify constraints and restrictions about the usage that will be done of their information once released to a third party.
- *Interactive enforcement.* A novelty of our framework is that we do not assume anymore that all credentials are collected before an access request is evaluated. Instead, the access control component may not have all the information it needs to decide whether or not an access should be granted. On the other side, the requester may not know in advance which information will be asked to get the access to the service. As a consequence, a new way of enforcing the access control process has been defined based on a negotiation protocol aimed at establishing the least set of information that the requester has to disclose in order to access the desired service.

To take all these issues into account, a new privacy-aware access control model together with an access control protocol for the communication of policies and of identity information among parties have been defined and the following different types of privacy policies have been introduced:

- traditional *access control policies* governing access/release of data/services managed by the party [20];
- *release policies* governing the release of properties, credentials, and personal identifiable information of the party [7];
- *data handling policies* defining how personal information released by a third party have to be managed [8];

– *sanitized policies* filtering the response to be returned to the counterpart to avoid release of sensitive information related to the policy itself.

In the following, we focus on access control and release policies.

4.1 Privacy-Aware Access Control Rules

Although it is not in the scope of this paper to discuss the details of the access control language, a brief introduction of its basic elements is necessary to describe the different sub-systems that must be coordinated together with the ACDF. In short, the main elements of PRIME's authorization rules are as follows.

– *Subject expression*: a boolean formula of terms that allows the reference to a set of subjects depending on whether they satisfy or not certain conditions, where conditions can evaluate the user's profile, location predicates, or the user's membership in groups, roles, and so on.
– *Object expression*: a boolean formula of terms that allows the reference to a set of objects depending on whether they satisfy or not certain conditions, where conditions evaluate membership of the object in categories, values of properties on metadata, and so on.
– *Actions*: the action (or class of actions) to which the rule refers.
– *Purposes*: a statement, certified or not, representing how the data is going to be used by the recipient.
– *Conditions*: a boolean formula of terms that express additional conditions, for example, dictated by legislation, location-based conditions, and trust conditions.
– *Obligations*: conditions defined by the users and attached to corresponding data when they are disclosed to third parties. Receiving parties must comply with obligations coming along with data and the framework is able to enforce it.

Each access request results in an *access decision* that can take three different forms:

– *Yes*: the access request is granted;
– *No*: the access request is denied;
– *Undefined*: the access request provides insufficient information to determine whether the request can be granted or denied. The negotiation phase between the requester and the service provider is entered.

5   ACDF Architecture

The PRIME's Access Control component is composed by two parts: the Access Control Decision Function (ACDF) responsible for taking an access decision for all access requests directed to PRIME resources, like data and services, and the Access Control Enforcement Function (ACEF) responsible for the enforcing of access control decisions by intercepting accesses to resources and granting them only if they are part of an operation for which a positive decision has been taken. From an architectural point of view, the ACDF is a unique module composed by different sub-modules associated with specific tasks of the decisional process or in charge of interacting with external components. More precisely, the submodules are the following.

- *Decision Maker*: produces the final response possibly combining different access decisions coming from different sub-components;
- *Policy Evaluator*: manages the evaluation of the applicable policies against an access request;
- *Policy Handler*: is in charge of managing all communications with the Policy Manager (an external component) to retrieve all policies applicable to an access request;
- *Reasoner Administrator*: manages communication with the Reasoner component to require reasoning operations about policies to calculate extended policies;
- *Context Administrator*: manages the access and the communication with the Context Manager component, which is the requestors information repository during a transaction;
- *PII Database Mediator*: manages the communication with the information (PII) repository that represents the storage system for personal information;

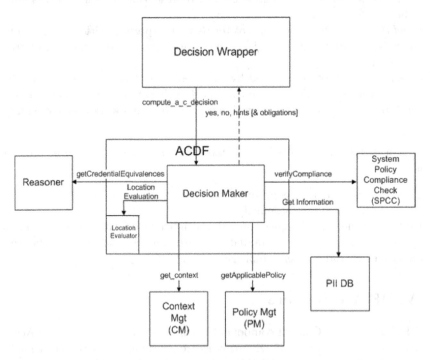

Fig. 1. The Access Control Decision Function and its interactions with other components

- *SPCC Handler*: manages all interactions with the System Policy Compliance Check (SPCC) component, the one in charge of evaluating special conditions based on assurance and trust predicates;
- *LBS Evaluator*: is the sub-module that evaluates special conditions based on location-based predicates;
- *Obligation Handler*: selects and attaches to the access decision all corresponding obligations.

5.1   ACDF Interactions

As illustrated in Figure 1, the ACDF component interacts with many other components of PRIME's Identity Management System (IDMS). Below we present a brief description of these components.

Context Manager (CM). The Context Manager component manages user's *session data* (see Figure 2). Session thereby denotes a single communication action, usually one connection established by an access requester. The context management acts as a database for the ACDF that can query it for retrieving credentials (*User PII*).

The data structure of a single context contains information on the following two aspects:

- data disclosed to and by the communication party such as pseudonym and personal information, either certified or not;
- certified proofs about negotiation, disclosure, and exchange of personal information.

Policy Manager (PM). The Policy Manager component handles the life cycle management of policies by providing functionalities for policy administration (see Figure 3). Related to the access decision, the ACDF interacts with the

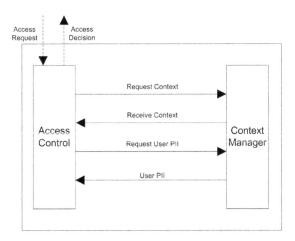

Fig. 2. Interactions with the Context Manager

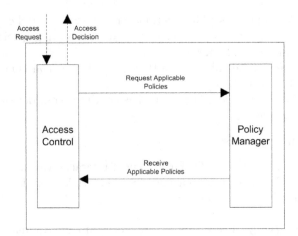

Fig. 3. Interactions with the Policy Manager

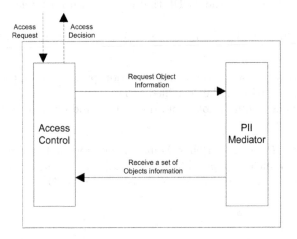

Fig. 4. Interactions with the PII Database Mediator

Policy Manager to collect all policies that can be applied to the access request being evaluated. The Policy Manager has a searching functionality that filters out policies based on access request attributes.

PII Database Mediator (PII DB). The PII Database Mediator component manages all accesses to the database containing personal information (*PII*) (see Figure 4). The access to PII information stored into the PII Database is handled by the Mediator component so that no special privilege is granted to internal modules of PRIME. The ACDF interacts with the PII Database Mediator by invoking a specific method and passing all parameters needed for querying PII data.

Reasoner. The Reasoner is the component that maintains and makes use of the ontologies defined in the project (see Figure 5). It provides deductions based

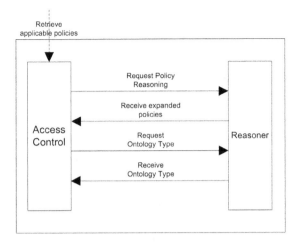

Fig. 5. Interactions with the Reasoner

on machine readable data and rules. In addition to data and prolog style rules and generic methods for producing all inferences from an ontology, the module also provides methods specific to some PRIME components. For the ACDF component, in particular, this includes *credentials equivalences*, which is a feature to verify equivalences between credential expressed according to different ontologies. The reasoner is based on the Jena API and as such requires data and ontologies to be expressed using Jena RDF models [16].

System Policy Compliance Check (SPCC). The SPCC module handles trust, assurance and accountability compliance conditions which requires the analy-

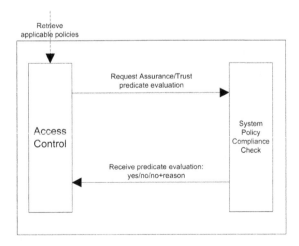

Fig. 6. Interactions with the SPCC

sis of the assurance information (see Figure 6). Although in certain cases trust and assurance constraints, specified by some policies, can be computed statically and independently of access control, in other cases (notably when dynamic constraints are involved) trust conditions need to be evaluated together with other conditions by the ACDF. In these cases, the ACDF recognizes the assurance constraint during the evaluation process and invokes the SPCC component to evaluate it.

5.2   Decision Maker

Having introduced all the components involved in the access control process, the core module of ACDF, the *Decision Maker*, can be fully described. The Decision Maker is the module responsible for all access control decisions and returns a *Yes, No,* or *Undefined* response. It handles applicable access control policies and proceeds evaluating all different components of the rules, like subject expressions, object expressions, and so on. Such an evaluation requires the Decision Maker to interact and coordinate with both sub-modules internal to the ACDF and external components. The ACDF execution flow prescribes that, first, the ACDF receives an access request and selects the context associated with the current session through a *Context Manager* API. After that, information related to the requested object is collected from the *PII Database Mediator* and all the applicable policies are retrieved from the *Policy Management* module by means of access request attributes. When applicable policies are acquired, the evaluation process can start and proceeds as follows:

1. predicates based on trust/assurance properties are communicated to the *System Policy Compliance Check (SPCC)* that is in charge of evaluating them;
2. predicates about the subject are evaluated based on context information;
3. similarly, predicates about the object of the request are evaluated by interacting with the PII Database Mediator;
4. location-based predicates represent a special case and their evaluation is delegated to a specialized sub-module of ACDF, called *Location Evaluator*;
5. with all partial evaluations generated by sub-modules and external systems, the Decision Manager produces a final access control decision by composing all partial decisions:
    (a) if the decision is *positive* (response *Yes*) obligations and constraints need to be returned. Obligation defines how released data must be handled after disclosure, constraints provide directives to the PII Database Mediator when the access is enforced;
    (b) if the decision is *negative* (response *No*) a reason for that can be returned attached to the answer;
    (c) if a decision cannot be reached (response *Undefined*) obligations and additional requests are returned to the subject, possibly sanitized for preventing disclosure of access control policies details.

Finally, the ACDF produces a message for the *Decision Wrapper*, which acts as a mediator between the ACDF and the ACEF module, to communicate to the ACEF component how to handle the corresponding access request.

```
<policy>
 <subject>any</subject>
 <action>http://.../action#rent_a_car</action>
 <object>http://.../object#sport_car</object>
 <purpose>http://.../purpose#any_purpose</purpose>
 <subjectExpr>
  <condition>
   <Lval>Idemix-EU-DriversLicence.Issuer.Country</Lval>
   <op>=</op>
   <rVal>IT</rVal>
  </condition>
  <condition>
   <Lval>
    Idemix-EU-DriversLicence.Permit.CarPermit.Allowed
   </Lval>
   <op>=</op>
   <rVal>true</rVal>
  </condition>
  <condition>
   <Lval>User.Age</Lval>
   <op>></op>
   <rVal>21</rVal>
  </condition>
 </subjectExpr>
 <objectExpr/>
 <trust>http://.../assurance#HasWorkingTMP</trust>
 <lbs>in_area("Italy")</lbs>
 <genCond>
  <condition>
   <Lval>Idemix-Ecoin.Value</Lval>
   <op>=</op>
   <rVal>80</rVal>
  </condition>
 </genCond>
 <ns>http://.../prime-PII-lite</ns>
 <obligation ref="OBL1">
</policy>
```

Fig. 7. A simple example of policy

As an example, consider a rent-a-car scenario and suppose that a policy states that "an anonymous user with a valid Italian driver license can rent a sport car with a special price of 80 euro per day, if she is in Italy, she is more than 21 years old, and if the rent-a-car service provider has a working trusted platform management".

Figure 7 illustrates a representation of this policy using our privacy-aware access control language.

At server-side, suppose now that an access request stating that "Mary want to rent a sport car" arrives together with her credentials. The ACDF can query the context from the Context Manager to verify the age, the location, and the availability of an ecoin card of Mary. Assume that, among the required credentials, the driver license is missing.

The Decision Maker decomposes the policy and sends the location-based predicate (lbs element) to the LBS Evaluator, the assurance predicate (trust element) to the SPCC Handler, and evaluates the remaining conditions. After the evaluation, the LBS evaluator returns a positive response (Mary is in Italy), the SPCC handler returns a positive response (the server has a working TPM), and the Policy Evaluator calculates an undefined response due to the fact that Mary has not previously released her driver license. The Decision Maker collects all these responses and returns a final undefined decision together with a request for the driver license. At this point, Mary based on her privacy preferences can decide whether to disclose her driver license or to terminate the transaction.

6   Conclusions and Future Work

To protect the privacy of parties in today's global infrastructure we need to combine solutions from technology, legislation, and organizational practices. This paper showed a first proposal towards the solution of this problem developed in the context of our ongoing activity in the framework of the PRIME project. In particular, with respect to previous privacy-aware access control frameworks, this solution fully takes into account the possibility for the user to negotiate the credentials to be released and actually permits to enforce the principle of minimal disclosure. The solution, moreover, is not strictly targeted to Web-based transactions and to data handling policies, as for P3P. Future work include the development of negotiation policies to be applied to the parties; the extension of the notion of subject ontology to capture more complex assertions on subjects, as well as the notion of object and credential ontology; the support of variables into the language to achieve a higher degree of expressiveness.

Acknowledgments

This work was supported in part by the European Union within the PRIME Project in the FP6/IST Programme under contract IST-2002-507591 and by the Italian MIUR within the KIWI and MAPS projects.

References

1. C.A. Ardagna, E. Damiani, S. De Capitani di Vimercati, P. Samarati. A Web Service Architecture for Enforcing Access Control Policies. *In Proc. of the First International Workshop on Views On Designing Complex Architectures (VODCA 2004)*, Bertinoro, Italy, September 11-12, 2004.
2. C.A. Ardagna, E. Damiani, S. De Capitani di Vimercati and P. Samarati. Towards Privacy-Enhanced Authorization Policies and Languages. In *Proc. of the 19th Annual IFIP WG 11.3 Working Conference on Data and Applications Security (IFIP)*, Nathan Hale Inn, University of Connecticut, Storrs, USA, August 7-10, 2005.

3. C.A. Ardagna and S. De Capitani di Vimercati. A comparison of modeling strategies in defining XML-based access control languages. *Computer Systems Science & Engineering Journal*, 2004.
4. P. Ashley, S. Hada, C. Powers and M. Schunter. Enterprise Privacy Authorization Language(EPAL). *IBM Research*, 2003.
5. P. Ashley, S. Hada, G. Karjoth and M. Schunter. E-P3P privacy policies and privacy authorization. *In Proc. of the ACM workshop on Privacy in the Electronic Society (WPES 2002)*, Washington, DC, USA, November 21, 2002.
6. P. A. Bonatti and D. Olmedilla. Driving and monitoring provisional trust negotiation with metapolicies. *In Proc. of the IEEE 6th International Workshop on Policies for Distributed Systems and Networks (POLICY 2005)*, Stockholm, Sweden, 6-8 June 2005.
7. P. Bonatti and P. Samarati. A unified framework for regulating access and information release on the web. *Journal of Computer Security*, 10(3):241–272, 2002.
8. L. Cranor and M. Langheinrich and M. Marchiori and M. Presler-Marshall and J. Reagle. The Platform for Privacy Preferences 1.0 (P3P1.0) Specification. `http://www.w3.org/TR/P3P/`.
9. E. Damiani, A. Corallo, G. Elia. A Knowledge Management System Enabling Regional Innovation. *In Proc. of the VI international conference on Knowledge-Based Intelligent Information & Engineering Systems (KES 2002)*, Crema, Italy, September 16-18 2002.
10. S. De Capitani di Vimercati, S. Paraboschi, and P. Samarati. Access control: Principles and solutions. *Software – Practice and Experience*, 33(5):397–421, April 2003.
11. S. Farrell and R. Housley. An Internet Attribute Certificate for Authorization. Request For Comments 3281, *Internet Engineering Task Force*, 2002.
12. C. A. Gunter, M. J. May and S. G. Stubblebine. A Formal Privacy System and its Application to Location Based Services. *In Proc. of the 4th Workshop on Privacy Enhancing Technologies (PET 2004)*, Toronto, Canada, May 26-28, 2004.
13. International Security, Trust, and Privacy Alliance (ISTPA), `http://www.istpa.org/`
14. ITU Telecommunication Standardization Sector (ITU-T). Information Technology - Open Systems Interconnection - The Directory: Authentication Framework. Recommendation X.509 (03/00), *International Telecommunication Union*, 2000.
15. S. Jajodia, P. Samarati, M. Sapino, and V. Subrahmanian. Flexible support for multiple access control policies. *ACM Transactions on Database Systems*, 26(2):18–28, June 2001.
16. Jena. `http://jena.sourceforge.net`.
17. G. Karjoth, M. Schunter and M. Waidner. Privacy-enabled Services for Enterprises *In Proc. of the 13th International Conference on Database and Expert Systems Applications (DEXA'02)*, Aix-en-Provence, France, September 2-6, 2002.
18. PRIME (Privacy and Identity Management for Europe). `http://www.prime-project.eu.org`.
19. Reasoning on the Web (REWERSE), `http://www.pms.ifi.lmu.de/rewerse-wga1/index.html`
20. P. Samarati and S. De Capitani di Vimercati. Access control: Policies, models, and mechanisms. In R. Focardi and R. Gorrieri, editors, *Foundations of Security Analysis and Design*, LNCS 2171. Springer-Verlag, 2001.
21. Truste, `http://www.truste.org/about/index.php`
22. XACML - (eXtensible Access Control Markup Language), `http://www.oasis-open.org/committees/tc_home.php?wg_abbrev=xacml#XACML20`

Mobile Resource Guarantees and Policies

David Aspinall and Kenneth MacKenzie

LFCS, School of Informatics, The University of Edinburgh, UK

Abstract. This paper introduces notions of *resource policy* for mobile code to be run on smart devices, to integrate with the proof-carrying code architecture of the *Mobile Resource Guarantees* (MRG) project. Two forms of policy are used: *guaranteed* policies which come with proofs and *target* policies which describe limits of the device. A guaranteed policy is expressed as a function of a methods input sizes, which determines a bound on consumption of some resource. A target policy is defined by a constant bound and input constraints for a method. A recipient of mobile code chooses whether to run methods by comparing between a guaranteed policy and the target policy. Since delivered code may use methods implemented on the target machine, guaranteed policies may also be provided by the platform; they appear symbolically as assumptions in delivered proofs. Guaranteed policies entail proof obligations that must be established from the proof certificate. Before proof, a policy checker ensures that the guaranteed policy refines the target policy; our policy format ensures that this step is tractable and does not require proof. Delivering policies thus mediates between arbitrary target requirements and the desirability to package code and certificate only once.

1 Introduction

The *Mobile Resource Guarantees* project has built a proof-carrying code (PCC) infrastructure for ensuring resource bounds on mobile code (for an overview, see [AGH+05]). The infrastructure uses a certifying compiler from a high-level functional language called *Camelot* to a low-level language *Grail*, which is a functional presentation of a sub-language of the Java Virtual Machine Language (JVML). Thus, Grail programs are executed on a JVM but transmitted as standard class files, packaged together with PCC certificates. The architecture (with our extension) is shown below:

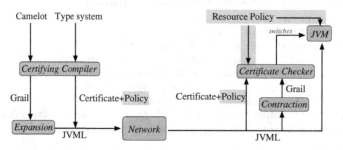

G. Barthe et al. (Eds.): CASSIS 2005, LNCS 3956, pp. 16–36, 2006.
© Springer-Verlag Berlin Heidelberg 2006

This is a fairly usual picture for proof-carrying code, except that we highlight the role of a *guaranteed resource policy* which is delivered as part of the certificate and a *target resource policy* which is the instance of the safety policy for code to meet resource usage restrictions imposed by the target machine.

The guaranteed resource policy is a specification, ultimately generated by the certifying compiler. It contains concrete bounds on the resource usage of the compiled Camelot program, in a standard format; it is guaranteed because it comes with a proof. The idea of the standard format is to allow mediation with an arbitrary target policy. In a general setting where the code delivery to a smart device takes place off-line (i.e. without communication back to the code producer), the recipient cannot communicate its target policy; it is therefore unrealistic to hope that the delivered code comes with a certificate stating exactly the required behaviour.

The certificate checker has responsibility (1) to check that the delivered policy would meet or exceed the target policy, and then (2) to check that the code indeed meets its guaranteed policy. Our design is to use the proof evidence in the certificate to establish (2), but allow the target certificate checker to use its own mechanism to establish (1), ideally as an efficient operation not involving proof checking or running a VCG. In more advanced scenarios, the certificate checker might use claimed policies to select between several possible implementations of a method supplied, for example, selecting the more favourable alternative in a time-space trade-off according to local conditions.

The target resource policy is an input both to the certificate checker and to the modified JVM. Usually in a PCC scenario, the safety check is entirely static. The certificate checker immediately denies execution to code which does not satisfy the target resource policy, switching off execution in the JVM. But the resource policy is also shown in the diagram as an input to the modified JVM: this is to allow, in principle, the possible *run-time monitoring* of resource usage to check conformance with the policy. A checker may decide to defer some resource bounds to dynamic checks if they cannot be ensured by the delivered policy, or, indeed, if the delivered proof certificate lacks static evidence that a particular claimed policy is met.

Contributions. Until now in our work on MRG and the closely related work, resource policies have not been considered explicitly. In MRG, we have used a fixed type system technology to express schematic constraints on Grail functions and methods which impose a single space bound on the overall program (linear on input size). This paper designs a significant extension, introducing:

- the extension of certificates with resource policies that can express complex bounds on several resources for individual methods;
- a language describing resource policies and its formal semantics;
- the specification of target resource policies on the target device;
- extended certificate checking to relate target resource policies to claimed guarantees, as well as the check that claimed guarantees are indeed satisfied.

As a simple example of a guaranteed policy, we are able to express statements such as:

"for positive integer inputs n and m, the method call `calc(int m,int n)` requires at most $16+42*m+9*m*n$ JVM instructions to be executed."

More complex concrete bounds statements constructed with polynomials, logarithms, and exponentials, are allowed, providing they satisfy some reasonable restrictions described later. As well as time costs, we consider heap space consumption, maximum stack depth, and costs related to specific method calls. The latter is useful, for example, to bound the number of calls to expensive or security critical library methods made by client code: e.g., a program to be run on a mobile phone may be allowed to send two text messages but no more. Formally, we consider cost metrics, such as heap space consumption, to be supplied with an ordering. This allows us to relate different policies in the checking process.

Guaranteed policies are checked against target policies which express limits of constrained devices. An example is:

"for all inputs n < 10 and m < 10, executing the `calc(int m,int n)` method must take no more than 2000 instructions."

Here the client of the delivered code provides a promise about the way the code will be invoked, and asks for a hard limit on resource consumption in turn. Fixing the format of both forms of policy allows us to use a simple checking process.

Code that is run on a target machine is often a combination of delivered methods and methods supplied by the platform. In this case, the resource consumption of the delivered methods may depend on the precise behaviour of the platform library functions, which is unknown at the time that the mobile code is certified. To deal with this scenario, we allow delivered policies to refer symbolically to *provided* functional bounds on platform functions whose implementation is unknown. We may express statements such as:

"for a positive integer input m, the method `throwdice(m)` takes at most $m * F(6)$ JVM instructions to execute, where $F(x)$ is the number of instructions taken by the platform function `rand(int x)`."

In this case, the delivered certificate will contain a proof of the guaranteed bound under the *assumption* that the symbolic bound is satisfied. To (soundly) compute an overall worst case bound the platform must supply a (guaranteed and proven) bound which can be used during certificate checking.

Resource usage statements such as the above may not always hold unless particular safety conditions are met; or the resource usage may depend on non-functional (intensional) factors, such as the layout of data in memory. Consider, for example, the different space behaviour between deep and shallow copying of objects in memory, or a method whose complexity depends on the length of a list represented as a linked list sequence of objects. To deal with (and in particular, to prove) such cases, our preferred approach is to combine resource statements with *high-level typing invariants* which are maintained by our compiled methods. This has been done for heap space usage bounds in the existing fixed policy scheme of MRG [BHMS05] based on the specialised type system of Hofmann and Jost [HJ03] for inferring space usage. In this paper we focus instead on new forms of resource statement not previously considered in the implementation of MRG, and how such statements can be expressed and related in our PCC architecture. The generation and proof of resource statements is beyond the scope of what is considered here, although in certain cases automatic generation of bounds for resources other than heap usage is feasible by extending existing techniques (for example, inferring stack depth by an extension of Hofmann-Jost is considered by Campbell [Cam05]).

Outline. In the next section we introduce Grail and the semantic notions for resource policies expressed on the Grail operational semantics, which is a simplified abstraction of the JVML semantics. Resource policies are statements in the Grail program logic, which is also introduced in Sect. 2. In Sect. 3 we introduce a simple language for describing two forms of resource policies, one for guaranteed policies delivered with code and the other for the target policy of a smart device. We use the standard format of Java security policy files augmented with dedicated forms of permission. In Sect. 4 we describe some mechanisms for checking policies and how this interacts with the usual proof checking process. Finally, Sect. 5 concludes with a summary of the status of our work on policies and a comparison with related work.

2 Resource Policies for Grail

We want to make our resource policies precise and formalise their meaning. To do this, we first recall the Grail syntax, semantics and program logic, before considering the semantics of policies in Sect. 2.3.

2.1 Grail Syntax and Semantics

Grail is a functional language for writing imperative low-level code; we sketch a simplified version here. Together with intuition based on knowledge of the JVM, this sketch should suffice for an understanding of this paper; full details of Grail and its compilation scheme appear elsewhere [BMS03, MW04].

The simplified abstract syntax of Grail is as follows:

$$
\begin{aligned}
v &::= \texttt{null} \mid i \\
a &::= v \mid x \\
e &::= a \mid op\ a\ a \mid \texttt{new}\ C \mid x.t \mid x.t := a \\
&\quad \mid \texttt{let val}\ x = e\ \texttt{in}\ e \mid \texttt{let val}\ () = e\ \texttt{in}\ e \mid \texttt{if}\ e\ \texttt{then}\ e\ \texttt{else}\ e \\
&\quad \mid \texttt{call}\ f \mid C.m(\overline{a}) \\
op &::= \texttt{add} \mid \texttt{sub} \mid \texttt{mul} \mid \texttt{div} \mid = \mid \texttt{<=} \mid < \mid \texttt{<=}
\end{aligned}
$$

A Grail program consists of a sequence of class definitions for class names C. Each class definition may contain declarations for fields t and for methods m. Each method m in turn declares a number of mutually recursive functions f together with an overall expression body.

Expressions e include arguments, which may be values v (the null reference and integer literals) or variables x. Integers 1 (or any non-zero value) and 0 are

```
class List {
      field int hd
      field List tl

      method static List emptylist(int n) =
        let
          val l = null[List]

          fun emptylist(int n,List l) =
            if n>0 then empty_aux(n,l) else l

          fun empty_aux(int n,List l) =
            let val cell = new <List()>()
                val ()   = putfield cell <int List.hd> 0
                val ()   = putfield cell <List List.tl> l
                val n    = sub n 1
                val l    = cell
            in
                emptylist(n,l)
            end
        in
            emptylist(n,l)
        end
}
```

Fig. 1. Grail List class

also used to represent boolean values `true` and `false` as on the JVM. The remaining expressions are formed from: binary operations, object construction, field selection and field update, binding and sequential composition (written as in SML, by binding to the unit value), function and method invocations. Strong syntactic restrictions ensure that all functions are tail recursive, so a function in Grail can be compiled directly into a branch instruction in the underlying virtual machine: this is reflected in the abstract syntax above by using the `call` expression which does not pass any arguments. Method invocation is different, and a method may have a number of arguments a which can be variables or literal values. To keep the presentation brief, we will only consider class (static) methods, although the full language includes instance methods, as well as many other features of JVML.

An example Grail program is shown in Fig. 1. This program defines a class `List` to represent linked lists, and a method `List.emptylist` which constructs a list of a given length whose `hd` fields all contain zero. The method is defined using two tail recursive functions `emptylist` and `emptylist_aux`. Programs in concrete Grail syntax are more verbose than the simplified abstract syntax shown above: we use the extra keywords `putfield`, `getfield` and `invokestatic` and some additional typing information is included, for example, on the `null` value and the `putfield` instruction. We will return to extend this example later.

Semantics. The semantics of Grail is given in terms of a *resource algebra* $\mathcal{R}$, extending a big-step evaluation relation based on the functional interpretation:

$$E \vdash h, e \Downarrow h', v, r$$

where E is an environment, h and h' are heaps (partial maps from locations to values), v is the result value (or () indicating the absence of a value) and r is a *resource value* from $\mathcal{R}$. The semantics is deterministic: whenever e evaluates in some E, h then v, h' and r are uniquely determined. Moreover, the resources r are a purely non-invasive annotation on the ordinary operational semantics; evaluation of an expression is not affected by the resources consumed in subexpressions (this is reminiscent of effects [TJ94]).

A resource algebra $\mathcal{R}$ has a carrier set R consisting of *resource values* $r \in R$, together with:

- A cost ordering $\leq \subseteq R \times R$
- For the atomic expressions, families of constants $\mathcal{R}^{\texttt{null}} \in R$, $\mathcal{R}^{\texttt{int}} \in R$, etc.
- For compound expressions, families of operations, e.g. $\mathcal{R}^{\texttt{let}} \in R \times R \rightarrow R$.

The cost ordering expresses when one resource value is considered cheaper or better than another. The resource constants and operators are used to calculate costs by annotating the operational semantics; there is a constant or operator for each component of the syntax. An example rule is the rule for let-bindings (sequential composition with assignment):

$$\frac{E \vdash h, e_1 \Downarrow h_1, v_1, r_1 \qquad E[x := v_1] \vdash h_1, e_2 \Downarrow h_2, v, r_2}{E \vdash h, \texttt{let val } x = e_1 \texttt{ in } e_2 \Downarrow h_2, v, \mathcal{R}^{\texttt{let}}(r_1, r_2)}$$

For this paper we do not require additional properties of the resource algebra, although it is natural to impose further structure. For quantitative costs, for example, we may define the compound resource operators such as $\mathcal{R}^{\texttt{let}}$ in terms of an associative and commutative addition operator corresponding to sequential composition, as in the standard resource algebra described in Sect. 2.2.

The full definition of the semantics is in Table 2 at the end of the paper.

Program logic. Grail has a program logic which is formulated to take advantage of the functional semantics. Statements in the Grail Logic are written:

$$G \rhd e : P[E, h, h', v, r]$$

where e is a program expression and P is a predicate over the components of the operational semantics; G is a collection of assumptions of statements of the form $e' : P'$. This statement has a partial correctness reading: it states that whenever e evaluates in input environment E and heap h, then P holds for E, h, and the resulting heap h', value v, and resources consumed r.

Here is the rule in the logic for let-bindings:

$$\frac{G \rhd e_1 : P_1 \qquad G \rhd e_2 : P_2}{G \rhd \texttt{let } x \; e_1 \; e_2 : \{\exists \, h_1 \, v_1, r_1 \, r_2. \; P_1[E, h, h_1, v_1, r_1] \land}$$
$$P_2[E[x := v_1], h_1, h', v, r_2] \land$$
$$r = \mathcal{R}^{\texttt{let}}(r_1, r_2)\}$$

This rule says that a let expression satisfies the assertion which is formed by combining two assertions P_1 and P_2 for the subexpressions, whenever there is an intermediate result state and result h_1, v_1, r_1 and the overall resource r consumed is given by the let operator applied to the component costs r_1 and r_2.

The full definition of the logic is shown in Table 3 at the end of the paper. Predicates in the logic are like post-assertions in VDM: they range over both input and output without needing auxiliary variables as would be necessary in Hoare logic. This allows powerful but comparatively simple rules for adaptation, derived from the second consequence rule shown in Table 3. The main power of the logic comes with the last two rules for recursive function and procedure calls; these allow one to establish the correctness of a function or method body under the assumption that recursive calls are already correct.

The program logic enjoys good meta-theoretic properties; in particular, it is sound and relative complete. Grail's syntax, semantics, program logic and meta-theory have been all formalised in the theorem prover Isabelle; the formalisation serves both to provide strong confidence in the meta-theoretical results and to provide an experimental PCC environment. The program logic does not define a notation for predicates: these are written in the ambient higher-order logic of the theorem prover; this allows powerful specifications which can directly use the available library functions for arithmetic, etc. Our work here extends the Isabelle formalisation which is presented elsewhere [ABH+05, ABH+04]. In the overview here we elide some of the technicalities of the Isabelle encoding (for further details see *loc. cit.*).

2.2   A Standard Resource Algebra

We will suppose that a standard resource algebra is fixed by the application framework, which implies that the producer and consumer of mobile code have some agreement over which costs are of interest and how they are calculated.

As an example resource algebra which collects four costs of interest, we consider resource quadruples:

$$r = (clock, \ space, \ depth, \ methcnts)$$

where the first three components range over natural numbers, and the last over multisets of method names.

The costs have the following meaning:

- *clock* is a JVM instruction counter, counting bytecodes executed;
- *space* is the cumulative size of allocated objects on the heap;
- *depth* is an approximation of the maximum frame stack depth;
- *methcnts* counts how many times each method is invoked.

The resource operators for this standard algebra are given in Table 1.

The time and space resources measured here have a standard meaning. For *clock*, we count JVM instructions under the Grail to JVML translation.[1] For

---

[1] The details of this translation explain why if expressions are apparently free: the guard in the conditional is compiled into a test-and-branch instruction which is already accounted for by $\mathcal{R}^{\mathrm{prim}}$; similarly, sequential composition is just juxtaposition.

Table 1. Standard resource algebra

$$\mathcal{R}^{\texttt{null}} = \mathcal{R}^{\texttt{int}} = \mathcal{R}^{\texttt{var}} = (1, 0, 0, \{\})$$
$$\mathcal{R}^{\texttt{prim}}(r_1, r_2) = r_1 + r_2 + (1, 0, 0, \{\})$$
$$\mathcal{R}^{\texttt{new}}_C = (3, size(C), 0, \{\})$$
$$\mathcal{R}^{\texttt{getf}} = (2, 0, 0, \{\})$$
$$\mathcal{R}^{\texttt{putf}}(r) = r + (2, 0, 0, \{\})$$
$$\mathcal{R}^{\texttt{let}}(r_1, r_2) = r_1 + r_2 + (1, 0, 0, \{\})$$
$$\mathcal{R}^{\texttt{comp}}(r_1, r_2) = r_1 + r_2$$
$$\mathcal{R}^{\texttt{if}}(r_1, r_2) = r_1 + r_2$$
$$\mathcal{R}^{\texttt{call}}(r) = r + (1, 0, 0, \{\})$$
$$\mathcal{R}^{\texttt{meth}}_{C.m, \overline{a_i}}(r) = r + (2 + |\overline{a_i}|, 0, 1 + |\overline{a_i}|, \{C.m\})$$

$$(t_1, s_1, d_1, ms_1) + (t_2, s_2, d_2, ms_2) = (t_1 + t_2, s_1 + s_2, max(d_1, d_2), ms_1 \cup_+ ms_2)$$

$$(t_1, s_1, d_1, ms_1) \leq (t_2, s_2, d_2, ms_2) = t_1 \leq t_2 \wedge s_1 \leq s_2 \wedge d_1 \leq d_2 \wedge ms_1 \subseteq ms_2$$

Note: resource values r_k have the form $r_k = (t_k, s_k, ms_k, d_k)$ for $k = 1, 2$.
A tuple (t, s, d, ms) stands for $(clock, space, depth, methcnts)$.
The notation $|\overline{a_i}|$ denotes the length of the list $a_1 \ldots a_n$ and $\cup_+$ is multiset union.

space we measure memory usage based on the sizes of instance fields in a Java class (the function $size(C)$). For *depth* we approximate frame stack space based on the number of method parameters. The stack space calculation could easily be made more precise by incorporating the size needed for the local variables of each method. Finally, the method invocation counter *methcnts* accumulates method names invoked.

For a particular JVM implementation, these measures could be used to calculate approximate real time and space bounds, for example, based on empirical measurements of timings and knowledge of object overhead used in heap layout.

Notice that values in this resource algebra are composed of four independent components that could each be calculated separately within separate resource algebras. Each kind of resource has different properties, and will be expressed separately in our policy language described in Sect. 3.

This example algebra is similar to the one considered in the main MRG prototype described in [ABH+04], although there the heap size and method count components were not included. Many other interesting resource algebras can be given in this general scheme; see [ABH+05] for some particular examples and [ABM05] for an application of a more constrained form of resource algebra than that considered here. The important fact is that the soundness and completeness of the Grail Logic hold for any resource algebra.

2.3 Formal Notions of Resource Policy

Given a notion of resource consumption and a way to calculate it, we can go on to define a formal notion of resource policy. With respect to the Grail semantics, a *resource policy RP* for expressions is a predicate on environments E, heaps h and resource values r, written as:

$$RP[E, h, r]$$

Intuitively, the policy determines acceptable resource limits for expressions executed in the given environment and heap. This is simply a restricted form of assertion in the program logic: a policy for an expression is a specification of its resource consumption in terms of its input taken from the environment E and heap h. In the mechanised Isabelle implementation we again express these predicates in Isabelle HOL, the meta-logic used to formalise the Grail syntax, semantics and logic rules.

Note that in general the policy may rely on a type safety invariant (or more generally, some invariant involving object containment and separation), as mentioned on page 18. In this case we must use specifications in the program logic which are conditional on type safety before evaluating expressions, and ensure type safety of the output afterwards. A resource policy would be embedded as:

$$P_{RP}[E, h, h', v, r] \quad \triangleq \quad TS[E, h] \implies TS'[E, h, h', v] \land RP[E, h, r]$$

where TS and TS' are domain-specific safety invariants supplied by the certifying compiler. If the input environment and heap do not satisfy the safety invariant the policy is satisfied vacuously. For Camelot and its space-aware type system, the type safety invariant refers to the integrity of heap representations of high-level Camelot datatypes and the free list used for space reuse; the translation of this into *derived assertions* [BHMS05] in the Grail Logic may be understood as a special case of the above where the resource policy states that no heap space is consumed.

Definition 1. *An expression e conforms to a policy RP, written $e \models RP$, just in case:*
$$\forall E\, h\, r. \quad E \vdash h, e \Downarrow h', v, r \implies RP[E, h, r].$$

Notice that this is a *partial correctness* interpretation, in that conformance is only considered for terminating expressions. Termination may be treated as an orthogonal issue, using a related logic as proposed in [ABH+05], or we may impose run-time monitoring to ensure that programs do not diverge and violate their resource bounds.

Policy conformance is a special case of validity of assertions in the program logic, which means that we have a sound and complete logic for establishing conformance of resource policies.

Theorem 1 (cf. [ABH+05]). $\{\} \rhd e : RP[E, h, r]$ *if and only if* $e \models RP$.

Of course, we are ultimately interested in resource policies for method bodies; the environment declares the parameters of the method.

Example. The resource policy for the standard resource algebra given by

$$RP_{calc}[E, h, (t, s, d, ms)] = t \leq 16 + 42 * E(\mathbf{m}) + 9 * E(\mathbf{m}) * E(\mathbf{n})$$

formalises the example policy described in words for the calc method in Sect. 1. We claim that it is satisfied by the implementation of the calc method shown

```
method static void addthrow(List l, int n) =
   let
      fun update_pos(List l) =
         let val i  = getfield l <int List.hd>
             val i  = add i 1
             val () = putfield l <int List.hd> i
         in () end

      fun addthrow(int n,List l) =
         if n=0 then update_pos(l) else addthrow_aux(l,n)

      fun addthrow_aux(List l, int n) =
         let val l   = getfield l <List List.tl>
             val n   = sub n 1
         in addthrow(n,l) end
   in addthrow(n,l) end

// Throw n-sided dice m times and count results in a list
method static List calc(int n,  int m) =
   let
      val l = invokestatic <List List.emptylist (int)> (n)

      fun make_throws (List l, int n,  int m) =
         if m=0 then l
                else next_throw(l,n,m)

      fun next_throw (List l, int n,  int m) =
         let val r  = invokestatic <int Platform.Random.rand(int)> (n)
             val () = invokestatic <void List.addthrow(List,int)> (l, r)
             val m  = sub m 1
         in make_throws(l,n,m) end
   in make_throws(l,n,m) end
```

Fig. 2. Grail program to count dice throws

in Fig. 2, which shows a Grail program to count the results of m throws of an n-sided dice. The result of throwing a dice is represented by a call to a platform function Platform.Random.rand(n). To establish the bound above we must assume additionally that the platform function satisfies a policy:

$$RP_{Platform.Random.rand}[E, h, (t, s, d, ms)] = t \leq 20$$

i.e., that the number of instructions executed in the random method is at most 20.

For a given resource algebra, we can relate different policies in a refinement ordering.

Definition 2. *A resource policy RP_1 refines another policy RP_2, if*

$$\forall e.e \models RP_1 \Longrightarrow e \models RP_2$$

If RP_1 refines RP_2, then by definition any expression which conforms to the first policy also conforms to the second (more permissive) policy.

Example. A refinement for RP_{calc} is the policy given by:

$$RP'_{calc}[E, h, (t, s, d, ms)] = t \leq 16 + 42 * E(\mathtt{m}) + 9 * E(\mathtt{m}) * E(\mathtt{n}) \wedge s \leq 2 * E(\mathtt{n})$$

which requires additionally that the `calc` method allocates no more than $2 * \mathtt{n}$ words of heap space during its execution, which is also satisfied by the example program in Fig. 2, which allocates a list of length n.

Apart from adding requirements for further kinds of resource, one policy refines another of the form of RP_{calc} if it places a tighter bound on the resource consumption. We are interested in policies which place bounds on resource consumption in the manner of RP_{calc} above, but the form of resource policy allowed so far is much more general. For the framework here we at least want policies to respect the ordering of resources (downward closure):

Definition 3. *A resource policy RP respects $\leq$ for R, if for all E and h,*

$$\forall r, r' \in R. \quad r \leq r' \wedge RP[E, h, r'] \implies RP[E, h, r].$$

Clearly our example policies respect the resource ordering of the standard resource algebra. From now on we restrict to policies which respect resource ordering on the resource algebra of interest. This ensures that alternative implementations of methods with better resource behaviour may be selected to implement any policy. It rules out, for example, policies which describe a minimum resource usage.

Based on these definitions we can define a simple theory of policy refinement and its implementation in Isabelle. But this semantic notion of policy is still too general: we introduce further restrictions in the next section, by introducing our two specific forms of policy liable to be useful in practice on constrained devices.

3   Expressing Resource Policies

Resource policies can be written in our formal logic in the same way as program logic assertions, but this is an internal format and it is too rich: it is more useful to consider a way of expressing policies that is meaningful for the user. For this we need to investigate a *policy language*. Since we have an infrastructure for the Java platform, we will extend Java's existing notion of *permissions* and *security policy*. Security policies in Java are specified in files created with the `policytool` program or otherwise. For example, the trivial policy file:

```
grant {
  permission java.security.AllPermission;
};
```

describes a policy which grants all permissions. More interestingly, the policy file:

```
grant codeBase "file:${user.dir}/" {
  permission java.io.FilePermission "/etc/passwd", "read";
};
```

gives special permissions to code executed from the user's home directory, to read the contents of the password file.

To express resource policies for our application, we will introduce new forms of permission for the guaranteed policy and for the target policy. Permissions in Java are usually associated with running code: the security manager will raise an exception if some method does not possess appropriate permissions. However, our overloading of the concept will be useful: we can extend the built-in mechanisms for loading policy files and comparing between them, as well as allow a mechanism for run-time instrumentation.

The starting point is the `Permission` class, which defines an abstract method `implies` that compares two permissions. If permission p_1 implies p_2, then code which is granted permission p_1 also has permission p_2. If we can implement this method in a way which is consistent with our formal interpretation of resource permissions, we can integrate some parts of our policy refinement checking into the Java security model.

Guaranteed policies. Guaranteed policies deliver a parametrised bound on resource consumption, expressed as a nondecreasing function of a measure on each of the inputs. For integer inputs, the measure takes the input parameter unchanged; for other types we define a type-dependent coercion into the integers, in a standard way. For example:

```
permission ClockGuarantee  "List.calc(int m, int n)"
                           "16 + 42*m + 9*m*n"
permission SpaceGuarantee  "List.calc(int m, int n)" "2*n"
```

expresses the time and space bounds of the earlier example. Several permissions together define a resource policy for a method; resource policies for several methods define an overall guaranteed policy for a delivered program.

Target policies. The second form of policy is simpler and expresses some fixed hard limits of the particular target machine. For example:

```
permission ClockTarget "List.calc(int m, int n)"
                       "500, m<=3, n<=4"
permission SpaceTarget "List.calc(int m, int n)" "100"
```

Here, the absolute maximum execution time allowed for the `calc` method is 500 steps, and the target environment is providing a promise that the input parameters will satisfy the constraints shown. For heap space, the maximum new space consumed when evaluating the method is 100 words, irrespective of the input parameters to the method.

3.1   Permissions Language

Formally, Java methods are selected by a *method descriptor*. Method descriptors are described by the following grammar:

$$mdesc ::= mspec\,(type\ x, \ldots, type\ x)$$
$$mspec ::= C\#m \quad | \quad C.m$$

A method descriptor can disambiguate overloaded methods. A static method has its usual Java name (e.g., `java.lang.Integer.parseInt`), whereas an instance method has a name of the form `java.lang.Integer#toString`.

Guaranteed policies delivered with the code are described by the following grammar (for clarity we elide the quotation marks required for Java policy files):

$$G ::= \textbf{permission}\ gdesc\ bound$$
$$gdesc ::= ClockGuarantee\ mdesc$$
$$| \quad SpaceGuarantee\ mdesc$$
$$| \quad DepthGuarantee\ mdesc$$
$$| \quad MethcntGuarantee\ mdesc, mdesc$$
$$bound ::= f$$
$$f ::= K \quad | \quad x \quad | \quad f+f \quad | \quad f*f \quad | \quad f\hat{\ }f$$
$$| \quad \log(f) \quad | \quad \min(f,f) \quad | \quad \max(f,f)$$
$$| \quad gdesc\,(v, \ldots, v)$$
$$v ::= K \quad | \quad x$$

while target policies are given by the grammar:

$$T ::= \textbf{permission}\ tdesc\ limit, constraints$$
$$tdesc ::= ClockTarget\ mdesc$$
$$| \quad SpaceTarget\ mdesc$$
$$| \quad DepthTarget\ mdesc$$
$$| \quad MethcntTarget\ mdesc, mdesc$$
$$limit ::= K$$
$$constraints ::= x <= K, \ldots, x <= K$$

where K denotes a non-negative integer constant and x denotes a variable occurring in the method descriptor or (in the case of instance methods only) the keyword `this`.

The permissions defined above mirror the four classes of cost defined in Sect. 2.2 and describe guaranteed and target bounds for these costs. The `Clock`, `Space` and `Depth` permissions take a single method descriptor, specifying the method to which the bounds apply. In contrast the `Methcnt` permissions take two method descriptors m_1 and m_2 say; the meaning is that when m_1 is invoked, it will cause no more than the specified number of invocations of m_2 to occur.

In the final expression former for f, we allow the bounds in guaranteed policies to refer to other guaranteed policies. For example, we may have a policy such as:

permission *ClockGuarantee* C.m(int n)
    4*n + 3*(*ClockGuarantee* D.rand(int k) (n))

which states that the execution time of the method C.m depends on that of D.rand.

Note that we do not allow arbitrary bounding functions in guaranteed policies, but only ones of the form f above. It is not hard to see that functions which are generated by the grammar above are all nondecreasing. This will be important in our policy-checking procedure.

3.2   Semantics of Resource Policies

So far, resource policies are purely symbolic; we now give their semantic interpretation. Recall that a guaranteed policy for a resource R consists of a method signature (for the method m say) followed by a bound f. The intention is that f describes a function which is an upper bound on the amount of R which is consumed by any invocation of m, the bound being given as a function of the inputs to m. To this end, we require that the variables appearing in f are a subset of the variables appearing in the signature of m (with the addition of this if m is an instance method). Since not all of the arguments of m may influence its resource consumption we do not insist that all arguments appear in f. For example, if we have a method pow(int p, int q) which calculates p^q by repeated multiplication then it is probable that the execution time of pow would only depend on q.

In order to interpret the bounding expressions appearing in policies, we assume that every Java type t has an associated *measure* $\|\cdot\| : t \to \mathbb{N}$. For x of type int or long, $\|x\| = |x|$, the absolute value of x. For floating-point types, we put $\|x\| = \lceil|x|\rceil$. For heap-allocated objects o, we define $\|o\|$ to be the size of the object allocated in memory ($size(C)$ when o is of class C).[2]

We will sometimes wish to deal with unbounded quantities: to facilitate this we consider values lying in the set $\widehat{\mathbb{N}} = \mathbb{N} \cup \{\infty\}$. Arithmetic operators are extended from $\mathbb{N}$ to $\widehat{\mathbb{N}}$ in the obvious way: for example, $x + \infty = \infty$ and $\min(x, \infty) = x$ for all $x \in \widehat{\mathbb{N}}$. Given a bounding expression f and an environment E mapping identifiers to values (in $\widehat{\mathbb{N}}$), we define an interpretation $[\![f]\!]_E \in \widehat{\mathbb{N}}$ as follows:

$$[\![K]\!]_E = K$$
$$[\![x]\!]_E = \|E(x)\|$$
$$[\![f_1 + f_2]\!]_E = [\![f_1]\!]_E + [\![f_2]\!]_E$$
$$[\![f_1 * f_2]\!]_E = [\![f_1]\!]_E[\![f_2]\!]_E$$
$$[\![f_1 \hat{\ } f_2]\!]_E = [\![f_1]\!]_E^{[\![f_2]\!]_E}$$
$$[\![\texttt{log}f]\!]_E = \begin{cases} 0 & \text{if } [\![f]\!]_E = 0 \\ \max\{k : 2^k \leq [\![f]\!]_E\} & \text{otherwise} \end{cases}$$
$$[\![\min(f_1, f_2)]\!]_E = \min([\![f_1]\!]_E, [\![f_2]\!]_E)$$
$$[\![\max(f_1, f_2)]\!]_E = \max([\![f_1]\!]_E, [\![f_2]\!]_E)$$
$$[\![g(v_1, \ldots, v_n)]\!] = [\![T_g]\!]_{[x_i \mapsto [\![v_i]\!]_E]}$$

where, in the last line, the x_i are the variables appearing in the first method descriptor inside g, and T_g stands for the bounding expression for the permission g.

---

[2] This size function is not flexible enough for richer forms of resource specification such as those expressed by the Camelot type system; for such cases we would want to allow additional user-defined size functions as part of a proof certificate.

To interpret expressions involving other permissions, we first collect together all guaranteed policies from the delivered code and platform. We must disallow circular references between guarantee policies, as this could lead to infinite recursion while evaluating bounding expressions.

Note that if f is a bounding expression in the variables $\{x_1, \ldots, x_n\}$ then there is an induced function $\bar{f} : \widehat{\mathbb{N}}^n \to \widehat{\mathbb{N}}$ defined by

$$\bar{f}(u_1, \ldots, u_n) = [\![f]\!]_{\{x_1 \mapsto u_1, \ldots, x_n \mapsto u_n\}}.$$

Every such $\bar{f}$ is a nondecreasing function on $\widehat{\mathbb{N}}^n$.

Given this semantic interpretation for new forms of permission, it is straightforward to convert Java policies to their formal equivalents in the Isabelle program logic, so that policy conformance and refinement can be checked formally. However, we have designed the format of policies so that refinement can be checked simply, without needing arbitrary proof. This means that we must trust an implementation of the checking procedure, described next.

4   Checking Policies

Suppose that we have been supplied with a guaranteed policy G for a static method m stating that a resource R is bounded by the function f.

Let the variables occurring in the expression f be $x_1, \ldots, x_n$, which are a subset of the set of formal arguments appearing in the signature for m.

Now suppose that we have a target policy T for the method m and the resource R. Recall that T consists of a signature for m (without loss of generality we assume that the formal arguments appearing in the signatures for m in G and T are identical) followed by a constant b and a sequence of constraints for the formal arguments of m. The interpretation of T is that the code consumer requires that no more than b units of R are consumed, provided that the inputs to m do not exceed the given bounds.

By eliminating redundant constraints and adding vacuous constraints $x_j \leq \infty$ for variables not explicitly constrained in T we form a set of constraints $\{x_1 \leq b_1, \ldots x_n \leq b_n\}$ (with $b_i \in \widehat{\mathbb{N}}$) where each x_i appears precisely once.

Recall that f induces a function $\bar{f} : \widehat{\mathbb{N}}^n \to \widehat{\mathbb{N}}$. The code producer has supplied a proof that the resource usage of m when applied to a given set of arguments is bounded above by the value of $\bar{f}$ applied to the appropriate subset of the arguments of m. Since $\bar{f}$ is nondecreasing it follows that the maximum resource usage of m subject to $\{x_i \leq b_i\}$ is

$$\sup \{\bar{f}(u_1, \ldots, u_n) : u_i \in \widehat{\mathbb{N}}, u_i \leq b_i\} = \bar{f}(b_1, \ldots, b_n) = [\![f]\!]_E$$

where E is the environment $\{x_1 \mapsto b_1, \ldots, x_n \mapsto b_n\}$ (the resource usage is unbounded if $[\![f]\!]_E = \infty$). Thus to check the validity of T we need merely check whether $[\![f]\!]_E \leq b$.

For instance methods we follow the same procedure, but one must also consider the variable this.

4.1 Remarks

The policy-checking strategy described above depends crucially on the fact that the bounding functions given in guaranteed policies are nondecreasing. Note that the grammar for bounding functions makes this property manifest; a simple syntactic check suffices to show that a purported bound is nondecreasing, and so no extra overhead of proof-checking is required to establish this. This is a particular advantage in the scenario mentioned in the introduction, where we may ship several possible implementations of library functions with different resource behaviour which are used by the target device; it would be possible try to optimise resource usage by rearranging its choice of methods within given target policies. More importantly, this step can be done more quickly than VCG and proof checking, avoiding the need to check proofs when a policy cannot be met.

We have considered policy-checking with more general policy formats. For example, the code producer might supply code with some certified bounding function f and the consumer may require to know that some other bounding function g is satisfied for some set of inputs (the case we consider above is when g is constant). In this case, the consumer has to check that $g - f$ is positive for some set of inputs, and since $g - f$ could essentially be any function, this is a difficult problem. Furthermore, it is not possible for the code producer to provide any help (in the form of proof, for instance) since it has no *a priori* knowledge of the bounds that the consumer will require to be satisfied. Policy-checking in this general situation thus appears to be infeasible.

5 Conclusions

We have described a way of generalising the present proof-carrying code infrastructure of the MRG project to include resource policies based on assertions on bytecode expressed in the Grail program logic. Policies are naturally treated as special cases of assertions in the logic, but we want to express them in a simpler and more uniform way, in particular, to allow an efficient check of whether mobile code supplied with a guaranteed policy implements the target policy of particular device. To this end, we introduced syntax and semantics for two forms of policy embedded as Java permissions in Java security policy files. Using the Java file format and permissions mechanism allows us to implement a sound test for policy refinement inside Java. Then checking policy conformance is reduced to checking that the code satisfies the guaranteed policy claimed for it (delivered with the certificate) and that the guaranteed policy implies the policy desired by the client.

The security model here is quite analogous to the present security mechanisms in Java, where code is implicitly supplied with its "code base" (origin) which may be checked against permitted code bases, and where code may be supplied with cryptographic signatures and these signatures may be accepted according to the policy.

More work is required to implement our policies inside the full MRG architecture and try full-sized examples. So far we have constructed necessary extensions to the Grail Logic, conducted experimental verifications and implemented a prototype parser and a checker for resource policies. It remains to integrate with the Java platform (perhaps following the technique described in [GP05]), and to embed guaranteed policies in certificates — ultimately with automation extending that provided for the current fixed policy derived from the Camelot type system.

Related Work. Other researchers have worked on inferring and proving static bounds on different kinds of resources both for high-level languages and low-level ones, using type-based and logical techniques e.g., [CW00, VH04, HP99, BPS05]. Recent work [CEI05] has explored combinations of static and dynamic methods, which would also be useful in our setting. In this paper we concentrated on the mechanism of describing policies rather than the mechanism of inferring, proving or dynamically checking them; our approach would still be applicable if we used other techniques for those steps. Moreover, the basic ideas for the PCC architecture based on delivering policies with code are not specific to resource usage policies. Although important for general adoption, there seems to be relatively little published work on how policies are described and delivered in other PCC settings. One of the original PCC architectures described by Necula [Nec98] proposed the negotiation of policy between code producer and code consumer, in principle allowing the certificate to be specially adapted to the target requirements. In later work this was simplified to a fixed type-safety policy which would also work for a store-and-forward network.

Away from PCC, there is other related work on specification of resource behaviour for compiled Java programs. Most developments focus on dynamic checking. The Java Resource Management API (RM API)[CHS+03] (a development of the JRes interface [CvE98]) is a flexible mechanism which allows Java-based platforms to manage and monitor resource consumption. Resource policies are implemented via *resource domains*, which supply units of a given resource to applications (more precisely, to Java *isolates*) and also allow client applications to query availability of resources. To expose a resource through the RM API, the implementation of the resource includes code which records consumption and destruction, requiring modification of system classes. CPU time is monitored by a separate thread which periodically polls the operating system. Another resource accounting system for Java is J-SEAL2 [BHV01, J-S], which performs its resource accounting via bytecode instrumentation to insert calls to record resource allocations; CPU time again requires special handling, but in this case an estimate is calculated from the number of bytecode instructions executed. In both Java RM API and J-SEAL2, resource monitoring is dynamic; this can result in more accurate tracking and allocation of resources than static prediction as in our approach, but it requires runtime overhead and the need for recovery mechanisms in the case of resource exhaustion.

We have introduced a very simple policy language here. There are connections to work on policy languages in other domains of computer security, such as the use of Datalog, or the generation of large databases from policies, as in SELinux [LS01]. It would be interesting to consider whether one may usefully express our policies in languages such as these. However, the fundamental problem here is different: rather than querying some policy database to see if some access should be granted, the central question we have considered is *refinement* between policies, given that we already have guaranteed conformance for some program and a particular given policy.

Future work. There are several directions for further work. Most importantly, we need more automated mechanisms to provide the resource bound guarantees which are delivered with mobile code, and ways to analyse and predict the resource behaviour of existing platform library functions. We also need to undertake practical experiments on a particular platform to calibrate our cost model, and ensure that our resource guarantees can indeed be fulfilled on a particular architecture. Knowledge of an architecture and in particular additional hooks (such as provided by the Real-Time Java Specification [B+00]) could help provide sharper guarantees, including modelling of garbage collection, for example. Concerning the certificate checking mechanism, it would be interesting to investigate the combination of static and dynamic techniques, as outlined in the introduction. We plan to pursue some of these activities in the recently started EPSRC Project ReQueST, which is investigating resource bound certification for Grid computing.

Acknowledgements. We're grateful to our colleagues working on the MRG project for discussions on the topic of this paper, in particular to Lennart Beringer, Martin Hofmann, Alberto Momigliano, and Ian Stark for collaboration on resource algebras and to Lennart, Martin, Alberto, and Hans-Wolfgang Loidl for their collaboration on the Grail Logic. Our work was supported by the European Community as part of the MRG and Mobius projects (IST-2001-33149 and FP6-015905), as well as by the EPSRC ReQueST project (EP/C537068/1). This paper reflects only the authors' views and neither the Community nor EPSRC is liable for any use that may be made of the information contained within it.

References

ABH+04. David Aspinall, Lennart Beringer, Martin Hofmann, Hans-Wolfgang Loidl, and Alberto Momigliano. A program logic for resource verification. In *Proc. of 17th Int. Conf. on Theorem Proving in Higher Order Logics (TPHOLs 2004)*, Lecture Notes in Computer Science, Heidelberg, September 2004. Springer.

ABH+05. David Aspinall, Lennart Beringer, Martin Hofmann, Hans-Wolfgang Loidl, and Alberto Momigliano. A program logic for resources. Technical Report EDI-INF-RR-0296, Informatics, University of Edinburgh, July 2005.

ABM05. David Aspinall, Lennart Beringer, and Alberto Momigliano. Optimisation validation. Technical report, Informatics, University of Edinburgh, December 2005.

AGH+05. David Aspinall, Stephen Gilmore, Martin Hofmann, Donald Sannella, and Ian Stark. Mobile resource guarantees for smart devices. In *Construction and Analysis of Safe, Secure, and Interoperable Smart Devices: Proceedings of the International Workshop CASSIS 2004*, number 3362 in Lecture Notes in Computer Science, pages 1–26. Springer-Verlag, 2005.

B⁺00. Greg Bollella et al. *The Real-time Specification for Java*. Addison-Wesley, 2000.

BHMS05. Lennart Beringer, Martin Hofmann, Alberto Momigliano, and Olha Shkaravska. Automatic certification of heap consumption. In Andrei Voronkov Franz Baader, editor, *Proc. Logic for Programming, Artificial Intelligence, and Reasoning: 11th International Conference, LPAR 2004*, volume 3425 of *Lecture Notes in Computer Science*, pages 347–362. Springer, Feb 2005.

BHV01. Walter Binder, Jane G. Hulaas, and Alex Villazón. Portable resource control in Java. In *OOPSLA '01: Proceedings of the 16th ACM SIGPLAN conference on Object oriented programming, systems, languages, and applications*, pages 139–155, New York, NY, USA, 2001. ACM Press.

BMS03. Lennart Beringer, Kenneth MacKenzie, and Ian Stark. Grail: a functional form for imperative mobile code. *Electronic Notes in Theoretical Computer Science*, 85(1), June 2003.

BPS05. G. Barthe, M. Pavlova, and G. Schneider. Precise analysis of memory consumption using program logics. In B. Aichernig and B. Beckert, editors, *Proceedings of SEFM'05*. IEEE Press, 2005.

Cam05. Brian Campbell. Folding stack memory usage prediction into heap. In *Proceedings of Quantitative Aspects of Programming Languages Workshop, ETAPS 2005*, April 2005.

CEI05. Ajay Chander, David Espinosa, and Nayeem Islam. Enforcing resource bounds via static verification of dynamic checks. In *Proc. ESOP 2005*, Lecture Notes in Computer Science, Heidelberg, 2005. Springer-Verlag LNCS.

CHS⁺03. Grzegorz Czajkowski, Stephen Hahn, Glenn Skinner, Pete Soper, and Ciaran Bryce. Sun Microsystems Technical Report TR-2003-124: A resource management interface for the Java platform, May 2003.

CvE98. Grzegorz Czajkowski and Thorsten von Eicken. JRes: a resource accounting interface for Java. In *OOPSLA '98: Proceedings of the 13th ACM SIGPLAN conference on Object-oriented programming, systems, languages, and applications*, pages 21–35, New York, NY, USA, 1998. ACM Press.

CW00. K. Crary and S. Weirich. Resource bound certification. In *Proc. 27th Symp. Principles of Prog. Lang. (POPL)*, pages 184–198. ACM, 2000.

GP05. Stephen Gilmore and Matthew Prowse. Proof-carrying bytecode. In *Proceedings of First Workshop on Bytecode Semantics, Verification, Analysis and Transformation (BYTECODE '05)*, Edinburgh, Scotland, April 2005.

HJ03. M. Hofmann and S. Jost. Static prediction of heap space usage for first-order functional programs. In *Proceedings of the 30th ACM Symposium on Principles of Programming Languages*, volume 38 of *ACM SIGPLAN Notices*, pages 185–197, New York, January 2003. ACM Press.

HP99. J. Hughes and L. Pareto. Recursion and dynamic data structures in bounded space: towards embedded ML programming. In *Proc. International Conference on Functional Programming (ACM). Paris, September '99*, 1999.

J-S. J-SEAL2 website. See www.jseal2.com.

LS01. Peter Loscocco and Stephen Smalley. Integrating flexible support for security policies into the linux operating system. In Clem Cole, editor, *USENIX Annual Technical Conference, FREENIX Track*. USENIX, 2001.

MW04. Kenneth MacKenzie and Nicholas Wolverson. Camelot and grail: resource-aware functional programming on the JVM. In *Trends in Functional Programing*, volume 4, pages 29–46. Intellect, 2004.

Nec98. George C. Necula. *Compiling with Proofs*. PhD thesis, Carnegie Mellon University, October 1998. Available as Technical Report CMU-CS-98-154.

TJ94.   Jean-Pierre Talpin and Pierre Jouvelot. The type and effect discipline. *Inf. Comput.*, 111(2):245–296, 1994.

VH04.   Pedro Vasconcelos and Kevin Hammond. Inferring costs for recursive, polymorphic and higher-order functional programs. In *IFL 2003: Proceedings of the 15th International Workshop on the Implementation of Functional Languages*, Lecture Notes in Computer Science. Springer-Verlag, 2004.

Appendix

Table 2. Grail operational semantics

$$E \vdash h,\ a \Downarrow h,\ eval_E(a),\ cost(a)$$

$$\frac{r_1 = cost(a_1) \qquad r_2 = cost(a_2)}{E \vdash h,\ op\ a_1\ a_2 \Downarrow h,\ op(eval_E(a_1),\ eval_E(a_2)),\ \mathcal{R}^{\mathrm{prim}}(r_1, r_2)}$$

$$\frac{l = \mathsf{freshloc}(h)}{E \vdash h,\ \mathtt{new}\ c \Downarrow h[l \mapsto (c, \{t_i := initval_i\})],\ l,\ \mathcal{R}^{\mathrm{new}}}$$

$$\frac{E\langle x \rangle = l \qquad l \in dom(h)}{E \vdash h,\ x.t \Downarrow h,\ h(l).t,\ \mathcal{R}^{\mathrm{getf}}}$$

$$\frac{E\langle x \rangle = l \qquad l \in dom(h)}{E \vdash h,\ x.t{:=}a \Downarrow h[l.t \mapsto eval_E(a)],\ (),\ \mathcal{R}^{\mathrm{putf}}(cost(a))}$$

$$\frac{E \vdash h,\ e_1 \Downarrow h_1,\ v_1,\ r_1 \qquad E \vdash h_1,\ e_2 \Downarrow h',\ v,\ r_2}{E \vdash h,\ \mathtt{let\ val}\ () = e_1\ \mathtt{in}\ e_2 \Downarrow h',\ v,\ \mathcal{R}^{\mathrm{comp}}(r_1, r_2)}$$

$$\frac{E \vdash h,\ e_1 \Downarrow h_1,\ v_1,\ r_1 \qquad E\langle x := v_1 \rangle \vdash h_1,\ e_2 \Downarrow h',\ v,\ r_2}{E \vdash h,\ \mathtt{let\ val}\ x = e_1\ \mathtt{in}\ e_2 \Downarrow h',\ v,\ \mathcal{R}^{\mathrm{let}}(r_1, r_2)}$$

$$\frac{E \vdash h,\ e_1 \Downarrow h_1,\ v_1,\ r_1 \qquad v_1 \neq \mathtt{false} \qquad E \vdash h_1,\ e_2 \Downarrow h',\ v,\ r_2}{E \vdash h,\ \mathtt{if}\ e_1\ \mathtt{then}\ e_2\ \mathtt{else}\ e_3 \Downarrow h',\ v,\ \mathcal{R}^{\mathrm{if}}(r_1, r_2)}$$

$$\frac{E \vdash h,\ e_1 \Downarrow h_1,\ \mathtt{false},\ r_1 \qquad E \vdash h_1,\ e_3 \Downarrow h',\ v,\ r_2}{E \vdash h,\ \mathtt{if}\ e_1\ \mathtt{then}\ e_2\ \mathtt{else}\ e_3 \Downarrow h',\ v,\ \mathcal{R}^{\mathrm{if}}(r_1, r_2)}$$

$$\frac{E \vdash h,\ f_{body} \Downarrow h',\ v,\ r}{E \vdash h,\ \mathtt{call}\ f \Downarrow h',\ v,\ \mathcal{R}^{\mathrm{call}}(r)}$$

$$\frac{\{x_i := eval_E(a_i)\} \vdash h,\ C.m_{body} \Downarrow h',\ v,\ r}{E \vdash h,\ C.m(\overline{a}) \Downarrow h',\ v,\ \mathcal{R}^{\mathrm{meth}}(r)}$$

Notes:

- argument evaluation is defined by $eval_E(x) = E(x)$ and $eval_E(v) = v$;
- argument costs are defined as $cost(\mathtt{null}) = \mathcal{R}^{\mathrm{null}}$, $cost(i) = \mathcal{R}^{\mathrm{int}}$, $cost(x) = \mathcal{R}^{\mathrm{var}}$;
- the function $\mathsf{freshloc}(h)$ returns a fresh location l not in the domain of h;
- $initval_i$ stands for the initial value of the field t_i in class c;
- f_{body} and $C.m_{body}$ denote the definition of function f and method $C.m$ respectively.

Table 3. Grail Logic

$$\frac{e : P \in G}{G \triangleright e : P} \qquad\qquad \frac{G \triangleright e : P \quad P \Longrightarrow Q}{G \triangleright e : Q}$$

$$\overline{G \triangleright a : \{h' = h \;\wedge\; v = eval_E(x) \;\wedge\; r = cost(a)\}}$$

$$\overline{G \triangleright op\; a_1\; a_2 : \{h' = h \;\wedge\; v = op(eval_E(a_1), eval_E(a_2)) \;\wedge \atop r = \mathcal{R}^{\mathrm{prim}}(cost(a_1), cost(a_2))\}}$$

$$\overline{G \triangleright \mathbf{new}\; C : \{v = \mathrm{freshloc}(h) \;\wedge\; h' = h[v \mapsto (C, \{t_i := initval_i\})] \;\wedge\; r = \mathcal{R}^{\mathrm{new}}\}}$$

$$\frac{G \triangleright e_1 : P_1 \qquad G \triangleright e_2 : P_2}{G \triangleright \mathbf{let\ val}\; x = e_1\ \mathbf{in}\ e_2 : \{\exists\, h_1\, v_1, r_1\, r_2.\ P_1[E, h, h_1, v_1, r_1] \wedge \atop P_2[E[x := v_1], h_1, h', v, r_2] \;\wedge \atop r = \mathcal{R}^{\mathrm{let}}(r_1, r_2)\}}$$

$$\frac{G \triangleright e_1 : P_1 \qquad G \triangleright e_2 : P_2}{G \triangleright \mathbf{let\ val}\; () = e_1\ \mathbf{in}\ e_2 : \{\exists\, h_1\, r_1\, r_2.\ P_1[E, h, h_1, (), r_1] \wedge \atop P_2[E, h_1, h', v, r_2] \;\wedge \atop r = \mathcal{R}^{\mathrm{comp}}(r_1, r_2)\}}$$

$$\frac{G \triangleright e_1 : P_1 \qquad G \triangleright e_2 : P_2 \qquad G \triangleright e_3 : P_3}{G \triangleright \mathbf{if}\ e_1\ \mathbf{then}\ e_2\ \mathbf{else}\ e_3 : \{\exists\, h_1\, v_1\, r_1\, r_2.\ P_1[E, h, h_1, v_1, r_1] \wedge \atop (v_1 \neq \mathbf{false} \Longrightarrow P_2[E, h_1, h', v, r_2]) \;\wedge \atop (v_1 = \mathbf{false} \Longrightarrow P_3[E, h_1, h', v, r_2]) \;\wedge\; r = \mathcal{R}^{\mathrm{if}}(r_1, r_2)\}}$$

$$\frac{G, \mathbf{call}\; f : P \;\;\triangleright\; f_{body} : \{P[E, h, h', v, \mathcal{R}^{\mathrm{call}}(r)]\}}{G \triangleright \mathbf{call}\; f : P}$$

$$\frac{G, c.m(y) : P \triangleright m_{body} : \{P[E, h, h', v, \mathcal{R}^{\mathrm{meth}}(r)]\}}{G \triangleright c.m(y) : P}$$

Note: assertions in braces $\{\ldots\}$ have standard free variables E, h, h', v, r. The notation $P[E_1, h_1, h'_1, v_1, r_1]$ indicates the instantiation of a predicate.

Information Flow Analysis for a Typed Assembly Language with Polymorphic Stacks

Eduardo Bonelli[1], Adriana Compagnoni[2], and Ricardo Medel[2]

[1] LIFIA, Fac. de Informática, Univ. Nac. de La Plata, Argentina
[2] Stevens Institute of Technology, Hoboken NJ 07030, USA
eduardo@sol.info.unlp.edu.ar, {rmedel, abc}@cs.stevens.edu

Abstract. We study secure information flow in a stack based Typed Assembly Language (TAL). We define a TAL with an execution stack and establish the soundness of its type system by proving *non-interference*. One of the problems of studying information flow for a low-level language is the absence of high-level control flow constructs that guide information flow analysis in high-level languages. Furthermore, in the presence of an execution stack, code that frees space on the stack must be constrained in order to avoid illegal flows. Finally, in the presence of stack polymorphism, we must ensure that type variables are instantiated without observable differences. These issues are addressed by introducing *junction points* into the type system, ensuring that they behave as ordered linear continuations, and that they interact safely with the execution stack. We also discuss several limitations of our approach and point out some remaining open issues.

1 Introduction and Motivation

The increasing need to guarantee the confidentiality of electronically stored information has prompted the academic community to study confidentiality from different points of view. Although access control regulates who can access information, it does not regulate the proper manipulation of sensitive data, i.e. the flow of information. In contrast, the theory of programming languages provides powerful techniques that have proven successful in studying information flow security.

In a multilevel security architecture, information can range from having low (public) to high (secret) security level. Information flow analysis studies whether an attacker can obtain information about the secret data by observing the public output of the system. The *non-interference* property states that any two executions of the same program, where only the high-security inputs differ in both executions, do not exhibit any observable difference in their outputs.

The example in Fig. 1(a) shows a program that has the non-interference property only if the variable y is secret. Otherwise, information about the secret (labelled ⊤) value stored in x is revealed by the different values that y can have, depending on the branch of the **if-then-else** instruction executed. This breach of security is called *implicit* information flow. In order to statically detect

G. Barthe et al. (Eds.): CASSIS 2005, LNCS 3956, pp. 37–56, 2006.
© Springer-Verlag Berlin Heidelberg 2006

pc level	$x : \text{int}^\top ; z : \text{int}^\perp$
low	if x = 0
high	then y := 1
high	else y := 2;
low	z := 3

(a) High-level language

```
L1 : bnz r1,L2
     mov r2, 1
     jmp L3
L2 : mov r2, 2
L3 : mov r3, 3
```

(b) Assembly language

```
L1 : pushJP L3
     bnz r1,L2
     mov r2, 1
     jmpJP L3
L2 : mov r2, 2
     jmpJP L3
L3 : mov r3, 3
```

(c) SIFTAL

Fig. 1. Example of implicit information flow

this kind of information flow, a security level is associated with the program counter at each program point. This association is shown in the left column of the example, and it can be verified that at each program point no variable with a lower security level than the program counter is updated. Notice that the assignment in the last line of code does not depend on the value of x. Therefore, the level of the program counter becomes low again and the public (labelled $\perp$) variable z can be updated without compromising confidentiality.

Motivated by the desire to obtain secure information flow results for low-level code without trusting the compiler, and the fact that most mobile programs are distributed in some low-level format, we study confidentiality for assembly programs using a language-based approach to security via type theory.

Information flow analysis in low-level languages presents a number of difficulties typically not present in high-level ones. As already noted in several articles on information flow for low-level languages [3, 14], the absence of high-level control flow constructs dictates the need for some alternative mechanism for retrieving high-level program structure. For example, the program in Fig. 1(b) is a standard translation of the high-level program of Fig. 1(a) to assembly language. Notice that the security level of the program counter can be raised after the execution of the **bnz** instruction, but there is no way of knowing where it can be lowered again, in order to allow the update of the public variable z represented by register **r3**.

In [15] we introduced the notion of *junction point*, which represents a program point where execution of different branches of computation converge. Our *Typed Assembly Language* SIFTAL uses junction points and typing directives to manipulate a stack of junction points and reflect the control flow structure of the programs. These junction points are instrumental during typechecking to prove non-interference; however, they bear no meaning during execution, and are therefore removed after typechecking.

The code in Fig. 1(c) is a translation to SIFTAL of the high-level program in Fig. 1(a). The SIFTAL program uses the code label *L3* as a junction point, in order to signal where the security level can be lowered. During typechecking, the typing directive **pushJP** *L3* pushes the label *L3* onto a stack, introducing a *linear obligation* that has to be met by using a **jmpJP** *L3* instruction. Moreover, the program is well-typed only if there are no modifications of public registers inside the branches of the **bnz** instruction. Note that **pushJP** has no effect at run-time and it is discarded after typechecking, while **jmpJP** will be replaced by a **jmp** instruction.

L_{start} CODE$\langle\{r1 : int^\perp, r2 : int^\top\} \mid \perp\rangle$
```
    salloc 2
    mov r1,0
    sst sp[0],r1
    mov r1,1
    sst sp[1],r1
    bnz r2, Lhigh
    jmp LJP
```

L_{high} CODE$\langle\{r1 : int^\perp\} \mid \top\rangle$
```
    sfree 1
    jmp LJP
```

L_{JP} CODE$\langle\{r1 : int^\perp\} \mid \perp\rangle$
```
    sld r1,sp[0]
    ...
```

(a)

L_{start} CODE$\langle\{r1 : int^\perp, r2 : int^\top\} \mid \perp\rangle$
```
    salloc 3
    mov r1,0
    sst sp[2],r1
    mov r1,1
    sst sp[1],r1
    sst sp[0],r2
    bnz r2, Lhigh
    jmp LJP
```

L_{high} CODE$\langle\{r1 : int^\perp\} \mid \top\rangle$
```
    sfree 1
    jmp LJP
```

L_{JP} CODE$\langle\{r1 : int^\perp\} \mid \perp\rangle$
```
    sfree 1
    sld r1,sp[0]
    ...
```

(b)

Fig. 2. Insecure information flow in the presence of stacks

SIFTAL is a RISC *load-store* assembly language, and it includes instructions to allocate (`salloc`) and deallocate (`sfree`) space on the stack, and instructions to load (`sld`) and store (`sst`) words from and onto the stack. In order to verify the non-interference of a program that manipulates the stack, we must ensure the absence of explicit illegal flows via the stack: elements that are pushed onto the stack while the **pc** has a security level l must be popped while the **pc** has at least security level l.

However, other more subtle forms of information leaks may arise. Consider the code in Fig. 2. The expression CODE$\langle\Gamma \mid \mathbf{pc}\rangle$ that appears alongside a code label is the type of the code block, where Γ is the type of the registers before execution starts, and **pc** indicates the initial security level of the program counter. For simplicity, in these programs we do not include the type of the stack pointer.

Fig. 2(a) shows that it is possible to leak confidential information by allowing to pop a public stack component during the execution of a high-security branch. The first five lines of the program push a 0 and a 1 onto the stack using the auxiliary register `r1`. Then, in line 6 a branching operation based on the secret value stored in `r2` is performed. One branch (line 7) is empty, and only jumps to the junction point L_{JP}. The second branch pointed to by L_{high} eliminates one element from the stack with `sfree`. Thus, the top of the stack is erased, leaving 1 as the new top, and the branch ends with a jump to L_{JP}. At the junction point L_{JP}, the security level of the **pc** is low again, allowing the public register `r1` to learn information about the secret value in the register `r2` by reading the top of the stack. Now, if `r1` contains 1 the attacker knows that `r2` is not 0, if `r1` contains 0 the attacker knows that `r2` contains 0.

The previous problem stems from the fact that a high-security branch has freed the public stack component on the top of the stack. However, as the next example shows, it is not sufficient to restrict the free operation to components whose security level is at least that of the program counter at that point. The code in Fig. 2(b) pushes two public values on the stack and then a secret one.

It then branches on the secret value of r2. One branch does nothing and the other frees the top of the stack. It is legal to do it because at the top of the stack there is a secret value and the program counter is high-security at that point. Once the junction point L_{JP} has been reached, the topmost item of the stack is freed. Again, this is legal because the security level of the program counter is low. Therefore, any public or secret value can be erased from the stack. However, depending on the public value of the top of the resulting stack, information may be inferred about the secret value of r2. The conclusion is that the type system must guarantee that high branches free the same amount of items from the stack.

Stack types in SIFTAL are polymorphic. That is, type variables can be included in a stack type to abstract part of the type. This is required to implement multiple calls to code sections, as in procedure calls. The new format of the type for a piece of code will be $\text{CODE}\langle \forall[\Theta]\Gamma \mid \mathbf{pc}\rangle$, with Θ being the list of variables (usually denoted by the capital letters X, Y, etc.), Γ being the type of the registers, including a stack pointer register named sp, and $\mathbf{pc}$ being the expected security level of the program counter in such code.

In order to jump to a piece of code that has a polymorphic stack type, the type variables must be instantiated. For example, code of type $\text{CODE}\langle \forall[X]\{sp : int^{\perp} \cdot X\} \mid \mathbf{pc}\rangle$ requires a stack with type $int^{\perp} \cdot X$ to be executed safely. If that code is at label L then the jump instruction $\mathtt{jmp}\ L\,[int^{\top} \cdot \epsilon]$ instantiates, for this particular call, the type of the stack to $int^{\perp} \cdot int^{\top} \cdot \epsilon$.

```
L_start  CODE⟨∀[X]{r1 : int^⊥, r2 : int^⊤, sp : X} | ⊥⟩
         salloc 2
         mov r1,0
         sst sp[0],r1
         mov r1,1
         sst sp[1],r1
         pushJP L_JP
         bnz r2,L_high[X]
         jmpJP L_JP[int^⊥ · X]  % requires L_JP on top

L_high   CODE⟨∀[Y]{r1 : int^⊥, sp : int^⊥ · L_JP · int^⊥ · Y} | ⊤⟩
         sfree 1
         jmpJP L_JP[Y]          % requires L_JP in the middle

L_JP     CODE⟨∀[Z]{r1 : int^⊥, sp : int^⊥ · Z} | ⊥⟩
         sld r1,sp[0]
         ...
```

Fig. 3. Implicit information flow detected in SIFTAL

By translating the code in Fig. 2(a) to SIFTAL, we obtain the program in Fig. 3. This code fails to typecheck since the occurrence of jmpJP in L_{start} requires that L_{JP} be at the top of the stack, but the one in L_{high} requires that it be in the middle, since L_{high} frees the topmost component.

This paper presents an extension of our previous work on information flow for assembly languages [7, 15] to address the issues that arise by the inclusion of an execution stack. The examples in this section illustrate that stack constructs are *not* orthogonal to junction point constructs. Indeed, the main technical contribution of this work is the explicit treatment of junction points as a tool to address the problems that arise in the presence of polymorphic stacks.

Additional benefits of dealing explicitly with junction points in the type system are: 1) well-typed programs must "consume" all of their junction points, which, in the vision of junction points as ordered linear continuations [28], is equivalent to requiring that all linear obligations are met; and 2) whenever a jump to a code block is performed, the type system ensures that the current pending junction points are passed on as obligations to the destination code block. Complete definitions and detailed proofs of the results in this paper appear in the preliminary version of the technical report [6].

2   An Overview of SIFTAL

2.1   Syntax of Terms and Type Expressions

SIFTAL is a Typed Assembly Language (TAL) [17] based on STAL [16]. It has an execution stack and constructs that support stack allocation. The syntax of the types for SIFTAL is given in Fig. 4, and the syntax of SIFTAL programs is given in Fig. 5. We assume the following pairwise disjoint sets: an infinite enumerable set of code labels $L_1, L_2, \ldots$, an infinite enumerable set of memory tuple labels $p_1, p_2, \ldots$, an infinite enumerable set of stack variables $X_1, X_2, \ldots$ and a finite set of registers $\{r_0, \ldots, r_n, \mathbf{sp}\}$.

security labels	$l, \mathbf{pc} \in \mathfrak{L}_{\mathbf{sec}}$
security types	$\sigma ::= \tau^l$
types	$\tau ::= int \mid \text{CODE}\langle \forall[\Theta]\Gamma \mid \mathbf{pc}\rangle \mid \langle \sigma_0, \ldots, \sigma_n \rangle$
register bank types	$\Gamma ::= \{r_1 : \sigma_1, \ldots, r_n : \sigma_n, \mathbf{sp} : \Sigma\}$
stack types	$\Sigma ::= X \mid \epsilon \mid \hat{\sigma} \cdot \Sigma \mid L \cdot \Sigma$
stack component types	$\hat{\sigma} ::= \sigma \mid ns$
type assignment	$\Theta ::= \cdot \mid X, \Theta$
heap types	$\Psi ::= \{\ell_1 : \sigma_1, \ldots, \ell_n : \sigma_n\}$
machine configuration types	$\Omega ::= [\Psi, \Gamma, \mathbf{pc}]$

Fig. 4. Types in SIFTAL

Since type expressions in SIFTAL may include annotations for security levels, we assume given a lattice $\mathfrak{L}_{\mathbf{sec}}$ of *security labels*. The least and greatest elements of this lattice are $\bot$ and $\top$, respectively. We use $\sqsubseteq$ for the lattice ordering and $\sqcup$ for the lattice join operation. *Security types* are types annotated with a security label (τ^l). The type of integer constants is int, while $\text{CODE}\langle \forall[\Theta]\Gamma \mid \mathbf{pc}\rangle$ is the type of code blocks. The type of tuple labels is denoted by $\langle \sigma_0, \ldots, \sigma_n \rangle$ or $\langle \overline{\sigma} \rangle$. The type of a code block $\text{CODE}\langle \forall[\Theta]\Gamma \mid \mathbf{pc}\rangle$ consists of the register context Γ, a *register bank type* that maps registers to types; the security label of the program counter $(\mathbf{pc})$; and a type assignment (Θ) of stack type variables that binds all free stack variables in Γ. *Execution stack types* (Σ) are sequences of stack component types: security types, nonsense types, and code labels. The nonsense type is used when allocating space on the stack. Letters α, α_i are used for stack component types. We use $FV(\Sigma)$ for the free variables in Σ (and similarly for the free variables in security types, code blocks, etc.). A *heap type* (Ψ) is a mapping from

machine configuration	$\Pi ::= (H, R, B)$
heap	$H ::= \{\ell_1 : h_1, \ldots, \ell_n : h_n\}$
heap labels	$\ell ::= p \mid L$
heap values	$h ::= \langle w, \ldots, w \rangle \mid \mathrm{CODE}\langle \forall[\Theta]\Gamma \mid \mathbf{pc}\rangle^l.B$
register bank	$R ::= \{r_1 : w_1, \ldots, r_n : w_n, \mathbf{sp} : S\}$
code blocks	$B ::= \mathtt{halt} \mid \mathtt{jmp}\ v \mid \mathtt{jmpJP}\ L[\Sigma] \mid \iota; B$
instructions	$\iota ::= aop\ r_d, r_s, v \mid \mathtt{bnz}\ r, v \mid \mathtt{mov}\ r, v \mid \mathtt{ld}\ r_d, r_s[i]$
	$\quad \mathtt{st}\ r_d[i], r_s \mid \mathtt{pushJP}\ L \mid \mathtt{salloc}\ i \mid \mathtt{sfree}\ i$
	$\quad \mathtt{sld}\ r_d, \mathbf{sp}[i] \mid \mathtt{sst}\ \mathbf{sp}[i], r_s$
arithmetic operations	$aop ::= \mathtt{add} \mid \mathtt{sub} \mid \mathtt{mul}$
operands	$v ::= r \mid w \mid v[\Sigma]$
word values	$w ::= i \mid p \mid L \mid w[\Sigma]$
stack component values	$\hat{w} ::= w \mid ns$
stack	$S ::= \epsilon \mid \hat{w} \cdot S$

Fig. 5. Syntax of SIFTAL

heap addresses to security types. We assume that Ψ maps code block security types to code labels L and tuple security types to tuple pointers p.

A *machine configuration* is a tuple (H, R, B), where H is the *heap* (mapping heap labels to heap values), R is a *register bank* (mapping registers to word values), and B is the currently executing *code block*. A heap label ℓ is either a code label L or a tuple label p. A heap value h is either a code block (annotated with a security type) $\mathrm{CODE}\langle \forall[\Theta]\Gamma \mid \mathbf{pc}\rangle^l.B$ or a tuple of word values $\langle w_1, \ldots, w_n \rangle$, also denoted $\langle \overline{w} \rangle$.

A word value is either an integer constant (i), a heap label $(p$ or $L)$ or a heap label followed by a series of stack types of the form $L[\Sigma_1] \ldots [\Sigma_n]$, (expressions of the form $p[\Sigma_1] \ldots [\Sigma_n]$ and $i[\Sigma_1] \ldots [\Sigma_n]$ are ruled out by the type system). The register bank is a finite set of registers r_i, including a designated stack pointer $\mathbf{sp}$ which points to the top of the stack. A stack is modeled as a sequence of stack components: either word values or the special "nonsense" value ns, used for newly allocated stack space.

Besides standard assembly instructions, SIFTAL has instructions to manipulate the execution stack (salloc, sfree, sst, and sld) and to handle the junction points (pushJP and jmpJP). Note that both jmp and jmpJP may instantiate the stack variables of the destination code. For example, jmp $L[\Sigma]$ instantiates the stack variable of code block L with Σ before jumping to it (cf. Sec. 2.3).

2.2   Type System

In order to present the type system of SIFTAL, we need to define some notation first: if $\Gamma = \{r_1 : \sigma_1, \ldots, r_n : \sigma_n, \mathbf{sp} : \Sigma\}$, then $Dom(\Gamma)$ is the set $\{r_1, \ldots, r_n, \mathbf{sp}\}$, and $\Gamma[r := \sigma]$ is the register bank type resulting from updating Γ with $r : \sigma$. We define $\mathtt{label}(\tau^l) = l$. We use $\Gamma\{X \leftarrow \Sigma\}$ for the result of substituting all free occurrences of the stack type variable X in Γ with Σ. A similar notation is used for substituting inside word values, operands, types, code blocks, etc. If Θ is a sequence of stack type variables $X_1, \ldots, X_n$ and $\overline{\Sigma}$ is a sequence of stack types

$$\boxed{\Theta \mid \Gamma \mid \mathbf{pc} \rhd_{\psi} B \text{ blk}}$$

$$\frac{\Theta \rhd \Gamma \text{ ok} \quad \Gamma(\mathbf{sp}) = Halt \cdot \Sigma}{\Theta \mid \Gamma \mid \mathbf{pc} \rhd_{\psi} \mathtt{halt} \text{ blk}} \text{ T\_Halt}$$

$$\frac{\Theta \mid \Gamma \rhd_{\psi} v : \text{CODE}\langle \forall [\cdot] \Gamma' \mid \mathbf{pc}' \rangle^{l'} \text{ opnd} \quad \Theta \rhd \text{CODE}\langle \forall [\cdot] \Gamma' \mid \mathbf{pc}' \rangle \le \text{CODE}\langle \forall [\cdot] \Gamma \mid \mathbf{pc} \sqcup l' \rangle}{\Theta \mid \Gamma \mid \mathbf{pc} \rhd_{\psi} \mathtt{jmp}\ v \text{ blk}} \text{ T\_Jmp}$$

$$\frac{\Gamma'(\mathbf{sp}) = \alpha_1 \cdots \cdots \alpha_n \cdot X \quad \begin{array}{c} \Theta \rhd \text{CODE}\langle \forall [\cdot] \Gamma' \{X \leftarrow \Sigma\} \mid \mathbf{pc}' \rangle \le \text{CODE}\langle \forall [\cdot] \Gamma[\mathbf{sp} := \Sigma'] \mid l \rangle \\ \Theta \rhd \Sigma \text{ ok} \quad \Gamma(\mathbf{sp}) = L \cdot \Sigma' \quad \Psi(L) = \text{CODE}\langle \forall [X] \Gamma' \mid \mathbf{pc}' \rangle^{l} \end{array}}{\Theta \mid \Gamma \mid \mathbf{pc} \rhd_{\psi} \mathtt{jmpJPL}[\Sigma] \text{ blk}} \text{ T\_Jmpcc}$$

$$\frac{\Theta \mid \Gamma \rhd_{\psi} r_s : int^{l_1} \text{ opnd} \quad \Theta \mid \Gamma \rhd_{\psi} v : int^{l_2} \text{ opnd} \quad \mathbf{pc} \sqcup l_1 \sqcup l_2 \sqsubseteq \mathtt{label}(\Gamma(r_d)) \quad \Theta \mid \Gamma[r_d := int^{\mathtt{label}(\Gamma(r_d))}] \mid \mathbf{pc} \rhd_{\psi} B \text{ blk}}{\Theta \mid \Gamma \mid \mathbf{pc} \rhd_{\psi} \mathtt{aop}\ r_d, r_s, v; B \text{ blk}} \text{ T\_Arith}$$

$$\frac{\Theta \rhd \text{CODE}\langle \forall [\cdot] \Gamma' \mid \mathbf{pc}' \rangle \le \text{CODE}\langle \forall [\cdot] \Gamma \mid \mathbf{pc} \sqcup l_1 \sqcup l_2 \rangle \quad \Theta \mid \Gamma \rhd_{\psi} r : int^{l_1} \text{ opnd} \quad \Theta \mid \Gamma \rhd_{\psi} v : \text{CODE}\langle \forall [\cdot] \Gamma' \mid \mathbf{pc}' \rangle^{l_2} \text{ opnd} \quad \Theta \mid \Gamma \mid \mathbf{pc} \sqcup l_1 \rhd_{\psi} B \text{ blk}}{\Theta \mid \Gamma \mid \mathbf{pc} \rhd_{\psi} \mathtt{bnz}\ r, v; B \text{ blk}} \text{ T\_CondBrnch}$$

$$\frac{\Theta \mid \Gamma \rhd_{\psi} v : \tau_1^{l_1} \text{ opnd} \quad \mathbf{pc} \sqcup l_1 \sqsubseteq \mathtt{label}(\Gamma(r)) \quad \Theta \mid \Gamma[r := \tau_1^{\mathtt{label}(\Gamma(r))}] \mid \mathbf{pc} \rhd_{\psi} B \text{ blk}}{\Theta \mid \Gamma \mid \mathbf{pc} \rhd_{\psi} \mathtt{mov}\ r, v; B \text{ blk}} \text{ T\_Mov}$$

Fig. 6. Typing rules for code blocks (part I)

$\Sigma_1, \ldots, \Sigma_n$, then we write $\Gamma\{\Theta \leftarrow \overline{\Sigma}\}$ for $\Gamma\{X_1 \leftarrow \Sigma_1\}\{X_2 \leftarrow \Sigma_2\} \ldots \{X_n \leftarrow \Sigma_n\}$, if $\{X_i, \ldots, X_n\} \cap FV(\Sigma_{i-1}) = \emptyset$, for $2 \le i \le n$.

The typing judgments that determine when a code block B is well-typed under type assignment Θ, register type Γ, program counter security level $\mathbf{pc}$ and heap type Ψ, are given in Figs. 6 and 7. A `halt` instruction is treated as a jump to a special junction point that halts the program execution. As a consequence, the stack type must have the label $Halt$ at the top. The judgment $\Theta \rhd \Gamma$ ok verifies that the register bank type is well-formed under type assignment Θ, that is, that the free variables in Γ are declared in the type assignment Θ (see [6] for a formal statement). In order for a `jmp` v instruction to be well-typed, the current register bank type must be compatible with that which is expected at the destination label denoted by v. This is enforced by means of the subtyping judgment. The subtyping relation is omitted here for reasons of space, but it includes the standard requirements that it be a partial order (on types, security types and register bank types) and uses width subtyping for register bank types. Moreover, in order to avoid illegal flows, a jump instruction can only jump to a code block with the same or higher security level. Therefore, the security level of the destination code label must be higher than or equal to the current level $\mathbf{pc}$ of the program counter together with the security label of the destination code label l'.

The `jmpJP` $L[\Sigma]$ instruction is similar, although not identical, to the `jmp` case. First of all, in order to jump to the next junction point L, it must appear at

$$\frac{\begin{array}{l} \Theta \mid \Gamma \rhd_\psi r_s : \langle \sigma_0, \ldots, \sigma_i, \ldots, \sigma_{n-1} \rangle^{l_1} \text{ opnd } \mathbf{pc} \sqcup l_1 \sqsubseteq \mathrm{label}(\sigma_i) \\ \mathrm{label}(\sigma_i) \sqsubseteq \mathrm{label}(\Gamma(r_d)) \qquad\qquad \Theta \mid \Gamma[r_d := \sigma_i] \mid \mathbf{pc} \rhd_\psi B \text{ blk} \end{array}}{\Theta \mid \Gamma \mid \mathbf{pc} \rhd_\psi \text{ ld } r_d, r_s[i]; B \text{ blk}} \text{ T\_Ld}$$

$$\frac{\begin{array}{l} \Theta \mid \Gamma \rhd_\psi r_d : \langle \sigma_0, \ldots, \sigma_i, \ldots, \sigma_{n-1} \rangle^{l} \text{ opnd } \Theta \mid \Gamma \rhd_\psi r_s : \sigma_i \text{ opnd} \\ \mathbf{pc} \sqcup l \sqsubseteq \mathrm{label}(\sigma_i) \qquad\qquad \Theta \mid \Gamma \mid \mathbf{pc} \rhd_\psi B \text{ blk} \end{array}}{\Theta \mid \Gamma \mid \mathbf{pc} \rhd_\psi \text{ st } r_d[i], r_s; B \text{ blk}} \text{ T\_St}$$

$$\frac{\Psi(L) = \mathrm{Code}\langle \forall [X] \Gamma' \mid \mathbf{pc}' \rangle^{l'} \quad \mathbf{pc} \sqsubseteq \mathbf{pc}' \quad \Gamma(\mathbf{sp}) = \Sigma \quad \Theta \mid \Gamma[\mathbf{sp} := L \cdot \Sigma] \mid \mathbf{pc} \rhd_\psi B \text{ blk}}{\Theta \mid \Gamma \mid \mathbf{pc} \rhd_\psi \text{ pushJP } L; B \text{ blk}} \text{ T\_Push}$$

$$\frac{\Gamma(\mathbf{sp}) = \Sigma \quad \Theta \mid \Gamma[\mathbf{sp} := \overbrace{ns \cdots \ldots \cdot ns}^{i} \cdot \Sigma] \mid \mathbf{pc} \rhd_\psi B \text{ blk}}{\Theta \mid \Gamma \mid \mathbf{pc} \rhd_\psi \text{ salloc } i; B \text{ blk}} \text{ T\_Salloc}$$

$$\frac{\Gamma(\mathbf{sp}) = \hat{\sigma}_0 \cdot \ldots \cdot \hat{\sigma}_{i-1} \cdot \Sigma \quad \Theta \mid \Gamma[\mathbf{sp} := \Sigma] \mid \mathbf{pc} \rhd_\psi B \text{ blk}}{\Theta \mid \Gamma \mid \mathbf{pc} \rhd_\psi \text{ sfree } i; B \text{ blk}} \text{ T\_Sfree}$$

$$\frac{\begin{array}{l} \Gamma(\mathbf{sp}) = \hat{\sigma}_0 \cdot \ldots \cdot \hat{\sigma}_i \cdot \Sigma \ \mathbf{pc} \sqcup l \sqsubseteq \mathrm{label}(\Gamma(r_d)) \\ \hat{\sigma}_i = \tau^l \qquad\qquad \Theta \mid \Gamma[r_d := \tau^{\mathrm{label}(\Gamma(r_d))}] \mid \mathbf{pc} \rhd_\psi B \text{ blk} \end{array}}{\Theta \mid \Gamma \mid \mathbf{pc} \rhd_\psi \text{ sld } r_d, \mathbf{sp}[i]; B \text{ blk}} \text{ T\_Sld}$$

$$\frac{\begin{array}{l} \Gamma(\mathbf{sp}) = \hat{\sigma}_0 \cdot \ldots \cdot \hat{\sigma}_i \cdot \Sigma \ \mathbf{pc} \sqsubseteq l \\ \Theta \mid \Gamma \rhd_\psi r_s : \tau^l \text{ opnd} \quad \Theta \mid \Gamma[\mathbf{sp} := \hat{\sigma}_0 \cdot \ldots \cdot \hat{\sigma}_{i-1} \cdot \tau^l \cdot \Sigma] \mid \mathbf{pc} \rhd_\psi B \text{ blk} \end{array}}{\Theta \mid \Gamma \mid \mathbf{pc} \rhd_\psi \text{ sst } \mathbf{sp}[i], r_s; B \text{ blk}} \text{ T\_Sst}$$

Fig. 7. Typing rules for code blocks (part II)

the top of the current stack type $\Gamma(\mathbf{sp})$. Second, the current register bank type must be compatible with the one expected at the destination code. In particular, this includes passing on the pending junction points which appear in the type of the current execution stack $\Gamma(\mathbf{sp})$. The register bank type expected at the destination label L is given by $\Psi(L)$, where all occurrences of the stack type X have been instantiated with Σ. In order to deal with the problem mentioned in the introduction related to stack polymorphism, we assume that junction points have only one free stack variable (which may of course occur any number of times in Γ', the register bank type required by the destination code block) and that the type of the stack $\Gamma'(\mathbf{sp})$ has an occurrence of X at the end (cf. condition $\Gamma'(\mathbf{sp}) = \alpha_1 \cdot \ldots \cdot \alpha_n \cdot X$). This allows us to relate the type instantiated for X, namely Σ, to the type of the current execution stack (Σ') and this gives us a handle on Σ when dealing with non-interference. Finally, since the program counter level of the junction point is to be "reset" to $\mathbf{pc}'$, the label l' of the type of L becomes irrelevant. This is addressed by requiring $l' \sqsubseteq \mathbf{pc}'$, a condition which is easily met by defining l' appropriately.

T_Arith types the arithmetic operators. Since the result of the operation depends on the operands and the current program counter level, the register that holds the result (r_d) is required to have the appropriate security level. The rule for mov is similar to T_Arith. T_CondBrnch, T_Ld and T_St are as expected (see [6] for further details).

The pushJP L type directive simply adds the code label L to the top of the stack *type* and types the rest of the code block under this new stack type. The condition $\mathbf{pc} \sqsubseteq \mathbf{pc'}$ makes sure that when the junction point L is invoked, the label of the program counter does not drop below the current level $\mathbf{pc}$.

Regarding salloc, we simply add i nonsense types to the stack type and then typecheck the rest of the code under this new stack type. The instruction that frees the top i components of the stack, namely sfree i, simply drops the top i component types of the stack type and then types the rest of the program. Two comments are in order here. First, the stack components that are freed must not be code labels. This would interfere with the linear nature of the junction points (the only directives that may manipulate junction points are jmpJP and pushJP). Second, no condition on the security labels of the freed components is required. This is a consequence of our approach to junction points which, for example, guarantees that if components are freed before jumping to a low-level junction point, then the freed components must have been secret (and hence not observable to the low-level user). See the High-Step Invariant Lemma (Lemma 2) for details.

The typing rules for sld and sst follow similar patterns to those discussed above. T_Sld requires that the stack component to be loaded be initialized (i.e. not have nonsense type). We remark that it should be straightforward to extend both T_Sld and T_Sst so as to allow loading stack components that are under junction point labels, although the details remain to be verified.

Due to lack of space, we do not give here the typing rules for word values and operands. In the case of word values, they assign $int^{\perp}$ to integer constants and look up the type in Ψ for code and tuple pointers. Also, there is a subsumption rule that allows subtyping reuse: a word value of type σ may always be used at any supertype σ'. Finally, a rule allows word values of the form $w[\Sigma]$ to be typed. Similar comments apply to the typing rules for operands. Two typing rules are presented for typing heap values: one for typing a tuple $\langle w_1, \ldots, w_n \rangle$ with a tuple security type $\langle \sigma_1, \ldots, \sigma_n \rangle^l$ componentwise, and another for typing annotated code blocks.

The typing rules for execution stacks (Fig. 8) need no further comment except for T_ExeSLbl. This rule states that junction points in the execution stack type may be ignored at run-time. Regarding heaps and register banks, the former is well-typed if each of the labels in its domain is mapped to well-typed heap values and the latter if each register different from sp is mapped to a well-typed word value. Finally, a machine configuration (H, R, B) is well-typed if the heap, register bank, current code block and execution stack are all well-typed.

2.3   Operational Semantics

The operational semantics of SIFTAL is shown in Fig. 9. Each rule establishes the semantics of an instruction on the current machine configuration. We say that Π *reduces* to Π' if $\Pi \longrightarrow \Pi'$. We use $\twoheadrightarrow$ for the reflexive, transitive closure of $\longrightarrow$. The expression $\hat{R}(v)$ is defined as: $R(r)$ if $v = r$, w if $v = w$, and $\hat{R}(v_1)[\Sigma]$ if $v = v_1[\Sigma]$. The jmp v instruction is executed by first looking up the destination

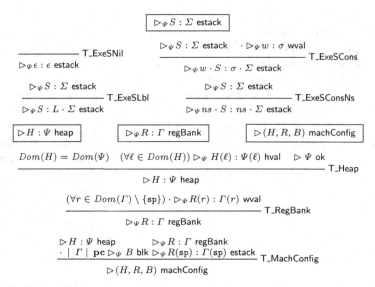

Fig. 8. Type rules for execution stacks, heaps, register banks and machine configurations

$$(H, R, B) \longrightarrow \Pi$$

where if $B =$	then $\Pi =$	
jmp v	$(H, R, B\{\Theta \leftarrow \overline{\Sigma}\})$ where $\hat{R}(v) = L[\overline{\Sigma}]$ and $H(L) = \text{CODE}\langle\forall[\Theta]\Gamma \mid \mathbf{pc}'\rangle^l.B$	OS_Jmp
jmpJP $L[\Sigma]$	$(H, R, B\{X \leftarrow \overline{\Sigma}\})$ where $H(L) = \text{CODE}\langle\forall[X]\Gamma \mid \mathbf{pc}'\rangle^l.B$	OS_Jmpcc
$aop\ r_d, r_s, v; B$	$(H, R[r_d := n], B)$ where $n = \hat{R}(v) \oplus \hat{R}(r_s)$	OS_Arith
bnz $r, v; B$	(H, R, B) where $\hat{R}(r) = 0$	OS_Bnz1
bnz $r, v; B$	$(H, R, B'\{\Theta \leftarrow \overline{\Sigma}\})$ where $\hat{R}(r) \neq 0$, $\hat{R}(v) = L[\overline{\Sigma}]$ and $H(L) = \text{CODE}\langle\forall[\Theta]\Gamma \mid \mathbf{pc}''\rangle^l.B'$	OS_Bnz2
mov $r, v; B$	$(H, R[r := \hat{R}(v)], B)$	OS_Mov
ld $r_d, r_s[i]; B$	$(H, R[r_d := w_i], B)$ where $\hat{R}(r_s) = p$ and $H(p) = \langle w_0, \ldots, w_i, \ldots, w_{n-1}\rangle$	OS_Load
st $r_d[i], r_s; B$	$(H[p := \langle w_0, \ldots, R(r_s), \ldots, w_{n-1}\rangle], R, B)$ where $\hat{R}(r_d) = p$ and $H(p) = \langle w_0, \ldots, w_i, \ldots, w_{n-1}\rangle$	OS_Store
pushJP $L; B$	(H, R, B)	OS_Push
salloc $i; B$	$(H, R[\text{sp} := \underbrace{ns \cdot \ldots \cdot ns}_{i} \cdot S], B)$ where $R(\text{sp}) = S$	OS_Salloc
sfree $i; B$	$(H, R[\text{sp} := S], B)$ where $R(\text{sp}) = \hat{w}_0 \cdot \ldots \cdot \hat{w}_{i-1} \cdot S$	OS_Sfree
sld $r_d, \text{sp}[i]; B$	$(H, R[r_d := w_i], B)$ where $R(\text{sp}) = \hat{w}_0 \cdot \ldots \cdot \hat{w}_i \cdot S$	OS_Sld
sst $\text{sp}[i], r_s; B$	$(H, R[\text{sp} := \hat{w}_0 \cdot \ldots \cdot \hat{w}_{i-1} \cdot R(r_s) \cdot S], B)$ where $R(\text{sp}) = \hat{w}_0 \cdot \ldots \cdot \hat{w}_i \cdot S$	OS_Sst

Fig. 9. Operational semantics

code label L in v, obtaining the destination code block from the heap and finally instantiating this code with the vector of stack types given in the operand. The rule for jmpJP $L[\Sigma]$ is the same as that of jmp v for $v = L[\Sigma]$. The remaining rules are self explanatory. Note that pushJP is a type directive: it has no effect at run-time. As a consequence, it could be erased once type checking has been completed. Finally, we would like to point out that the semantics of SIFTAL is exactly that of STAL, disregarding the malloc and pack instructions that are not treated in this work.

The operational semantics is sound with respect to the type system. If a typed machine configuration is not in a valid final state, then it can always progress towards one, as formalized by the Progress and Subject Reduction propositions. In order to formalize this, we use the notation $\rhd(H, R, B) : [\Psi, \Gamma, \mathbf{pc}]$ machConfig to mean that all of the judgments $\rhd H : \Psi$ heap, $\rhd_\Psi R : \Gamma$ regBank, $\rhd_\Psi R(\mathsf{sp}) :$ $\Gamma(\mathsf{sp})$ estack and $\cdot \mid \Gamma \mid \mathbf{pc} \rhd_\Psi B$ blk hold. A machine configuration Π is said to be *stuck* at type $[\Psi, \Gamma, \mathbf{pc}]$ if $\rhd \Pi : [\Psi, \Gamma, \mathbf{pc}]$ machConfig and Π is not of the form $(H, R, \mathtt{halt})$ with $\Gamma(\mathsf{sp}) = Halt \cdot \Sigma$ and there does not exist a machine configuration Π' such that $\Pi \longrightarrow \Pi'$.

Proposition 1 (Progress). *If $\rhd \Pi : [\Psi, \Gamma, \mathbf{pc}]$ machConfig then either there exists Π' such that $\Pi \longrightarrow \Pi'$, or Π is of the form $(H, R, \mathtt{halt})$ with $\Gamma(\mathsf{sp}) = Halt \cdot \Sigma$.*

Proposition 2 (Subject Reduction). *If $\rhd \Pi$ machConfig and $\Pi \longrightarrow \Pi'$ then $\rhd \Pi'$ machConfig.*

3   Non-interference

Non-interference is a semantic property that states that computed low security level values should not be affected by high security ones. Here, "low security" and "high security" are relative to an arbitrary, but fixed a priori, security level ζ that determines what an observer can see (*low security values*) and what he cannot (*high security values*). A low security value or typ) is thus one whose security level is less than or equal to ζ; a high security value or type is one whose security level is *not* less than or equal to ζ. The formalization of non-interference proceeds by defining a notion of indistinguishable machine configuration with respect to the observer (we call this ζ-indistinguishability) and then showing that given any two runs of a program that start at indistinguishable machine configurations, if they terminate[1] then they both reach indistinguishable machine configurations. These two issues are studied in this section.

3.1 ζ-Indistinguishability

An appropriate notion of ζ-indistinguishability for machine configurations requires taking into account each of its components, namely heap, register bank

---

[1] Termination sensitive information flow analysis is an active topic of research. However, it is not considered in this paper.

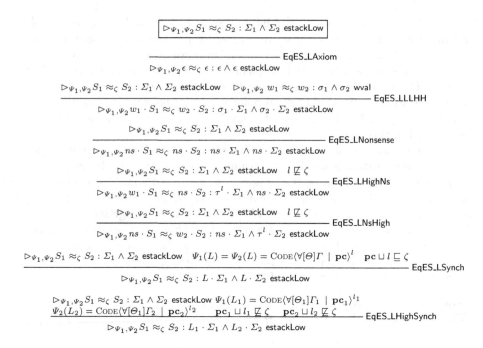

Fig. 10. Indistinguishable execution stacks at low level program counter

(including the execution stack) and currently executing code block. We begin our discussion with the execution stack. Clearly, when two runs of the same program are considered, they are seen to execute in lock-step fashion as long as no branching instruction appears. Moreover, the execution stack of each run is seen to have the same size and contain either the same low level values or high level ones. In this case we say that the stacks are *low level indistinguishable* and formalize this notion in Fig. 10. Once a branching instruction appears, say **bnz** **r,v**, the register **r** may either contain a low level value (in which case both programs are, once again, seen to execute in lock-step fashion) or it may be a high level value. In this last case, each run may take a different path (we talk about different *high level branches*) since this high level value may not coincide in both machine configurations. As a consequence, the execution stacks may begin to vary as a result of the execution of the subsequent instructions. In this case we say that the stacks are *high level indistinguishable* and formalize this notion in Fig. 11. However, note that before any further instruction is executed, the execution stacks of the two machine configurations are low level indistinguishable (cf. EqES_HAxiom in Fig. 11).

We have yet to clarify the meaning of $\triangleright_{\Psi_1,\Psi_2} w_1 \approx_\zeta w_2 : \sigma_1 \wedge \sigma_2$ wval, which relates to the indistinguishability of word values, used when defining low level indistinguishability of stacks. The naïve approach would be to state that two word values are low indistinguishable if σ_1, σ_2 are low security, $\sigma_1 = \sigma_2$ and $w_1 = w_2$, and high indistinguishable if σ_1 and σ_2 are high security. However, the presence

$$\boxed{\triangleright_{\psi_1,\psi_2} S_1 \approx_\zeta S_2 : \Sigma_1 \wedge \Sigma_2 \text{ estackHigh}}$$

$$\frac{\triangleright_{\psi_1,\psi_2} S_1 \approx_\zeta S_2 : \Sigma_1 \wedge \Sigma_2 \text{ estackLow}}{\triangleright_{\psi_1,\psi_2} S_1 \approx_\zeta S_2 : \Sigma_1 \wedge \Sigma_2 \text{ estackHigh}} \text{ EqES\_HAxiom}$$

$$\frac{\triangleright_{\psi_1,\psi_2} S_1 \approx_\zeta S_2 : \Sigma_1 \wedge \Sigma_2 \text{ estackHigh} \quad l \not\sqsubseteq \zeta}{\triangleright_{\psi_1,\psi_2} w \cdot S_1 \approx_\zeta S_2 : \tau^l \cdot \Sigma_1 \wedge \Sigma_2 \text{ estackHigh}} \text{ EqES\_HLeft}$$

$$\frac{\triangleright_{\psi_1,\psi_2} S_1 \approx_\zeta S_2 : \Sigma_1 \wedge \Sigma_2 \text{ estackHigh} \quad l \not\sqsubseteq \zeta}{\triangleright_{\psi_1,\psi_2} S_1 \approx_\zeta w \cdot S_2 : \Sigma_1 \wedge \tau^l \cdot \Sigma_2 \text{ estackHigh}} \text{ EqES\_HRight}$$

$$\frac{\triangleright_{\psi_1,\psi_2} S_1 \approx_\zeta S_2 : \Sigma_1 \wedge \Sigma_2 \text{ estackHigh}}{\triangleright_{\psi_1,\psi_2} ns \cdot S_1 \approx_\zeta S_2 : ns \cdot \Sigma_1 \wedge \Sigma_2 \text{ estackHigh}} \text{ EqES\_HLeftNs}$$

$$\frac{\triangleright_{\psi_1,\psi_2} S_1 \approx_\zeta S_2 : \Sigma_1 \wedge \Sigma_2 \text{ estackHigh}}{\triangleright_{\psi_1,\psi_2} S_1 \approx_\zeta ns \cdot S_2 : \Sigma_1 \wedge ns \cdot \Sigma_2 \text{ estackHigh}} \text{ EqES\_HRightNs}$$

$$\frac{\triangleright_{\psi_1,\psi_2} S_1 \approx_\zeta S_2 : \Sigma_1 \wedge \Sigma_2 \text{ estackHigh} \quad \Psi_1(L) = \text{CODE}\langle \forall[\Theta]\Gamma \mid \mathbf{pc}\rangle^l \quad \mathbf{pc} \sqcup l \not\sqsubseteq \zeta}{\triangleright_{\psi_1,\psi_2} S_1 \approx_\zeta S_2 : L \cdot \Sigma_1 \wedge \Sigma_2 \text{ estackHigh}} \text{ EqES\_HLeftSynch}$$

$$\frac{\triangleright_{\psi_1,\psi_2} S_1 \approx_\zeta S_2 : \Sigma_1 \wedge \Sigma_2 \text{ estackHigh} \quad \Psi_2(L) = \text{CODE}\langle \forall[\Theta]\Gamma \mid \mathbf{pc}\rangle^l \quad \mathbf{pc} \sqcup l \not\sqsubseteq \zeta}{\triangleright_{\psi_1,\psi_2} S_1 \approx_\zeta S_2 : \Sigma_1 \wedge L \cdot \Sigma_2 \text{ estackHigh}} \text{ EqES\_HRightSynch}$$

Fig. 11. Indistinguishable execution stacks at high level program counter

of stack polymorphism complicates matters. Consider the following SIFTAL program, where B is the current code block and $\sigma_X = \text{CODE}\langle \forall[\Theta]\{\mathbf{sp} : X\} \mid \mathbf{pc}\rangle^\perp$.

$$
\begin{array}{ll}
 & L1 \quad \text{CODE}\langle \forall[X]\{\mathbf{r1} : \sigma_X, \mathbf{sp} : X\} \mid \top\rangle^\top \\
B = \text{pushJP } L_{JP} & \quad\quad \text{jmpJP } L_{JP}[\Sigma_2] \\
\quad\quad \text{bnz } r, L1 & \\
\quad\quad \text{jmpJP } L_{JP}[\Sigma_1] & L_{JP} \quad \text{CODE}\langle \forall[Y]\{\mathbf{r1} : \sigma_Y, \mathbf{sp} : Y\} \mid \perp\rangle^\perp \\
 & \quad\quad \cdots
\end{array}
$$

Suppose that we have two runs of this program. Moreover, suppose that the initial machine configuration of each run satisfies the following conditions:

1. they both assign the program counter some (one) low level value,
2. they assign low level indistinguishable execution stacks to $\mathbf{sp}$, and
3. the register bank of the first configuration assigns 0 to the register r while the register bank of the other machine configuration assigns 1 to r. Note that these values are high indistinguishable.

At the bnz instruction one run shall jump to $L1$ while the other shall continue with the following instruction. At some point, both runs shall "synchronize" once they reach the junction point L_{JP}. Moreover, this junction point resets the program counter to a low security level, namely $\perp$. Note, however, that at this point in time the current machine configuration of each run differs in the type of $r1$, since X has been instantiated with different types (Σ_1 and Σ_2). Hence they cannot be low indistinguishable according to the aforementioned naïve definition.

As a result, when defining low indistinguishability of word values we must allow the types of these values (σ_1 and σ_2 in $\triangleright_{\Psi_1, \Psi_2} w_1 \approx_\zeta w_2 : \sigma_1 \wedge \sigma_2$ wval) to differ by instantiation of stack variables with different execution stack types. Furthermore, these execution stack types may not be arbitrary, they should also be low indistinguishable. For this reason, in order to formalize the definition of the judgment $\triangleright_{\Psi_1, \Psi_2} w_1 \approx_\zeta w_2 : \sigma_1 \wedge \sigma_2$ wval we first introduce the notion of low-indistinguishable security and stack types

$$\triangleright_{\Psi_1, \Psi_2} \sigma_1 \approx_\zeta \sigma_2 \text{ secTypeEq and } \triangleright_{\Psi_1, \Psi_2} \Sigma_1 \approx_\zeta \Sigma_2 \text{ stackTypeEq}$$

These notions are defined by simultaneous induction. Informally, types σ_1 and σ_2 are low indistinguishable if there is some security type σ and substitutions s_1, s_2 on stack variables such that $\sigma_1 = s_1(\sigma)$, $\sigma_2 = s_2(\sigma)$ and s_1 and s_2 assign low indistinguishable stacks to the same variables. The same applies to the notion of low indistinguishable stack types.

With this in place we can now complete our development of indistinguishability of machine configurations by defining the notion for word values, heap values, heaps, register banks and code blocks (Fig. 12). In the case of word values the judgment $\triangleright_{\Psi_1, \Psi_2} w_1 \approx_\zeta w_2$ wvalEq holds iff there exist substitutions s_1, s_2 and word value w such that:

1. $Dom(s_1) = Dom(s_2) = FV(w)$,
2. $w_1 = s_1(w)$ and $w_2 = s_2(w)$, and
3. for every $X \in Dom(s_1)$, $\Psi_1, \Psi_2 \triangleright s_1(X) \approx_\zeta s_2(X)$ stackTypeEq.

In Fig. 12 we write $Dom_\cup(\Psi_1, \Psi_2)$ as an abbreviation for $Dom(\Psi_1) \cup Dom(\Psi_2)$. Likewise, $Dom_\cap(H_1, H_2, \Psi_1, \Psi_2)$ abbreviates $Dom(H_1) \cap Dom(H_2) \cap Dom(\Psi_1) \cap Dom(\Psi_2)$.

Finally, we address ζ-indistinguishability of machine configurations. Both are required to be well-typed and their heaps and register banks ζ-indistinguishable. Furthermore, if their program counters are low level, then we are in the case that both programs are executing in lock-step fashion and, as a consequence, their program counters should have identical security levels, and both their currently executing code blocks and their stacks should be low indistinguishable. If their program counters are high level, then no condition applies to their currently executing code blocks, but their stacks must be high indistinguishable.

Definition 1 (ζ-indistinguishability of machine configurations). *Assume machine configurations $\Pi_i = (H_i, R_i, B_i)$ and machine types $\Omega_i = [\Psi_i, \Gamma_i, \mathbf{pc}_i]$, $i \in 1..2$. Then the judgment $\triangleright \Pi_1 \approx_\zeta \Pi_2 : \Omega_1 \wedge \Omega_2$ machConfig holds iff*

1. *$\triangleright \Pi_1 : \Omega_1$ machConfig and $\triangleright \Pi_2 : \Omega_2$ machConfig,*
2. *$\triangleright H_1 \approx_\zeta H_2 : \Psi_1 \wedge \Psi_2$ heap,*
3. *$\triangleright_{\Psi_1, \Psi_2} R_1 \approx_\zeta R_2 : \Gamma_1 \wedge \Gamma_2$ regBank,*
4. *(a) either $\mathbf{pc}_1 = \mathbf{pc}_2 \sqsubseteq \zeta$ and $\triangleright_{\Psi_1, \Psi_2} B_1 \approx_\zeta B_2$ code and $\triangleright_{\Psi_1, \Psi_2} R_1(sp) \approx_\zeta R_2(sp) : \Gamma_1(sp) \wedge \Gamma_2(sp)$ estackLow,*
    (b) or $\mathbf{pc}_1 \not\sqsubseteq \zeta$ and $\mathbf{pc}_2 \not\sqsubseteq \zeta$ and $\triangleright_{\Psi_1, \Psi_2} R_1(sp) \approx_\zeta R_2(sp) : \Gamma_1(sp) \wedge \Gamma_2(sp)$ estackHigh.

$$\boxed{\rhd_{\Psi_1,\Psi_2} w_1 \approx_\zeta w_2 : \sigma_1 \wedge \sigma_2 \ \mathsf{wval}}$$

$$\frac{l_1 \not\sqsubseteq \zeta \quad l_2 \not\sqsubseteq \zeta}{\rhd_{\Psi_1,\Psi_2} w_1 \approx_\zeta w_2 : \tau_1^{l_1} \wedge \tau_2^{l_2} \ \mathsf{wval}} \ \mathsf{Eq\_wval\_L} \qquad \frac{l_1 = l_2 \sqsubseteq \zeta \quad \rhd_{\Psi_1,\Psi_2} \tau_1^{l_1} \approx_\zeta \tau_2^{l_2} \ \mathsf{secTypeEq} \quad \rhd_{\Psi_1,\Psi_2} w_1 \approx_\zeta w_2 \ \mathsf{wvalEq}}{\rhd_{\Psi_1,\Psi_2} w_1 \approx_\zeta w_2 : \tau_1^{l_1} \wedge \tau_2^{l_2} \ \mathsf{wval}} \ \mathsf{Eq\_wval\_H}$$

$$\boxed{\rhd_{\Psi_1,\Psi_2} h_1 \approx_\zeta h_2 : \sigma_1 \wedge \sigma_2 \ \mathsf{hval}}$$

$$\frac{l_1 \not\sqsubseteq \zeta \quad l_2 \not\sqsubseteq \zeta}{\rhd_{\Psi_1,\Psi_2} h_1 \approx_\zeta h_2 : \tau_1^{l_1} \wedge \tau_2^{l_2} \ \mathsf{hval}} \ \mathsf{Eq\_hval\_H} \qquad \frac{l_1 = l_2 \sqsubseteq \zeta \quad \rhd_{\Psi_1,\Psi_2} w_i \approx_\zeta w_i' : \sigma_i \wedge \sigma_i' \ \mathsf{wval}}{\rhd_{\Psi_1,\Psi_2} \langle \overline{w} \rangle \approx_\zeta \langle \overline{w}' \rangle : \langle \overline{\sigma} \rangle^{l_1} \wedge \langle \overline{\sigma}' \rangle^{l_2} \ \mathsf{hval}} \ \mathsf{Eq\_hval\_tpl\_L}$$

$$\frac{l_1 = l_2 \sqsubseteq \zeta \quad \kappa_1^{l_1}.B_1 = \kappa_2^{l_2}.B_2}{\rhd_{\Psi_1,\Psi_2} \kappa_1^{l_1}.B_1 \approx_\zeta \kappa_2^{l_2}.B_2 : \kappa_1^{l_1} \wedge \kappa_2^{l_2} \ \mathsf{hval}} \ \mathsf{Eq\_hval\_blk\_L}$$

$\boxed{\rhd H_1 \approx_\zeta H_2 : \Psi_1 \wedge \Psi_2 \ \mathsf{heap}}$ holds iff for all $\ell \in Dom_\cup(\Psi_1, \Psi_2)$:

$\mathtt{label}(\Psi_1(\ell)) \sqsubseteq \zeta$ or $\mathtt{label}(\Psi_2(\ell)) \sqsubseteq \zeta$, implies $\begin{cases} \ell \in Dom_\cap(H_1, H_2, \Psi_1, \Psi_2), \\ \rhd_{\Psi_1,\Psi_2} H_1(\ell) \approx_\zeta H_2(\ell) : \Psi_1(\ell) \wedge \Psi_2(\ell) \ \mathsf{hval}. \end{cases}$

$\boxed{\rhd_{\Psi_1,\Psi_2} R_1 \approx_\zeta R_2 : \Gamma_1 \wedge \Gamma_2 \ \mathsf{regBank}}$ holds iff for all $r \in Dom_\cup(\Gamma_1, \Gamma_2) \setminus \{\mathsf{sp}\}$:

$\mathtt{label}(\Gamma_1(r)) \sqsubseteq \zeta$ or $\mathtt{label}(\Gamma_2(r)) \sqsubseteq \zeta$, implies $\begin{cases} r \in Dom_\cap(R_1, R_2, \Gamma_1, \Gamma_2), \\ \rhd_{\Psi_1,\Psi_2} R_1(r) \approx_\zeta R_2(r) : \Gamma_1(r) \wedge \Gamma_2(r) \ \mathsf{wval}. \end{cases}$

$\boxed{\rhd_{\Psi_1,\Psi_2} B_1 \approx_\zeta B_2 \ \mathsf{code}}$ holds iff $\exists s_1, s_2, B$ such that :

1. $Dom(s_1) = Dom(s_2) = FV(B)$
2. $B_1 = s_1(B)$ and $B_2 = s_2(B)$ and
3. for every $X \in Dom(s_1)$, $\Psi_1, \Psi_2 \rhd s_1(X) \approx_\zeta s_2(X) \ \mathsf{stackTypeEq}$.

Fig. 12. ζ-indistinguishability of word, heap values, heaps, register banks, code blocks

3.2 Noninterference Theorem

This section addresses the formulation and proof of the non-interference theorem, the main result of this work. As mentioned, we consider two runs of the same program that start off from indistinguishable machine configurations. Moreover, we assume that the initial security level of the program counter is $\bot$ and that the execution stack has the *Halt* code label at the top.

Theorem 1 (Non-Interference). *For $i \in \{1, 2\}$, given machine configurations $\Pi_i = (H_i, R_i, B)$ and machine types $\Omega_i = [\Psi_i, \Gamma_i, \bot]$, if these conditions hold:*

- $\Gamma_1(\mathbf{sp}) = Halt \cdot \Sigma_1$ *and* $\Gamma_2(\mathbf{sp}) = Halt \cdot \Sigma_2$,
- $\rhd \Pi_1 \approx_\zeta \Pi_2 : [\Psi_1, \Gamma_1, \bot] \wedge [\Psi_2, \Gamma_2, \bot] \ \mathsf{machConfig}$,
- $\Pi_1' = (H_1', R_1', \mathtt{halt})$ *and* $\Pi_1 \twoheadrightarrow \Pi_1'$, *and*
- $\Pi_2' = (H_2', R_2', \mathtt{halt})$ *and* $\Pi_2 \twoheadrightarrow \Pi_2'$,

then there exist machine types $[\Psi_1, \Gamma_1', \mathbf{pc}_1']$ and $[\Psi_2, \Gamma_2', \mathbf{pc}_2']$ such that:

$$\rhd \Pi_1' \approx_\zeta \Pi_2' : [\Psi_1, \Gamma_1', \mathbf{pc}_1'] \wedge [\Psi_2, \Gamma_2', \mathbf{pc}_2'] \ \mathsf{machConfig}.$$

The proof first considers one step reduction sequences and then weaves these together by means of an inductive argument on the length of the reduction sequences. Moreover, two kinds of one step reduction steps are considered, one where the program counter is low (*Low PC Lemma*) and one where the program counter is high (*High PC Lemma*). The proof of the Low PC Lemma does not present difficulties. It consists of showing that each step of the first machine configuration Π_1 can be mimicked by one step of the second machine configuration Π_2 such that ζ-indistinguishable machine configurations are reached.

Lemma 1 (Low PC Lemma). *Given machine configurations $\Pi_i = (H_i, R_i, B_i)$ and machine types $\Omega_i = [\Psi_i, \Gamma_i, \mathbf{pc}_i]$, $i \in 1..2$. Suppose $\rhd\Pi_1 \approx_\zeta \Pi_2 : \Omega_1 \wedge \Omega_2$ machConfig, $\mathbf{pc}_1 \sqsubseteq \zeta$ and $\mathbf{pc}_2 \sqsubseteq \zeta$, and $\Pi_1 \longrightarrow \Pi_1'$. Then there exists a machine configuration Π_2' and machine configuration types $\Omega_1' = [\Psi_1, \Gamma_1', \mathbf{pc}_1']$ and $\Omega_2' = [\Psi_2, \Gamma_2', \mathbf{pc}_2']$ such that $\Pi_2 \longrightarrow \Pi_2'$ and $\rhd\Pi_1' \approx_\zeta \Pi_2' : [\Psi_1, \Gamma_1', \mathbf{pc}_1'] \wedge [\Psi_2, \Gamma_2', \mathbf{pc}_2']$ machConfig.*

On the other hand, the key case in the proof of the High PC Lemma is when the reduction step $\Pi_1 \longrightarrow \Pi_1'$ lowers the level of the program counter by jumping to a junction point with low level program counter. A machine configuration Π_2' must be found such that $\Pi_2 \twoheadrightarrow \Pi_2'$ and such that Π_1' and Π_2' are ζ-indistinguishable. The main obstacle is how to guarantee that the execution stacks of Π_1 and Π_2, previously *high* indistinguishable and possibly of different sizes, are now *low* indistinguishable and of the same size. Since we started off with a low security program counter (cf. statement of Non-Interference Theorem) we know that the stacks of Π_1 and Π_2 have a common, low indistinguishable substack. The point is that we must make sure that this substack becomes the current stack when the junction point is jumped to. This is possible because junction points are part of the execution stack types. More precisely, when $\Pi_1 \longrightarrow \Pi_1'$ jumps to a junction point L, it must be the case that the type of the execution stack of Π_1 is of the form $L \cdot \Sigma_1$. Furthermore, from the fact that the program counter in the type of $\Psi(L)$ is low and $\rhd_{\Psi_1, \Psi_k} S_1 \approx_\zeta S_2 : L \cdot \Sigma_1 \wedge \Sigma_2$ estackHigh, we deduce that, $\Sigma_2 = ? \cdots \cdots ? \cdot L \cdot \Sigma_2'$ and $S_2 = w_1 \cdots \cdots w_m \cdot S_2'$, $m \leq n$, where the question marks "?" may either be junction points, nonsense types or security types. Moreover,

$$\rhd_{\Psi_1, \Psi_k} S_1 \approx_\zeta S_2' : \Sigma_1 \wedge \Sigma_2' \text{ estackLow} \tag{1}$$

must hold by the definition of the **estackHigh** judgment. The fact that these question marks are high level types is necessary and is guaranteed by the following definition and result:

Definition 2. *An execution stack type Σ is said to be ζ-topped in Σ', if there exist labels $L_1, \ldots, L_n$ (possibly none) and stack component types $\hat{\sigma}_{i,1}, \ldots, \hat{\sigma}_{i,k_i}$, $i \in 1..n$ (possibly none) such that:*

- $\Sigma' = \hat{\sigma}_{1,1} \cdots \cdots \hat{\sigma}_{1,k_1} \cdot L_1 \cdot \hat{\sigma}_{2,1} \cdots \cdots \hat{\sigma}_{2,k_2} \cdot L_2 \cdots \cdots \hat{\sigma}_{n,1} \cdots \cdots \hat{\sigma}_{n,k_n} \cdot L_n \cdot \Sigma$,
- $\Psi(L_i) = \text{CODE}\langle\forall[X_i]\Gamma_i \mid \mathbf{pc}_i\rangle^{l_i}$ *implies* $\mathbf{pc}_i \sqcup l_i \not\sqsubseteq \zeta$, *for all* $1 \leq i \leq n$, *and*
- $\text{label}(\hat{\sigma}_{ij}) \not\sqsubseteq \zeta$, *for all* $1 \leq i \leq n$ *and* $1 \leq j \leq k_i$.

Lemma 2 (High-Step Invariant). *For $i \in 1..k$, assume that machine configurations $\Pi_i = (H_i, R_i, B_i)$ and machine types $\Omega_i = [\Psi_i, \Gamma_i, \mathbf{pc}_i]$ are such that:*

1. *$\Pi_1 \twoheadrightarrow \Pi_k$,*
2. *$\triangleright \Pi_i : \Omega_i$ machConfig, $i \in 1..k$, and Ω_i is given by the Subject Reduction Theorem, for $i \in 2..k$,*
3. *$\mathbf{pc}_1 \not\sqsubseteq \zeta$, and*
4. *$\Gamma_k(sp) = L \cdot \Sigma_k$, for some L and Σ_k, is ζ-topped in $\Gamma_i(sp)$, for each $i \in 1..k$.*

Then all of the following hold: $\triangleright H_1 \approx_\zeta H_k : \Psi_1 \wedge \Psi_k$ heap, $\triangleright_{\Psi_1,\Psi_k} R_1 \approx_\zeta R_k :$ $\Gamma_1 \wedge \Gamma_k$ regBank, $\triangleright_{\Psi_1,\Psi_k} R_1(sp) \approx_\zeta R_k(sp) : \Gamma_1(sp) \wedge \Gamma_k(sp)$ estackHigh, and $\mathbf{pc}_i \not\sqsubseteq \zeta$, for all $1 \le i \le k$.

Thus, if we know that the reduction starting from Π_2 terminates, we obtain the desired result that at some point the junction point L is invoked by a machine state reachable from Π_2. At this point, according to (1), the machine configurations "synchronize" at a low security level program counter. The proof of the High PC Lemma proceeds by case analysis on the definition of $\Pi_1 \longrightarrow \Pi_1'$, using the High Step Invariant Lemma in the case that this reduction step is a jump to a junction point that resets the program counter to low security level.

Lemma 3 (High PC Lemma). *For $i \in 1..2$, consider machine configurations $\Pi_i = (H_i, R_i, B_i)$ and machine types $\Omega_i = [\Psi_i, \Gamma_i, \mathbf{pc}_i]$. Suppose $\triangleright \Pi_1 \approx_\zeta \Pi_2 :$ $\Omega_1 \wedge \Omega_2$ machConfig, $\mathbf{pc}_1 \not\sqsubseteq \zeta$ and $\mathbf{pc}_2 \not\sqsubseteq \zeta$, $\Pi_1 \longrightarrow \Pi_1'$, and Π_2 terminates. Then there exist a machine configuration Π_2' and machine configuration types $\Omega_1' = [\Psi_1, \Gamma_1', \mathbf{pc}_1']$ and $\Omega_2' : [\Psi_2, \Gamma_2', \mathbf{pc}_2']$ such that $\Pi_2 \twoheadrightarrow \Pi_2'$ and $\triangleright \Pi_1' \approx_\zeta \Pi_2' :$ $[\Psi_1, \Gamma_1', \mathbf{pc}_1'] \wedge [\Psi_2, \Gamma_2', \mathbf{pc}_2']$ machConfig.*

Finally, the proof of the Non-interference Theorem (Theorem 1) follows by weaving reduction steps whose departing machine configurations have a low or high security level program counter using the Low PC or the High PC Lemmas (Lemmas 1 and 3), respectively.

4   Conclusions, Related Work and Future Research

We present a TAL with a polymorphic execution stack, a type system enforcing secure information flow, and a proof of non-interference. The problems stemming from the absence of control flow constructs and the challenges raised by polymorphic execution stacks are addressed by including explicit junction points in types and introducing appropriate type directives (pushJP and jmpJP) that manipulate them. As an added benefit, we are able to ensure that junction points are treated as linear continuations and that pending junction points are passed on as obligations. Since pushJP is a type directive, it may be eliminated during execution, while jmpJP may be replaced by a standard jump instruction at runtime. The type system keeps track of two stacks: the execution stack type and the junction points stack. In general, two separate stacks cannot be combined into one; however, in this case the type system enforces a discipline that allows this combination, where a jump to a junction point L can only be done if L is at the top of the execution stack type.

Information flow analysis has been an active research area in the past three decades [22]. Pioneering work by Bell and LaPadula [4], Feiertag et al. [12], Denning and Denning [10, 11], Neumann et al. [21], and Biba [5] set the basis of multilevel security by defining a model of information flow where subjects and objects have a security level from a lattice of security levels. A subject cannot read objects of level higher than its level, and it cannot write objects at levels lower than its level.

Non-interference was first introduced by Goguen and Meseguer [13], and there has been a significant amount of research on type systems for confidentiality for high-level languages, including Volpano and Smith [24] and Banerjee and Naumann [2]. Type systems for low-level languages have been an active subject of study for several years now, including TAL [17], STAL [16], DTAL [25], Alias Types [23], and HBAL [1].

In his PhD thesis [20], Necula already suggests information flow analysis as an open research area at the assembly language level. Zdancewic and Myers [28] present a low-level, secure calculus with ordered linear continuations. This low-level calculus, like the calculus developed by Crary et al. [9], possesses high-level control flow structures (such as `if-then-else`) that simplify the analysis but require an extra, unanalyzed, translation to obtain a real low-level executable program. Moreover, none of these calculi includes a register bank or an execution stack. Barthe et al. [3] define a JVM-like low-level language with a heap and an operand stack. Instead of expressing the control dependence regions in the language, as in SIFTAL, this work assumes the existence of trusted functions that obtain such regions. Moreover, when a high branch is executed, the security level of all the elements on the stack is raised and is never lowered back, even when the execution returns to a low-security region.

We have recently learned from personal communication with Dachuan Yu about independent work on information flow analysis for TAL-c [26], a calculus similar in spirit to SIFTAL. Based on a preliminary manuscript we can identify differences in the definitions of equivalence of machine configurations, where, for example, their definition forces stacks to be of equal length, preventing the stack from being manipulated in a high branch. TAL-c has primitives to raise and lower the security level of the **pc** that delimit security regions, similar to our pushJP and jmpJP. However, the interaction of these primitives with stack type variables may potentially pull such variables beyond their scope, unless some stringent closure condition is required on typing contexts.

We are currently developing a type preserving compilation scheme from a high-level imperative language to SIFTAL, and studying unrestricted *register reuse*. The community's opinion is divided on whether registers are observable or not. If they are, then the reuse of a register to store data of lower security level may be seen as a leak of information, even if the data itself is not accessible. Although SIFTAL allows the reuse of registers, the security level of a register remains fixed throughout execution. Lifting this restriction is the subject of current research.

Recent developments [27, 8, 18, 19] argue that mechanisms enforcing the absence of illegal information flows are too drastic to be practical. They study high-level languages with *declassification*, a controlled form of sidestepping of confidentiality policies. A notion of declassification for TALs is required for type preserving compilation of such languages. However, this area remains unexplored.

Acknowledgments. We are grateful to Pablo Garralda, Healfdene Goguen, David Naumann, and Alejandro Russo for enlightening discussions. We also thank Joëlle Despeyroux and Dachuan Yu for comments on earlier drafts. This work was partially supported by the *NSF* project *CAREER: A formally verified environment for the production of secure software* – #0093362 and the Stevens Technogenesis Fund.

References

1. D. Aspinall and A. B. Compagnoni. Heap bounded assembly language. *Journal of Automated Reasoning, Special Issue on Proof-Carrying Code*, 31(3-4):261–302, 2003.
2. A. Banerjee and D. Naumann. Secure information flow and pointer confinement in a Java-like language. In *Proceedings of Fifteenth IEEE Computer Security Foundations - CSFW*, pages 253–267, June 2002.
3. G. Barthe, A. Basu, and T. Rezk. Security types preserving compilation. In *Proceedings of VMCAI'04*, volume 2937 of *Lecture Notes in Computer Science*. Springer-Verlag, 2004.
4. D. Bell and L. LaPadula. Secure computer systems: Mathematical foundations and model. Technical Report Technical Report MTR 2547 v2, MITRE, November 1973.
5. K. Biba. Integrity considerations for secure computer systems. Technical Report ESD-TR-76-372, USAF Electronic Systems Division, Bedford, MA, April 1977.
6. E. Bonelli, A. Compagnoni, and R. Medel. Information flow analysis for a typed assembly language with polymorphic stacks.
   http://www.cs.stevens.edu/~rmedel/siftalTechReport.ps, 2005.
7. E. Bonelli, A. Compagnoni, and R. Medel. SIFTAL: A typed assembly language for secure information flow analysis.
   http://www.cs.stevens.edu/~rmedel/techReport.ps, 2005.
8. T. Chothia, D. Duggan, and J. Vitek. Type-based distributed access control. In *Proc. of IEEE Computer Security Foundations Workshop*, Asilomar, California, 2003.
9. K. Crary, A. Kliger, and F. Pfenning. A monadic analysis of information flow security with mutable state. Technical Report CMU-CS-03-164, Carnegie Mellon University, September 2003.
10. D. E. Denning. A lattice model of secure information flow. *Communications of the ACM*, 19(5):236–242, May 1976.
11. D. E. Denning and P. J. Denning. Certification of programs for secure information flow. *Communications of the ACM*, 20(7):504–513, July 1977.

12. R. J. Feiertag, K. N. Levitt, and L. Robinson. Proving multilevel security of a system design. In *6th ACM Symp. Operating System Principles*, pages 57–65, November 1977.
13. J. A. Goguen and J. Meseguer. Security policy and security models. In *Proceedings of the Symposium on Security and Privacy*, pages 11–20. IEEE Press, 1982.
14. D. Hedin and D. Sands. Timing aware information flow security for a JavaCard-like bytecode. In *Proceedings of the First Workshop on Bytecode Semantics, Verification, Analysis and Transformation (Bytecode 2005)*, volume 141(1) of *Electronic Notes in Theoretical Computer Science*, pages 163–182, December 2005.
15. R. Medel, A. Compagnoni, and E. Bonelli. A typed assembly language for non-interference. In M. Coppo, E. Lodi, and G. M. Pinna, editors, *Ninth Italian Conference on Theoretical Computer Science - ICTCS 2005*, volume 3701 of *LNCS*, pages 360–374, Certosa di Pontignano, Siena (Italy), October 2005. Springer.
16. G. Morrisett, K. Crary, N. Glew, and D. Walker. Stack-based typed assembly language. In *Second International Workshop on Types in Compilation*, pages 95–117, Kyoto, March 1998. Published in Xavier Leroy and Atsushi Ohori, editors, *Lecture Notes in Computer Science*, volume 1473, pages 28-52. Springer-Verlag, 1998.
17. G. Morrisett, D. Walker, K. Crary, and N. Glew. From System F to Typed Assembly Language. *ACM Transactions on Programming Languages and Systems*, 21(3):528–569, May 1999. This is the expanded version of a paper that appeared in Twenty-Fifth ACM SIGPLAN-SIGACT Symposium on Principles of Programming Languages, pages 85-97, San Diego, CA, USA, January 1998.
18. A. Myers and A. Sabelfeld. A model for delimited information release. In *International Symposium on Software Security*, volume 3233 of *LNCS*, Tokyo, Japan, 2003.
19. A. Myers, A. Sabelfeld, and S. Zdancewic. Enforcing robust declassification. 7th IEEE Computer Security Foundations Workshop, 2004.
20. G. Necula. *Compiling with Proofs*. PhD thesis, Carnegie Mellon University, September 1998.
21. P. G. Neumman, R. J. Feiertag, K. N. Levitt, and L. Robinson. Software development and proofs of multi-level security. In *Proceedings of the 2nd International Conference on Software Engineering*, pages 421–428. IEEE Computer Society, October 1976.
22. A. Sabelfeld and A. Myers. Language-based information-flow security. *IEEE Journal on Selected Areas in Communications*, 21(1), 2003.
23. F. Smith, D. Walker, and G. Morrisett. Alias types. In Gert Smolka, editor, *Ninth European Symposium on Programming*, volume 1782 of *LNCS*, pages 366–381. Springer-Verlag, April 2000.
24. D. M. Volpano and G. Smith. A type-based approach to program security. In *TAPSOFT*, pages 607–621, 1997.
25. H. Xi and R. Harper. A dependently typed assembly language. Technical Report OGI-CSE-99-008, Oregon Graduate Institute of Science and Technology, July 1999.
26. D. Yu and N. Islam. A typed assembly language for confidentiality. Personal Communication, July 2005.
27. S. Zdancewic and A. Myers. Robust declassification. In *Proc. of 14th IEEE Computer Security Foundations Workshop*, pages 15–23, Cape Breton, Canada, June 2001.
28. S. Zdancewic and A. Myers. Secure information flow via linear continuations. *Higher Order and Symbolic Computation*, 15(2–3), 2002.

Romization: Early Deployment and Customization of Java Systems for Constrained Devices[*]

Alexandre Courbot[1], Gilles Grimaud[1], and Jean-Jacques Vandewalle[2]

[1] Laboratoire d'Informatique Fondamentale de Lille,
IRCICA/LIFL, Univ. Lille 1, CNRS UMR 8022, INRIA Futurs,
59655 Villeneuve d'Ascq Cédex, France
Alexandre.Courbot@lifl.fr,
Gilles.Grimaud@lifl.fr
[2] Gemplus Systems Research Labs,
La Vigie - ZI Athélia IV,
13705 La Ciotat Cedex, France
Jean-Jacques.Vandewalle@research.gemplus.com

Abstract. Memory is one of the scarcest resource of embedded and constrained devices. This paper studies the memory footprint benefit of pre-deploying embedded Java systems up to their activation using romization. We find out that the more the system is deployed off-board, the more it can be efficiently and automatically customized in order to reduce its final size. This claim is validated experimentally through the production of memory images that are between 10% and 45% the size of their J2ME CLDC counterparts, while using the J2SE API and being ready-to-run without any further on-board initialization. Embedded solutions like J2ME degrade the Java environment and API right from their specification, limiting their usage perspectives. By contrast, our romization scheme generates and specializes a custom-tailored Java API for embedded applications deployed in a full-fledged J2SE environment.

1 Introduction

Embedded and constrained devices programming is evolving towards more sophisticated and secure programming languages. In particular, strong efforts have been made during the last years to allow embedded applications to be written in Java. However, the low amount of memory and safety constraints of these devices make heavy runtime environments such as J2SE inapplicable to them. For these reasons, stripped-down versions of the Java environment have been defined, like Java 2 Micro Edition or Java Card.

Unfortunately, these special editions of the Java environment are incompatible with J2SE. For instance, Java Card does not support floating point numbers

---

[*] This work is partially supported by grants from the CPER Nord-Pas-de-Calais TACT LOMC C21, the French Ministry of Education and Research (ACI Sécurité Informatique SPOPS), and Gemplus Research Labs.

G. Barthe et al. (Eds.): CASSIS 2005, LNCS 3956, pp. 57–76, 2006.

and features a firewall that restricts access to methods and data. Also, the APIs of these editions define new packages and are thus not compatible with J2SE.

These incompatibilities and restrictions over the original Java environment break the Java gold rule *"compile once, run everywhere"*. J2ME and Java Card have been tailored in order to support a pre-defined range of applications. Therefore, they are unable to run standard Java applications which requirements go beyond their restrictions. For instance, J2ME CLDC doesn't provide the JDBC API, that offers a standard way to access databases. However, embedding a local database or database client on a small device makes sense for some businesses; but in order to provide Java derivatives that fit on a given range of embedded devices, a choice has to be made as to which parts of the API are kept.

Obviously, embedding Java into small devices such as mobile phones or sensors implies a degradation of the environment at some point. Anyway, even if the whole J2SE environment would fit into an embedded device, it would still be desirable to avoid embedding unused packages and features in order to save silicon and production costs. Providing a pared-down version of Java for these devices is therefore inevitable. But conversely to the J2ME and Java Card approaches, we support the idea that the specialization of the Java environment should not be imposed by a specification. Instead, it should be done on a per-case basis, according to the applicative domain of the Java programs that will run on it.

This paper is about a new deployment scheme that allows J2SE-compliant applications to be embedded into closed, constrained devices. To allow this, the Java API of the system is tuned and reduced according to the applications needs during an off-board deployment phase called romization. This phase offers a complete view of the deployed system to the customization tools, which can thus perform much more efficiently than classical library extraction tools.

The remainder of this paper is organized as follows: in section 2, we discuss the deployment process and the specifics of Java applications deployment for embedded devices. Section 3 describes romization, an off-board form of deployment suitable for embedded devices, and section 4 presents our romization architecture that allows the Java API to be tailored according to the applications that are deployed. We discuss experimental results and compare with related work in section 5, before concluding on our approach.

2   Deployment Schemes for Embedded Devices

Software deployment can take various forms and interpretations. This section presents a simple yet comprehensive model of deployment that maps the Java class loading process. We then observe the limitations of the Java class loading scheme for small and constrained embedded devices, and consider the existing solutions addressing this issue.

2.1   Application Deployment Model

The deployment process covers all the steps that bring a software component from a state where it is ready to be loaded (usually a software package) to a

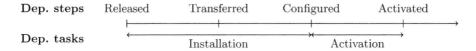

Fig. 1. The software deployment time-line. Before being used, a software component must go through installation and activation tasks. Note that the component starts being useful at step *Activated*.

state where it is ready to run on a particular environment. This includes the installation and configuration tasks, but also any kind of adaptation applied to the software being installed.

An exhaustive definition of the deployment process can be found in [1]. For the purpose of this paper, we only cover the deployment tasks that are needed to bring a software component up to a runnable state.

As shows figure 1, a software component needs to successfully go through several steps before being usable. After being *Released* (made available for installation by a software packager), a software component is *Transferred* into a target system and *Configured* in order to operate within its new environment. Put together, these two steps correspond to the *Installation* task. Finally, the component becomes operational by being *Activated* (*Activation* task). We name this state when a component is activated the *Useful Initial State* of the component, because it is from this state that its installation is complete and it can be used by the system without any other preparation.

The above-mentioned tasks have corresponding opposite operations: an activated component can be de-activated, then re-activated, and a component can be removed from the system by being uninstalled. The software packager can also choose to de-release the software by stopping its distribution and support.

This deployment model is mappable to the Java deployment scheme, which consists in loading classes into a Java virtual machine.

2.2 Java Applications Deployment Scheme

Several full-fledged software components deployment schemes are available for Java, like OSGi[2] or J2EE[3]. Because they all rely on the lower-level class loading mechanism, we center our deployment study on it.

Java Class Loading. The class loading process is one of the core mechanisms of Java. It can be seen as a classical software deployment solution that allows a software package (a Java class) to be deployed into an operational system (the Java virtual machine). We describe how the above-mentioned deployment tasks map with the class loading stages.

The Java Virtual Machine Specification[4] states that between the released .class file and the loaded and operational class, several distinct stages are passed over:

At first, a class loader is told to create a new class from a binary representation (the .class format). The class is read from a binary container (usually a file) and its internal representation in the JVM is created. This stage gives the state *LOADED* to the class, and corresponds to the transfer of the class within the virtual machine (*Transferred* step).

Then, the external references of the class are resolved during the linking stage. Linking can trigger the loading of several other classes that are referenced. This stage also verifies the bytecodes of every method for type-safety. The class is given state *LINKED* once this operation is finished, a state that is equivalent to the *Configured* step in our deployment model: the class is set up so that it can be used by the virtual machine. It should be noted, that the external references resolution can either be done once and for all during linking (*early linking*), or be delayed to be performed just-in-time when the bytecode is executed (*late linking*). Late linking can trigger the loading of classes during runtime, when an unlinked reference is met by the bytecode interpreter. Early linking prevents this, but at the cost of loading all the classes that are referenced in the code at once, regardless of whether the interpreter will actually meet them or not. On the contrary, late linking only loads the classes referenced if they are used at runtime. Desktop Java implementations run on comfortable machines and have all the necessary .class files at hand (either on disk, or from the network), so they usually adopt late linking. Embedded Java environments dispose of limited processing power, few storage space and intermittent (if any) network connections, and therefore tend to use early linking for their class loading model in order to avoid having to load classes during runtime.

Finally, the class is initialized by interpreting its static statements (or *class initializer*), which are mainly used to set the initial values of static variables. The class is *READY* (*Activated* step in our deployment model) once this stage is complete, and can be used thereafter. Contrary to loading and linking, the specification imposes a precise time for initialization to occur: right before the first *active use* of the class. The first active use is basically the first time the bytecode interpreter meets a reference to the class, for instance via a static method invocation or instance creation.

The figure 2 shows the mapping between the deployment and Java class loading steps.

Dep. steps   Released   Transferred   Configured   Activated

Java steps   .class   LOADED   LINKED   READY

Fig. 2. Java class loading steps mapped to their counterparts in our deployment model

It is only when the class loading is entirely done (i.e., when the class has reached the state *READY*) that a class can actually be used by the virtual machine. Just as the *Activated* step for a component, the *READY* state corresponds to the useful initial state of a Java class.

Java System Initialization Phase. Similar to a class, the whole Java virtual machine follows a time-line, which begins at its invocation. The Java virtual

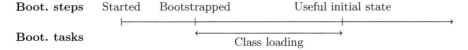

Fig. 3. The Java system time-line

machine first performs bootstrap activities to initialize itself. Then, in order to execute a program, it creates a Java thread and loads the class that contains the entry point of the program; typically, a static method named `main`. It is only once the entry point class reaches state *READY* that the system can start executing the `main` method and has reached its own useful initial state (figure 3).

We label the task performed before the virtual machine reaches its useful initial state the *system initialization task*. This definition embraces all the activities that are performed identically every time the virtual machine is invoked with the same program, before the program is actually run.

The system initialization task (especially class loading) is a quite heavy process, and can hardly (if at all) be performed by small and constrained devices [5]. Such devices have to turn to alternate class loading schemes.

Alternative Java Class Loading Schemes. The Java class loading process is so inadequate for embedded devices that research has been undertaken to provide smaller, easier to load class formats or loading schemes. EJVM[6] uses a client/server model to distribute the class loading burden and allow only useful methods of a class to be loaded. Several pre-loaded class formats have also been developed[7], and some have been made available on the market, like the `.cap` format of Java Card[8] or JEFF[9]. They define an almost ready-to-run format for sets of Java classes, where all the symbolic references are resolved and the constant pools are merged. In Java 2, Micro Edition, classes needed during runtime can also be pre-loaded into the virtual machine when the latter is being compiled. Such a process is called *romization*.

All these class loading schemes distribute the class loading process so that the hardest work has not to be performed in the target device. Romization in particular brings some interesting opportunities to efficiently tailor the system, that pre-loaded class formats cannot bring, as we will see in next section.

3   The Romization Process

Although widely used by the embedded devices industry, romization has evoked few interest from the scientific community so far. To our knowledge, no publication ever studied in depth or formalized romization. In this section, we define the general principles of romization and analyze the limitations of existing romization techniques.

3.1   Principles of Romization

Romization is the process by which a software system is pre-deployed by a specific tool (the *romizer*), running on a *deployment host*, for a *target device*. The

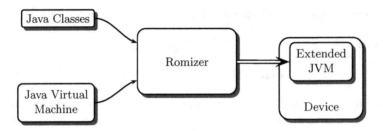

Fig. 4. The romization process applied to a Java virtual machine

inputs of romization are the bare system and a set of components to pre-deploy on it. From them, the romizer creates a memory image suitable for the target device that contains the system with the components already deployed on it. Romization can therefore be qualified an "in-vitro" form of deployment: the software is not deployed on its actual target, but rather inside a "test tube", before being transferred already-deployed to its runtime device.

Figure 4 illustrates the romization process applied to Java: the system is the embedded Java virtual machine, the components to deploy are the Java classes, and the resulting output is a virtual machine for which all the given classes are already loaded. This extended virtual machine can thereafter be transferred to the target device for being run.

The memory image produced by the romizer is completely ready-to-run and mappable to the physical memory of the device. It is intended to be placed in Read-Only Memory, hence the name *ROMization*, although other memories can be used. In the embedded devices industry, romization is used in order to instantiate the initial program of a device, that is invoked by the boot loader. The initial state of the system on the target device is the state of the system when it is dumped by the romizer (figure 5).

Ideally, the initial state on the device is as close as possible to the useful initial state. That way, the system is immediately active and useful when the device is powered on.

For Java systems, romization is mainly used to relieve the target device from loading the applications and system classes: as we said, this phase requires a lot of resources to be performed on a constrained device. Moreover, the class loading would unnecessarily be identically repeated every time the device is

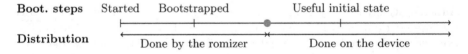

● Initial state of the system on the device

Fig. 5. Example distribution of the Java system initialization between the romizer and the target device. The romization process let the system be started on a deployment host before being transferred to the target device.

powered on, increasing startup times. Today's existing romization solutions for Java are designed to address this issue.

3.2   Available Romization Solutions

All the romization solutions studied hereafter are industry responses to the need of deploying Java applications on small and limited devices. They aim at preventing the embedded device to load the classes, by providing them already loaded within the embedded virtual machine.

Java 2 Micro Edition (J2ME). J2ME[10] is a configurable derivative of Java targeted at embedded devices with at least 128KB of memory. It features the Kilobyte Virtual Machine (KVM), a low-footprint Java virtual machine.

J2ME is divided into several *configurations* that reflect the differences between ranges of constrained devices. The Connected Device Configuration (CDC) is designed towards strong PDAs and set-box boxes, while the Connected Limited Device Configuration (CLDC) is more adapted for devices like mobile phones. The CLDC API is a strict subset of CDC API, which is itself a (non-strict) subset of the J2SE API. In addition to API restrictions, CLDC also limits the virtual machine capabilities by removing support for reflection, objects finalization and by limiting error handling.

J2ME also provides a romization tool called *JavaCodeCompact* (JCC), that is capable of pre-loading classes against the KVM so that they are immediately available upon invocation. JCC performs the loading and linking operations of the classes (figure 6). The classes initializers still have to be executed on the target system in order to finalize class loading, and there is no way to request the execution of code during romization.

As output, JCC produces a C file representing the loaded and linked form of the classes for the KVM. This file is thereafter compiled and linked with the KVM binary.

Fig. 6. The class loading activities covered by JCC

Java Card. As the tiniest flavor of the Java technology, Java Card[11] is targeted towards devices so limited that they cannot even support the lightest configuration of J2ME. As its name suggests, it is primarily designed towards smart cards. Although based on Java by concept, Java Card only gives a slight taste of it. The restrictions on the virtual machine are very drastic (optional 32-bits integers, no automatic memory collection, multithreading, 64-bits or floating point operands), and the high safety needs of smart cards applications led to the addition of new security mechanisms such as the firewall. The system API, which need to exploit the resources of these tiny devices with poor communication capabilities, has also very few in common with J2SE. Nonetheless, Java Card met success in the smart card industry thanks to its high safety, portability and ease of programming when compared to past smart card development toolkits.

The deployment of classes into a Java Card requires an additional step to be performed outside the device: the classes are pre-loaded into a .cap file in a nearly ready-to-run, yet portable across Java Cards, representation of the classes. This chewed-up form is then given to the device which has little more to do than verbatim-copying the class data to memory. For this reason, it is quite easy to produce a Java Card virtual machine with classes already romized in it.

The .cap file format contains classes that are in state *READY*: The class initializers are evaluated by the .cap production tool, and static variables are initialized on the card after a data array. However, and because of this, the static initializers in Java Card are limited to (arrays of) primitive compile-time constant values. One cannot, for instance, create new objects using the class initializers, which strongly limits the pre-deployment possibilities.

3.3   Evaluation of Existing Romization Solutions

Both J2ME and Java Card are good answers to the romization problem for their respective range of devices, as their commercial success witness. However, they are not going far in the deployment process regarding our definition of romization.

In section 2, we defined the state where the system actually start to run applications as the *useful initial state*. Our definition of romization in section 3.1 then states that the purpose of romization is to approach this state as much as possible outside the target device, so that the latter doesn't suffer from the cost of deployment. J2ME and Java Card approach the useful initial state by pre-loading classes against the virtual machine. The motivations behind this are to avoid embedding the heavy class loading mechanism if not necessary, to reduce the virtual machine startup time, and to avert the need of having a copy of the classes available (either locally or from a network).

However, by limiting their romization capabilities to these sole points, J2ME and Java Card are unable to do complete software pre-deployment. The deployment cost is indeed reduced by the class pre-loading, but nothing is done regarding higher-level components initialization or activation. For instance, it is possible to pre-load the classes of an OSGi component during romization, but not install or activate it in the OSGi sense. Moreover, class loading is not even completely covered by JCC, which leaves the classes initialization to the target device, and by Java Card, which considerably limits the class initialization capabilities. In the end, and although the most costly part of the deployment is done by the romizer, a non-neglectable part of the system and applications deployment must still be performed on the target device (figure 7).

This incomplete system initialization during romization has more consequences on the final system than the minor annoyance of a longer startup time. Indeed, it is common to apply customizations to the system being deployed

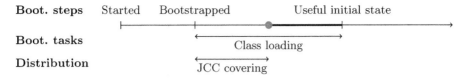

Fig. 7. The part of the Java system initialization covered by JCC. JCC only covers class loading partially, and leaves a consequent part of the initialization task to the target device.

during romization: JCC for instance can be given a list of the classes, methods and fields to romize. Elements not mentioned in this list are omitted in the system memory image. This selection allows the romized system to keep a reasonable memory footprint by not including useless elements of the system.

Let's consider that we want to romize the classical `HelloWorld` program, that uses the standard output stream (`System.out`) to display a constant string. The `System` class contains the standard output stream, but also refers to several other kinds of streams through `System.in` and `System.err`, to the system `Properties` and `SecurityManager`, and so on. Since the romizer works with early linking, all these references are recursively loaded when the romizer loads the `System` class. This means that for a single "Hello, World" displayed on the screen, one would need to load dozens of classes that are not used at runtime and occupy many kilobytes of precious memory. With JCC, the system producer can decide by hand to limit the romization of the class `System` to the static field `out`, disregarding useless references to other classes, fields and methods.

Determining which parts of the system and applications classes are needed can be done using a call-graph resolution algorithm[12], run from the entry points of the system. Many library-extraction tools[13, 14] use this technique to extract a minimal subset of a library, that will behave identically with respect to the original library for a given set of applications. Call graph analyzes are used to explore all the possible paths of a program and mark the classes, methods and fields that are likely to be accessed by it. A call graph analysis requires the knowledge of the program entry points, and give better results if it is provided static information about the system. For instance, knowing the initial values of some variables can help removing paths in the call graph, and thus keeping less elements. The romizer looks like a good place to perform call graph analyzes, because it has a complete view of the system being deployed: if the romizer were capable of going as far in the system initialization as creating the applications threads, it would know the entry points necessary to compute the call graphs. If it could initialize the classes and deployed software components, it would dispose of static information useful for further paths elimination and code simplification. Moreover, in addition to providing a great context for call graph analyzes, the romizer would also be the direct beneficiary of their results.

We can see that there is a great promise of system customizability for a romization scheme capable of handling deployment in a more complete manner. The next sections describes and evaluate a romization framework proposal that targets this purpose.

4   A New Romization Scheme

As we have seen, the romization solutions presented in the previous section limit their activities to part of class loading. By contrast, in order to increase the customization potential of the system, we need a solution that can not only handle the class loading completely, but also any software component layer that could be used on top of it. This way, the deployment could be covered in a more complete manner by the romizer, and the useful initial state of the system could effectively be approached off-board. Doing so would not only reduce the startup time, but more importantly would open the way to efficient call graph analyzes that allow to remove unused parts of the system and greatly reduce the final memory footprint.

4.1   System Initialization Task Distribution

The romization solutions studied earlier were simple class pre-loaders, that only perform a small part of the system initialization. In order to cover a larger range of initialization activities, a romizer has to include more features according to the additional operations it needs to support.

The following is a list of all the initialization tasks performed in order to reach the useful initial state of the system, and an evaluation of their applicability within a romizer:

Initializing the hardware: Since the romizer has no access to the hardware of the target device, it cannot perform this very first step. Anyway, the hardware loses its state when the device is switched off, so this operation needs to be done every time the device is powered on.

Bootstrapping the system: This operation consists in initializing the virtual machine internals in order to make it usable: for instance, setting up the heap or the bytecode interpreter. If the romizer can determine the suitable post-bootstrap system state, it can dump a binary image with these values already set up. Some system initializations may rely on the execution of Java code, especially if deep parts of the system are programmed in Java. In this case, the romizer must include a bytecode interpreter to execute them.

Loading, linking and initializing classes: This part is the only one covered by existing romization tools like JCC. However, without a bytecode interpreter, the classes cannot be initialized (which would involve executing the class initializers). Also, the class loading mechanism is often just a layer above which a real software component framework like OSGi relies. In this case, the components deployment is only partially covered by the romizer unless an execution environment is provided to cover the registration and activation of the software components.

Creating the threads: Once the classes of the applications are loaded, their threads can be created. The only requirements are properly initialized classes and objects creation capabilities from the romizer, so that a thread object can be created. This step is crucial for further system customizations: With the applications threads at its disposal, the romizer can infer information about the system that are useful for a customizer, like the call graph.

Running the threads: The Java threads might need to run until a given point before the useful initial state is reached. A common situation is a system for which the entry point is an OSGi implementation, which needs to be run in order to deploy the applications bundles. Executing the threads requires a full-fledged system to be performed safely: the romizer must have implementations for the native methods, and must be capable of running the Java code as if it was the target device itself.

In order to completely deploy the Java applications, the romizer thus needs to be able to perform runtime operations like executing bytecode or creating objects. A romization architecture covering the deployment activities we listed must therefore be based on a complete virtual execution environment.

4.2 General Architecture

We divide our romization architecture into three main parts that interact with each other (Figure 8). The *Environment* is a *virtual execution environment* (VEE), in which the system to romize is prepared. The *Dumper* takes the Java objects pool of the Environment as input and, as its name states, dumps them into a representation that is suitable to be used with the runtime environment. Finally, the *Builder* receives the output of the Dumper and creates the final system by assembling it with the runtime environment.

The Environment: A virtual execution environment that appears like a real Java runtime environment to the applications. It includes a class loader, a memory manager and a bytecode interpreter. The Environment allows the user to deploy and execute the system up to the point considered to be the "useful initial state". It also provides means to introspect the objects graph and to modify the objects of the system.

The Dumper: Its purpose is to create a memory representation of the objects contained in the Environment, correctly mapped with the physical memory of the target device. The Dumper must know about the device memory mapping (quantity, location, access means and properties of the different memories). It parses every object of the Environment and decides a destination memory for each of them according to placement policies. Then, it dumps a representation of the different memory sections and their objects that is passed to the builder for being linked with the runtime support layer of the target device.

The Builder: The Builder coordinates the actions of the two other romization parts with the building tools like the compiler to produce the memory image of the deployed system. It controls how the system is built according to the

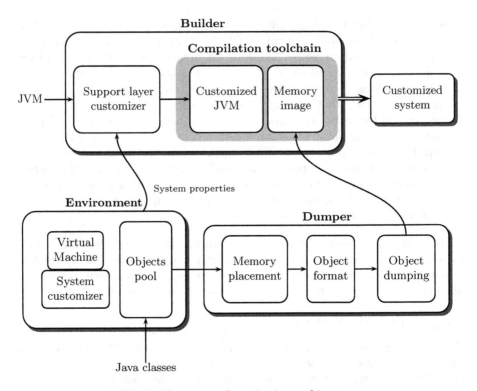

Fig. 8. The proposed romization architecture

target device: which compiler to invoke, with which options, which set of native methods to use, and so on. It also decides the parts of the runtime support layer to include and how to tune them according to system properties provided by the environment. For instance, if the environment asserts that the code it contains never allocates a single object during runtime, it is useless to include a memory manager in the generated system. The embedded bytecode interpreter can also be tuned in order not to support bytecodes that are absent in the code.

In a typical scenario, a user who wants to create a memory image of an embedded Java system that runs the `HelloWorld` OSGi bundle will proceed as follows: First of all, the building profile and memory mapping of the target device are given to the Builder and the Dumper. Then, the user asks the Environment to run the OSGi framework, by invoking the former with the latter as parameter, as with a regular Java runtime environment. The OSGi framework starts running into the Environment: the bundle can be loaded and initialized using the interaction means provided by the OSGi framework. The user then sets a "breakpoint" (similar to a debugger breakpoint) on the main method of the bundle (which marks the useful initial state of the bundle) and asks OSGi to activate the bundle. This action requests the execution of the main method, and causes the environment to freeze when meeting the breakpoint: the system has reached the state desired to be the initial state on the device. At this point, the bundle is totally deployed and the OSGi deployment facilities are no more used.

When the Environment has reached the initial state that the user wants for the target device, it can be dumped. But prior to doing so, it is opportune to take advantage of all the static informations that are provided by the fully-deployed system to customize it. The customization opportunities and their effects are described in detail in section 4.3. They affect the Environment by suppressing its useless parts, and by transforming some objects (for instance, objects for which an unused field can be removed, or methods that have been specialized to their calling context). The customized system also provides information to the Builder, like which classes are to be eventually included in the memory image, or which bytecodes are used (for tuning the embedded bytecode interpreter).

This final Environment state is given to the Dumper which, using the memory layout provided earlier and its memory placement policies, creates the memory image of the Environment objects, correctly spread between the different memories of the target device. It is then up to the Builder to tune the hardware support layer according to the Environment properties, and to compile the necessary part of the support layer along with the memory image given by the Dumper. The result of the compilation process is the ready-to-run memory image of the embedded system, at the state it had when the Environment was given to the Dumper. This memory image is finally burnt on the physical memory of the target device. When powered on, the target device immediately executes the main method of the `HelloWorld` bundle that has been deployed, as it simply continues the execution of the system from its final state within the Environment.

It should be noted that not all system states are safely dumpable. Typically, it has no purpose to dump states that contain non-serializable objects like opened network sockets or file descriptors.

The next subsection looks at the customization opportunities before the objects are passed to the dumper.

4.3   Customization Opportunities

As stated in the previous subsection and on figure 8, there are two kinds of customizations that can be performed on the romized system:

1. The customization of the Environment, done by tailoring or suppressing some of its objects,
2. The runtime virtual machine customization, done by the Builder, that selects and tailors the parts of the support layer to keep according to the Environment properties.

They are to be performed in the given order, since tailoring the Environment might influence on how the runtime virtual machine is to be customized. The customization of the virtual machine is planned for future work, we are concentrating in the present article on the customizations applied to the Environment.

Customization of the Environment occurs right before its objects are given to the Dumper: when the frozen system has reached its initial state on the device. The customizer figures out a transformation of the Environment that will perform the further execution of the system identically with respect to the original Environment, but is optimized for size and performance. The customization process starts by a call graph analysis from the current threads states to mark all the possible paths the embedded bytecode interpreter could go through. The advanced deployment state of the system helps removing unreachable paths: first, the call graph runs on live stacks, which contain objects of known type and known value. This allows, for instance, to resolve virtual methods invocations[15, 16]. Moreover, at the time the system is running, we have many instantiated static objects that won't change during the program execution, which allows their values to be inlined.

The call graph obtained also gives information about which classes, methods and fields are potentially needed by the program. All the fields, methods and classes not referenced in this call graph can safely be removed from the Environment, unless they are to be called later by dynamically loaded classes (in this case, the call graph can be completed with a list of "potential" entry points). The call graph can actually tell much more than just which objects are reached by the program flow: it can also provide additional information about the objects, like whether they may be written or not. Such information is useful for the placement manager of the Dumper to determine the destination memory of objects (objects that are never written can safely be placed in Read-Only Memory).

A second customization pass is then run on the remaining objects, in order to tailor them for their runtime usage. The most frequently concerned objects are Java methods, which can be simplified using partial evaluation with the static information of the Environment. For our `HelloWorld` example, the method `println` is only called from one context, with a static argument: it can therefore be specialized for this unique usage, and the string argument can be removed. Following the same principle, variables can be replaced by constants where applicable, conditionals on known values can be removed, virtual methods call can be turned into static ones, and so on.

Finally, decisions may be taken as to how the objects are to be outputted by the Dumper. Java methods which are found out to be critical (either by the code analyzer or the user) can be compiled into native code by an ahead-of-time compiler for maximum efficiency, at the cost of a larger memory footprint. The compiler can take advantage of all the static informations gathered during the call graph analysis to optimize the code, like omitting runtime exceptions checks for proven sites.

All these customizations affect the deployed Environment and aim at producing the most compact memory image of the Java system tailored for the applications that are (or are to be) deployed on it. The efficiency of applying these customizations at activation time is evaluated in the next section.

5   Experimental Results

Our romization architecture has been implemented into the Java In The Small (JITS[17]) platform. This section evaluates our approach by measuring the memory footprint of the image generated by the Dumper (including all the Java objects of the system, loaded classes, methods, etc.) at different stages of the deployment process.

5.1   Methodology

The memory footprint generated by JITS has been evaluated on three benchmarks. The `HelloWorld` benchmark is the typical example of a minimal program which final memory footprint should be very low. `AllRichards` is a much bigger benchmark (78 classes) that simulates 7 different implementations of an operating system kernel task dispatcher. Finally, `Dhrystone` is a small benchmark made of a few classes, mainly used for integer performance evaluation. Its interest for our measurements resides in its memory allocations within the class initializers.

The customizations implemented in the Environment customizer are the removal of unreferenced objects, classes, fields or methods, and the modification of the classes structure to suppress entries for unused fields and methods. The call graph computer implements constant propagation and static class hierarchy analysis[18] in order to detect inapplicable paths. It also marks all the objects likely to be accessed during runtime.

The measurements are performed as follows: for each benchmark, the main class is loaded into the Environment. The class loader then resolves and loads all the necessary dependencies. After this, the system is brought up to the desired state, and dumped into a C file containing the definition of all its Java objects. This C file is thereafter compiled using GCC 3.4.3 for the i386 platform with optimization level 2, and stripped. The final measurement is the size of the stripped object file.

We compare our measurements obtained using JITS with the equivalent memory image generated by running JCC on the CLDC configuration of J2ME, version 1.1, including the standard CLDC API as well as the benchmark classes. The C file generated by JCC is compiled and evaluated using the same protocol.

The measurements performed on JITS cover, for each benchmark, the size of the memory image generated by the Dumper at the following stages of the system deployment:

Transferred. All the classes have state *LOADED*,
Configured. All the classes have state *LINKED*,
Activated. All the classes have state *READY*, and the benchmark thread is created (but not started). This stage is considered to be the useful initial state of the system for these benchmarks.

5.2   Results

Table 1 shows the sizes of the memory images generated by JITS at the different deployment stages, as well as the equivalent images generated by JCC.

Table 1. Sizes (in Kbytes) of the memory images generated by JITS and J2ME CLDC

Benchmark	JITS		
	Transferred	*Configured*	*Activated*
HelloWorld	307	242	11
AllRichards	410	321	70
Dhrystone	314	248	86

The column labelled *Transferred* shows the size of the system when all the classes necessary for the benchmark are in state *LOADED*. The size of all the bare .class files necessary for the benchmarks to load and run is of 636 Kbytes for HelloWorld, 1014 Kbytes for AllRichards and 664 Kbytes for Dhrystone. We can see that the loaded form of the classes is much lighter than the original .class files, mainly because many constant pool entries containing symbolic references can be discarded at that point, depending on the class loading mechanism used[19]. However, at this stage no static information is available that would allow the customizer to suppress objects.

Linking the classes together brings the system to state *Configured*. This stage leaves more constant pool entries unreferenced (those whose sole purpose is to give the symbolic name of references), which can be suppressed. Another beneficial side-effect of this state is that more system objects reach their final state. This stage, which is the stage at which JCC dumps the classes it loaded, gives us memory images of 242 Kbytes for HelloWorld, 321 Kbytes for AllRichards and 248 Kbytes for Dhrystone.

The *Activated* column gives the size of the memory dump obtained when going further in the deployment process: the classes initializers are executed by the Environment, and the applications threads are created. This allows the customizer to compute the call graph, remove useless objects, and tailor the Environment. The final size obtained for HelloWorld is 11 Kbytes: the minimalist semantics of the program leads to a system of minimal size. AllRichards displays a size of 70 Kbytes, of which 58 Kbytes are made of its many classes and methods. Since all the code of this huge program is executed at runtime, it is romized entirely; however, we found out that the amount of system classes kept in the memory image is almost as low as for the HelloWorld benchmark. Dhrystone's final 86 Kbytes may seem surprising when considering that its memory footprint for the others deployment stages is very similar to HelloWorld's. They are however understandable regarding the class initializers: this benchmark, amongst other smaller allocations, allocates an array of 65 Kbytes in its class initializers. If we disregard this dynamically allocated data, we find a size of 14 Kbytes for all the others objects of the system. Would the system have been romized earlier, this memory would anyway have been allocated by the device.

These results are very supportive to our initial claim: going further in the deployment process during the romization of the system provides all the information needed to tailor it efficiently. In particular, the customization process allowed us to get rid of the useless references in the J2SE API, and to obtain the fitting derivative of it for the benchmark being deployed.

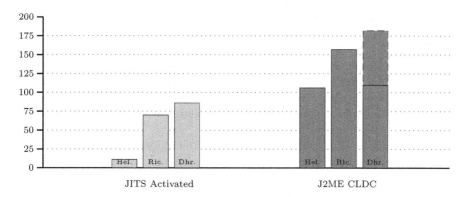

Fig. 9. Comparing the system size of JITS at state *Activated* with its J2ME CLDC counterpart

The graph of figure 9 compares the footprint of the memory images generated by JITS at state *Activated* against their J2ME CLDC counterparts. JITS generates closed memory images that are up to 90% smaller than their open J2ME equivalent: this is explained by the customization phase which tailors the API and benchmark code in order to extract and customize a minimal subset of it. The remaining Java API is finely adapted to the runtime needs, and therefore better-suited than the static J2ME API. It should be noted, that since J2ME doesn't initialize the romized classes, the memory allocated dynamically in the class initializers is not included in the dumped image. This detail is significant for the `Dhrystone` benchmark, so we represented this amount of memory, which is allocated on the target device, by the dashed part of its graph bar. We thus gain about 90 KBytes on J2ME for the `AllRichards` and `Dhrystone` benchmarks, while the J2ME systems retain the possibility to load classes.

Comparing our results at stage *Configured* against JCC is also interesting, because at this stage the classes have equivalent states on both systems. J2ME get better results, which is explained by several factors. First, JITS has many core parts of the system written in Java, which are therefore included in the memory image. For instance, the system class loader of JITS is written in Java, whereas the J2ME one is written in C and is therefore not counted in our measurements. The main reason, however, is that the system deployed by JITS uses the J2SE API, which has much more classes than J2ME and much more links between them. On the `HelloWorld` benchmark, JCC romized 99 classes, while loading and linking the `HelloWorld` class in JITS resulted in loading 142 classes. The customization phase, that frees the J2SE API from all the useless elements, can not be performed efficiently at this stage. Therefore, at this point of the deployment process, or for systems that need to remain open, using light APIs like J2ME is justified and indeed more efficient - besides, they have been specified to address these precise issues.

It is also pertinent to compare our results with classical library extractors. In[13], Rayside et al. obtained an extracted library size of 328 Kbytes for the HelloWorld program, using the J2SE API. While the entity measured (the unloaded bytecode) is not directly comparable with our results, the subset still comprehends 122 classes and one can predict that the loaded extracted library will still occupy between one or two hundreds of kilobytes in memory once loaded into the virtual machine. The library extractor operates on a non-deployed system and therefore has few clues about the possible runtime behavior of the system. On the opposite, the JITS customizer operates on a deployed system and knows all the types and values of entry points parameters (which are on the stack), as well as many static objects.

The conclusion of our experiments is that the more the system is deployed within the romizer, the more it can be tailored for its runtime needs. In particular, if the applications threads are available, the romizer is able to use this information to extract and customize the fitting subset of the system APIs that is necessary for runtime: in our experiments, the customization phase always leaded to a final memory image that is much lighter than its J2ME counterpart, while the romizer worked on the whole J2SE API. Contrary to J2ME, which restricts the system API right from its specification, our approach holds the API specialization until the deployment of the system, resulting in an per-case customization that is more adapted, and only comprehends the features useful for runtime. However, our approach forbids loading classes on a customized system that have not been evaluated (and therefore known) at the time of customization.

Our experiments also confirmed that, if the system is only partially deployed during romization, a dedicated API like J2ME clearly outperforms the J2SE API in terms of memory image footprint.

6   Conclusion

We presented a romization architecture capable of generating very small memory images of closed Java systems for applications written using J2SE. Experiments show that going further in the system deployment within the romizer allows the latter to perform very precise analyzes on the deployed Java system. These analyzes can then be used by a customizer to extract a custom-tailored subset of the large J2SE API for the applications being deployed. The resulting system is therefore broadly adapted to its runtime needs and shows a much smaller memory footprint than the equivalent system obtained with static solutions like J2ME, while preserving full J2SE compatibility for applications development.

Contrary to solutions like J2ME or Java Card, our architecture makes no initial assumption about the kind of applications that it will run, or the kind of device that will be used. Therefore, it imposes no upper-limit to the system capabilities: the generated system is the smallest possible Java subset that allows the deployed applications to run on the given device.

We see many perspectives from this work. They include the implementation of more customization tools (particularly code specializers), in order to study how they behave in the favorable romization environment. Another short-term study point is the efficient customization of the embedded Java virtual machine the romized applications are linked with. The system informations brought by the romizer could also probably be used in order to improve the results of other algorithms, like Worst Case Execution Time computation. Finally, an open problem is the extensibility of our solution. Our current implementation gives very small closed systems, yet it may be desirable to extend them.

Acknowledgments

The authors would like to thank Dorina Ghindici, who implemented the call graph analysis that allowed us to run our experiments.

References

1. A. Carzaniga, A. Fuggetta, R. S. Hall, A. van der Hoek, D. Heimbigner, and A. L. Wolf., "A characterization framework for software deployment technologies," Tech. Rep. CU-CS-857-98, Dept. of Computer Science, University of Colorado, April 1998.
2. OSGi Alliance, *OSGi Service Platform, Release 3*. IOS Press, Inc., 2003.
3. R. Searls, *Java 2 Enterprise Edition Deployment API Specification, Version 1.1*, August 2002.
4. T. Lindholm and F. Yellin, *Java Virtual Machine Specification*. Addison-Wesley Longman Publishing Co., Inc., 1999.
5. D. Mulchandani, "Java for embedded systems," *Internet Computing, IEEE*, vol. 2, no. 3, pp. 30 – 39, 1998.
6. D.-W. Chang and R.-C. Chang, "Ejvm: an economic java run-time environment for embedded devices," *Software Practice & Experience*, vol. 31, no. 2, pp. 129–146, 2001.
7. D. Rayside, E. Mamas, and E. Hons, "Compact java binaries for embedded systems," in *Proceedings of the 1999 conference of the Centre for Advanced Studies on Collaborative research*, p. 9, IBM Press, 1999.
8. Z. Chen, *Java Card Technology for Smart Cards: Architecture and Programmer's Guide*. Addison-Wesley Longman Publishing Co., Inc., 2000.
9. The J-Consortium, *JEFF Draft Specification*, March 2002.
10. Sun Microsystems, *J2ME Building Blocks for Mobile Devices*, 2000.
11. *The Java Card Virtual Machine Specification*, 2003.
12. D. Grove, G. DeFouw, J. Dean, and C. Chambers, "Call graph construction in object-oriented languages," in *OOPSLA '97: Proceedings of the 12th ACM SIGPLAN conference on Object-oriented programming, systems, languages, and applications*, (New York, NY, USA), pp. 108–124, ACM Press, 1997.
13. D. Rayside and K. Kontogiannis, "Extracting java library subsets for deployment on embedded systems," *Sci. Comput. Program.*, vol. 45, no. 2-3, pp. 245–270, 2002.
14. F. Tip, P. F. Sweeney, and C. Laffra, "Extracting library-based java applications," *Commun. ACM*, vol. 46, no. 8, pp. 35–40, 2003.
15. A. Diwan, K. S. McKinley, and J. E. B. Moss, "Using types to analyze and optimize object-oriented programs," *ACM Trans. Program. Lang. Syst.*, vol. 23, no. 1, pp. 30–72, 2001.

16. V. Sundaresan, L. Hendren, C. Razafimahefa, R. Vallée-Rai, P. Lam, E. Gagnon, and C. Godin, "Practical virtual method call resolution for java," in *OOPSLA '00: Proceedings of the 15th ACM SIGPLAN conference on Object-oriented programming, systems, languages, and applications*, (New York, NY, USA), pp. 264–280, ACM Press, 2000.

17. "Java In The Small." http://www.lifl.fr/RD2P/JITS/.

18. J. Dean, D. Grove, and C. Chambers, "Optimization of object-oriented programs using static class hierarchy analysis," in *ECOOP '95: Proceedings of the 9th European Conference on Object-Oriented Programming*, (London, UK), pp. 77–101, Springer-Verlag, 1995.

19. C. Rippert, A. Courbot, and G. Grimaud, "A low-footprint class loading mechanism for embedded java virtual machines," in *3rd ACM International Conference on the Principles and Practice of Programming in Java*, (Las Vegas (USA)), 2004.

Typed Compilation Against Non-manifest Base Classes

Christopher League[1] and Stefan Monnier[2]

[1] Long Island University
`christopher.league@liu.edu`
[2] Université de Montréal
`monnier@iro.umontreal.ca`

Abstract. Much recent work on proof-carrying code aims to build certifying compilers for single-inheritance object-oriented languages, such as Java or C#. Some modern object-oriented languages support compiling a derived class without complete information about its base class. This strategy—though necessary for supporting features such as mixins, traits, and first-class classes—is not well-supported by existing typed intermediate languages. We present a low-level IL with a type system based on the Calculus of Inductive Constructions. It is an appropriate target for efficient, type-preserving compilation of various forms of inheritance, even when the base class is unknown at compile time. Languages (such as Java) that do not require such flexibility are not penalized at run time.

1   Motivation

In most object-oriented languages, programmers factor their solutions over a hierarchy of *classes*. Since the classes in a hierarchy may appear in different compilation units, one question that the language designer (or implementer) must address is: how much information about a base class is needed to compile its derived class?

With its emphasis on efficient object layout and method dispatch, C++ requires *complete* information about the base class: the number, locations, and types of all its fields and methods. Indeed, it is because C++ depends on this information that a seemingly minor change to a base class triggers recompilation of all its descendents. Java is somewhat more flexible. To support binary compatibility, its class files are not committed to a particular object layout. A derived class depends only on the names and types of the base class fields and methods that it uses. Nevertheless, most Java implementations ultimately compile classes to lower-level code using the same layouts and techniques as C++.

A few modern object-oriented languages allow classes as module parameters (Moby [19], OCaml [31]) or as first-class values (Loom [4]). Other languages support more flexible forms of inheritance, such as mixins [27, 3] and traits [32]. If a base class is not available for inspection when a derived class is compiled, we say the base class is not *manifest*. Implementations of these languages use a *dictionary* data structure to map method and field names to their locations in the object layout. The dictionary may be applied at link time or at run time, as required by the language.

Here is a simple example in OCaml (although it could be expressed just as easily in Moby). We declare a signature for modules containing a `circle` class that implements

G. Barthe et al. (Eds.): CASSIS 2005, LNCS 3956, pp. 77–98, 2006.

three methods: center, radius, and area. The abstract type spec permits different implementations of this signature to have different constructor arguments.

```
module type CIRCLE =
sig type spec
    class circle : spec -> object
        method center : float*float
        method radius : float
        method area   : float
    end
end
```

Below, CircleBBox declares a class bbox that inherits from a (non-manifest) base class circle, overrides the area method (using a super call), and defines a new method bounds.

```
module CircleBBox = functor (C : CIRCLE) -> struct
    class bbox arg = object (self)
        inherit C.circle arg as super
        method area = super#area * 4.0 / pi (* area of bbox *)
        method bounds = let (x,y) = self#center in
            let r = self#radius in ((x-r,y-r), (x+r,y+r))
    end
end
```

To compile this functor, we must make do with relatively little information about the super class. We know it has the three methods specified in the signature, but not their positions nor whether there are other (hidden) methods, nor even the size of objects. We will return to this example throughout the paper.

Designing an effective *intermediate language* (IL) for compilers of these languages is challenging. Although method invocation is atomic at the source level, the IL should explicitly represent the dictionary search, method dereference, and (indirect) function call as separate operations. This way the operations may be independently optimized: combined, inlined, eliminated, or hoisted out of loops. To support such optimizations, Fisher, Reppy, and Riecke designed Links, a calculus for compiling and linking classes, based on the untyped λ-calculus. Its primitives can be combined "to express a wide range of class-based object-oriented features, such as class construction and various forms of method dispatch." [20]

In recent years, many researchers have based intermediate languages on *typed λ-calculi*. In addition to supporting type-directed optimizations, typed ILs are suitable for generating certified object code, such as typed assembly language [28] or proof-carrying code [29, 1]. Colby et al. [11] and League et al. [25, 26] have developed certifying compilers for Java, but more advanced class mechanisms are not yet well supported in this arena.

This paper presents a new intermediate language based on Links, but with a sound and decidable type system. We adopt the 'certified binaries' framework of Shao et al. [33], in which the types and proofs that govern computations are defined within the

Calculus of Inductive Constructions [13, 14]. Our language has the same primitive operators as Links, so it is an appropriate target for efficient, type-preserving compilation of various forms of inheritance, even when the base class is unknown at compile time.

In the next section, we review the primitives of Links and explain an untyped translation of our running example. Section 3 introduces the framework of our type language, and develops the semantics of LITL, our computation language. We revisit the example, now in a typed setting, in section 4. Section 5 explores techniques for extending the encoding to mixins and traits, and a discussion of related work appears in section 6.

2   A Review of Links

This section is a summary of the untyped Links representation by Fisher et al. [20]. The syntax of expressions appears in Fig. 1. Apart from the variables (x), abstractions $(\lambda x.e)$, and applications $(e\ e')$ inherited from the untyped λ-calculus, there are three new features: tuples $\langle e_1, ..., e_n \rangle$, dictionaries $\{l_1 = e_1, ..., l_n = e_n\}$, and natural numbers.

Tuples are indexed by natural numbers $(e\ @\ i)$. They also support functional update and extension. The expression $e\ @\ i \leftarrow e'$ produces a new tuple just like e, but with the value at offset i replaced by e'. The expression $e; \langle e_1, ..., e_n \rangle$ produces a new tuple containing all the values in tuple e followed by the values e_1 through e_n. Functional update will be used to implement *overriding*, while extension is helpful for *inheritance*.

Dictionaries map *labels* l to values. The expression $e\#l$ fetches the value corresponding to label l in dictionary e; this is a more expensive operation than fetching a value from a given offset in a tuple.

For the purpose of representing offsets (or *slots*) within tuples, we need only natural constants and addition. To write real programs, we would need more data types, conditionals, and recursive functions. These features are orthogonal, and omitted from the formal presentation for brevity (although we sometimes use them in examples). The primitive reductions in Fig. 2 may help to elucidate these operations. The original paper [20] includes more details, such as the definition of values (v) and evaluation contexts. We will recast these details in a typed setting in section 3.

The most general strategy for encoding objects is this: represent a method suite as a tuple of functions (also known as a virtual function table, or *vtable*), and use a

$$e ::= x \mid n \mid e_1 + e_2 \mid \lambda x.e \mid e_1\ e_2 \mid \langle e_1, ..., e_n \rangle \mid e_1\ @\ e_2 \mid e_1\ @\ e_2 \leftarrow e_3$$
$$\mid e; \langle e_1, ..., e_n \rangle \mid \{l_1 = e_1, ..., l_n = e_n\} \mid e\#l$$

Fig. 1. Links expression syntax

$$
\begin{array}{ll}
n_1 + n_2 \rightsquigarrow n_3 & \text{where } n_3 = n_1 + n_2 \\
(\lambda x.e)\ v \rightsquigarrow e[v/x] & \\
\langle v_0, ..., v_{n-1} \rangle\ @\ i \rightsquigarrow v_i & \text{where } i < n \\
\langle v_0, ..., v_{n-1} \rangle\ @\ i \leftarrow v' \rightsquigarrow \langle v_0, ..., v_{i-1}, v', v_{i+1}, ..., v_{n-1} \rangle & \text{where } i < n \\
\langle v_0, ..., v_{n-1} \rangle; \langle v'_0, ..., v'_{m-1} \rangle \rightsquigarrow \langle v_0, ..., v_{n-1}, v'_0, ..., v'_{m-1} \rangle & \\
\{l_0 = v_0, ..., l_{n-1} = v_{n-1}\}\#l \rightsquigarrow v_i & \text{where } l = l_i
\end{array}
$$

Fig. 2. Links reduction rules

let CircleBBox = $\lambda \langle sz, vt, dc \rangle$.
  let center_ind = dc#center **in**
  let radius_ind = dc#radius **in**
  let area_ind = dc#area **in**
  let dc' = { center=center_ind, radius=radius_ind, area=area_ind, bounds=sz } **in**
  let area_super = vt @ area_ind **in**
  let area = λ self. (area_super self) $* 4$ / **PI in**
  let bounds = λ self. **let** $\langle x, y \rangle$ = ((self @ 0) @ center_ind) self **in**
              let r = ((self @ 0) @ radius_ind) self **in**
              $\langle \langle x - r, y - r \rangle, \langle x + r, y + r \rangle \rangle$ **in**
  let vt' = (vt @ area_ind $\leftarrow$ area); $\langle$bounds$\rangle$ **in** $\langle sz + 1, vt', dc' \rangle$

Fig. 3. Translation of simple class generator into Links. We take several liberties with the syntax: **let** $x = e$ **in** e' is the obvious syntactic sugar for $((\lambda x.e') \, e)$, but we also permit pattern-matching on tuples.

dictionary d to map method labels to natural numbers, representing the corresponding slots in the vtable. Objects are tuples with a pointer to the vtable (shared by all objects created by that class). If the vtable is in the first slot (offset zero) of the object x, then the self-application expression for invoking a method named m would be $((x @ 0) @ (d\#m)) \, x$.

There is of course an important connection between the dictionary and the vtable in this representation, but they need not be packaged together. To compile a language (such as Moby or OCaml) in which base classes become known at link time, the dictionary would be a module parameter. All dictionary applications would be lifted to the top level of each module, so they occur at link time (i.e., functor application time). To compile Loom, in which classes are first-class values, a dictionary will need to be packaged with each object and passed around at run time. To compile Java, the dictionary is not needed at all, because the layout of the super class vtable is completely known at compile time.[1]

We can represent each class as a triple: the vtable and the dictionary, together with the *size* of the vtable. The size is needed so that when we extend non-manifest base classes, we can compute the offsets of new methods added to the vtable. We omit fields and constructors for convenience, but they pose no additional problems. A class that inherits from an unknown base class is therefore represented as a function that generates a new class triple from an existing one. The function is applied once the base class is provided. Figure 3 shows a rough translation of the example from section 1.

CircleBBox is a function whose argument is a triple representing a super class. We begin the function by looking up the offsets of all the methods in the super class, and then constructing the dictionary for the new class we are generating. It has one new method (bounds), so the new vtable will be larger by one slot. Next, we fetch the existing implementation of area from the super class's vtable vt; it will be called in the new implementation of area. In the implementation of bounds, we invoke two

---

[1] Here, we assume compilation to native code, which is done dynamically in many implementations. The observation is not true when producing JVM class files, which make extensive use of symbolic references and enjoy binary compatibility.

methods on self. We assume that an object is represented as a tuple with a pointer to its vtable at offset zero. In the final **let** expression, we create the new vtable using the functional update and tuple extension operators.

Fisher et al. [20] give further examples and justification for this encoding. Our goal in this paper is to achieve the benefits of Links in a typed representation. There appear to be two relatively independent problems here: (1) develop a sound but flexible type system for the Links primitives, and (2) reflect the various subtype relationships of the source language into the intermediate language.

Both of these problems are hard. In the first case, it is not just a matter of assigning standard types—such as those developed by Cardelli and Mitchell [7]—to dictionary lookup and tuple extension. The way the operators are used in Links, a given dictionary will map method names to offsets in some set of tuples. Although we know nothing about the size or structure of a tuple, we can use it anyway because some dictionary told us where to find the method we need. Subtle invariants govern how these data structures are linked to each other. To type-check Links, we must capture those invariants in the type system.

As for the second problem, Links is intended to be a common intermediate language for various class-based object-oriented languages. Such languages can have wildly different notions of subtyping and subsumption, from the simple name-based class and interface relationships in Java to explicit upward casts in OCaml to the matching relation and match types in Loom [4]. One thing working in our favor at the intermediate language level is that subsumption—where an object of one type may directly be treated as an object of another (super) type—is not strictly necessary. The compiler may insert explicit coercions that adjust the types of objects as needed—with no impact on the run-time behavior—as long as these coercions are proved sound.

3   A New Typed Intermediate Language

Shao et al. [33] introduced a framework "for explicitly representing complex propositions and proofs in typed intermediate and assembly languages." The set of types that classify computation terms is defined within the Calculus of Inductive Constructions (CIC) [14]. The semantics of the computation language can then incorporate propositions and proofs expressed in CIC.

As an example, Shao et al. define a language with an unchecked array access operator. One of its operands (apart from the array and the index) is a *proof* that the index is less than the length of the array. If both numbers are known at compile-time, generating these proofs as constants is quite easy. Otherwise, the if expression—used to check the index against the bound dynamically—provides proofs to its branches that relate to the semantics of its test expression. This language permits safe bounds check elimination.

The full power of CIC is available in generating the proofs, but they are (like types) compile-time phenomena only: once an expression is shown to be well-formed, the proofs and types may be erased and have no impact on the behavior and performance of the program.

The Calculus of Constructions [13] rests on the most powerful corner of the λ cube [2]. It can encode Church's higher-order predicate logic via the Curry-Howard isomorphism [23]. Extended with inductive definitions, it is the basis for the Coq Proof Assistant [12]. In this paper, we will use a typographically-enhanced variant of Coq 8 syntax.[2] In fact, the definitions in this paper are automatically extracted and sent to Coq for verification.

CIC is most conveniently expressed as a pure type system, where abstractions and applications at different levels are expressed in a uniform syntax, but classified under different *sorts*. The sorts of CIC include SET, PROP, and TYPE. We will use meta-variables τ, σ, κ, and f to range over CIC terms, where τ is usually used for terms corresponding to traditional types, κ for terms corresponding to traditional kinds, f for type functions, and σ for everything else. The dependent product type is written as $\Pi \alpha : \sigma_1 . \sigma_2$, or as $\sigma_1 \rightarrow \sigma_2$ if α does not appear free in σ_2. This type is introduced by abstractions of the form $\lambda \alpha : \sigma_1 . \sigma_2$ and eliminated by applications $\sigma_1 \, \sigma_2$. The calculus supports inductive definitions, constructors, and dependent elimination. We freely use the Coq `match` and `Fixpoint` syntax for eliminations, as well as other syntactic niceties like implicit arguments.

3.1 Syntax of Types and Terms

Our first task is to define a set of types for our computation language, LITL.[3] From the Coq library, we import the *option* constructor and the definition *nat* : SET of natural numbers in terms of zero (O) and the successor function (S). We will also need *sym* : SET to represent labels in the dictionary type. Symbols could be represented as natural numbers, or defined (as in the companion technical report [24]) as sequences of characters from some alphabet. Here is the inductive definition of types in LITL:

> **Inductive** *Ty* : SET $\equiv$
> | *arw* : $Ty \rightarrow Ty \rightarrow Ty$
> | *snat* : $nat \rightarrow Ty$
> | *tup* : $nat \rightarrow (nat \rightarrow Ty) \rightarrow Ty$
> | *dict* : $(sym \rightarrow option\ Ty) \rightarrow Ty$
> | *mu'* : Πk : SET. $(k \rightarrow Ty) \rightarrow Ty$
> | *all* : Πk : SET. $(k \rightarrow Ty) \rightarrow Ty$
> | *ex* : Πk : SET. $(k \rightarrow Ty) \rightarrow Ty$.
> **Definition** *mu* $\equiv$ *mu'* $(k \equiv Ty)$.

arw $\tau_1 \, \tau_2$ is the type of a function mapping values of τ_1 to values of τ_2. *snat* $\widehat{n}$ is the singleton type of the natural number n; that is, the value 0 has type *snat* O and the expression $1+1$ has type *snat* $(S\,(S\,O))$. *tup* $\widehat{n}\,f$ is the type of a tuple of size n where f is a type function which maps the index of each field to its type. *dict* f is the type of a dictionary where f is a type function that maps each label to the type of its corresponding value. *mu* f, *all* $\kappa\,f$, and *ex* $\kappa\,f$ are the *higher-order abstract syntax* encoding [30] of resp. the iso-recursive type $\mu x . f\,x$, the universally quantified type $\forall x : \kappa . f\,x$, and the existential type $\exists x : \kappa . f\,x$.

---

[2] With version 8, Coq moved to a weaker, predicative variant of CIC. We need the impredicative version, which is available with the command-line argument `-impredicative-set`.

[3] LITL Is Typed Links.

$$e ::= x \mid n \mid e_1 + e_2 \mid f \mid e_1 \, e_2 \mid e[\tau] \mid \langle e_1, ..., e_n \rangle \mid e_1 @ e_2 [\sigma] \mid e_1 @ e_2 [\sigma] \leftarrow e_3$$
$$\mid e; \langle e_1, ..., e_n \rangle \mid \{l_1 = e_1, ..., l_n = e_n\} \mid e\#l [\sigma] \mid \mathbf{cast}[\sigma] e \mid [\tau_1, e \rhd \tau_2]$$
$$\mid \mathbf{open} \, e_1 \, \mathbf{as} \, [\alpha, x] \, \mathbf{in} \, e_2 \mid \mathbf{fold} \, e \, \mathbf{as} \, \tau \mid \mathbf{unfold} \, e$$

$$f ::= \lambda x : \tau . e \mid \Lambda \alpha : \sigma . f$$

Fig. 4. LITL term syntax

To classify an unknown natural number, we hide its value using an existential type:

Definition *some_nat* : *Ty* ≡ *ex snat*.

(Thanks to Coq's implicit arguments feature, the k parameter of *ex* is inferred from the type of *snat*.) We can define syntactic sugar for the uninhabited *void* type:

Definition *void* : *Ty* ≡ *all* $(\lambda t. t)$.

Tuples are described by their size, and a (type-level) function that maps indices to component types. To specify the function, we will often build a list of types and pass it to the *ith* function:

Definition *ith* : *list Ty* → *nat* → *Ty* ≡ $\lambda l \, i. \, nth \, i \, l \, void$.

We are using *list* and *nth* from the Coq library. Lists are constructed from *nil* and *cons* (::), and *nth* has type $\Pi \alpha : \text{SET}. \, snat \rightarrow list \, \alpha \rightarrow \alpha \rightarrow \alpha$, where the α is implicit. We use *void* as the default case, for when the index is out of range. Pairs and triples are used fairly often in our encodings, so it is helpful to define more syntactic sugar:

Definition tup_2 : *Ty* → *Ty* → *Ty* ≡ $\lambda t \, u. \, tup \, 2 \, (ith \, (t :: u :: nil))$.
Definition tup_3 : *Ty* → *Ty* → *Ty* → *Ty* ≡ $\lambda t \, u \, v. \, tup \, 3 \, (ith \, (t :: u :: v :: nil))$.

Dictionaries are described by a (partial) function that maps labels to types. The function relies on the *option* : SET → SET type constructor of Coq, which is either *None* : $\Pi \alpha :$ SET. *option* α or *Some* : $\Pi \alpha :$ SET. $\alpha \rightarrow option \, \alpha$. Again, we specify the function using a list (in this case a list of pairs, representing a map) and a *lookup* function:

Definition *map* : SET ≡ *list* (*prod sym Ty*).
Fixpoint *lookup* $(m : map) \, (x : sym) \, \{struct \, m\}$: *option Ty* ≡
match m **with** $nil \Rightarrow None \mid (y, v) :: m \Rightarrow ifeq \, x \, y \, (Some \, v) \, (lookup \, m \, x)$ **end**.

The syntax of the type-annotated computation language appears in Fig. 4. It is essentially the same syntax as the untyped version in Fig. 1, but we add a few type operators and annotations.

The tuple selection and update operators now expect a CIC expression σ, representing a *proof* that the index is less than the size of the tuple. (We use $lt : nat \rightarrow nat \rightarrow$ PROP from the Coq library.) The labels in the dictionary construction and lookup syntax are CIC expressions of set *sym*. We also added standard type manipulation terms such as the type abstraction $\Lambda \alpha : \sigma . f$ and its corresponding type instantiation $e[\tau]$, existential package constructor $[\tau_1, e \rhd \tau_2]$ and its corresponding destructor (**open** e_1 **as** $[\alpha, x]$ **in** e_2), as well as recursive type folding (**fold** e **as** τ) and unfolding (**unfold** e). Finally, there is a cast expression (**cast** $[\sigma] \, e$). Here, σ should be a proof that $eq \, \tau_1 \, \tau_2$, where eq is the built-in (Leibniz) equality in Coq. Then, if e has type τ_1, the entire cast expression can be considered to have type τ_2. See the typing rules in section 3.3.

3.2   Dynamic Semantics

The dynamic semantics of LITL are defined in terms of a small-step reduction $\rightsquigarrow$. We distinguish a subset of the expressions as *values*. The primitive reduction rules are the only enlightening part; the definition of values and congruence rules are available in the extended technical report [24].

Primitive reductions $\boxed{e \rightsquigarrow e'}$

$$\frac{}{n_1 + n_2 \rightsquigarrow n_3 \quad \text{where } n_3 = n_1 + n_2} \ (1) \qquad \frac{}{(\lambda x{:}\_.e)\, v \rightsquigarrow e[v/x]} \ (2)$$

$$\frac{}{(\Lambda \alpha{:}\_.f)[\tau] \rightsquigarrow f[\tau/\alpha]} \ (3) \qquad \frac{}{\mathbf{cast}\,[\_]\,v \rightsquigarrow v} \ (4)$$

$$\frac{}{\mathbf{open}\,[\tau, v \triangleright \_]\,\mathbf{as}\,[\alpha, x]\,\mathbf{in}\,e \rightsquigarrow e[v/x][\tau/\alpha]} \ (5) \qquad \frac{}{\mathbf{unfold}\,(\mathbf{fold}\,v\,\mathbf{as}\,\tau) \rightsquigarrow v} \ (6)$$

$$\frac{}{\langle v_1, ..., v_n \rangle\, @\, i\,[\_] \leftarrow v' \rightsquigarrow \langle v_1, ..., v_i, v', v_{i+2}, ..., v_n \rangle} \ (7)$$

$$\frac{}{\langle v_1, ..., v_n \rangle; \langle v_1', ..., v_m' \rangle \rightsquigarrow \langle v_1, ..., v_n, v_1', ..., v_m' \rangle} \ (8) \qquad \frac{}{\langle v_1, ..., v_n \rangle\, @\, i\,[\_] \rightsquigarrow v_{i+1}} \ (9)$$

$$\frac{}{\{l_1 = v_1, ..., l_n = v_n\}\, \#\, l_i\,[\_] \rightsquigarrow v_i} \ (10)$$

3.3   Static Semantics

To specify the static semantics of this language, one more definition will be needed:

> **Fixpoint** *append* $(n : nat)\,(f\,g : nat \rightarrow Ty)\,(i : nat)\,\{\,struct\,i\,\} : Ty \equiv$
> **match** i **with** $O \Rightarrow (\mathbf{match}\,n\,\mathbf{with}\,O \Rightarrow g\,O \mid \_ \Rightarrow f\,O\,\mathbf{end})$
> $\mid S\,i \Rightarrow \mathbf{match}\,n\,\mathbf{with}\,O \Rightarrow g\,(S\,i)$
> $\qquad\qquad \mid S\,n \Rightarrow append\,n\,(\lambda x.f\,(S\,x))\,g\,i$
> $\qquad\quad \mathbf{end}$
> $\mathbf{end}.$

The judgments are $\Delta \vdash^{\mathrm{CIC}} \tau : \sigma$ from the type language and $\Delta; \Gamma \vdash e : \tau$ for term formation. The environment Δ maps type variables to their kinds, while Γ maps term variables to their types. LITL enjoys the subject reduction and progress properties; proofs are in the technical report.

Term formation $\boxed{\Delta; \Gamma \vdash e : \tau}$

$$\frac{\Delta \vdash^{\mathrm{CIC}} \Gamma(x) : Ty}{\Delta; \Gamma \vdash x : \Gamma(x)} \ (11) \qquad \frac{}{\Delta; \Gamma \vdash n : snat\,\hat{n}} \ (12)$$

$$\frac{\begin{array}{c}\Delta; \Gamma \vdash e_1 : snat\,\tau_1 \\ \Delta; \Gamma \vdash e_2 : snat\,\tau_2\end{array}}{\Delta; \Gamma \vdash e_1 + e_2 : snat\,(plus\,\tau_1\,\tau_2)} \ (13) \qquad \frac{\begin{array}{c}\Delta \vdash^{\mathrm{CIC}} \tau : Ty \\ \Delta, \Gamma, x{:}\tau \vdash e : \tau'\end{array}}{\Delta; \Gamma \vdash \lambda x{:}\tau.e : arw\,\tau\,\tau'} \ (14)$$

$$\frac{\Delta \vdash^{\mathrm{CIC}} \sigma : \mathrm{SET} \quad \Delta, \alpha{:}\sigma; \Gamma \vdash f : \tau \quad \alpha \notin \Delta}{\Delta; \Gamma \vdash \Lambda \alpha{:}\sigma.f : all\,(\lambda \alpha{:}\sigma.\tau)} \ (15)$$

$$\frac{\Delta;\Gamma \vdash e_1 : arw \; \tau' \; \tau \quad}{\Delta;\Gamma \vdash e_2 : \tau'} \quad (16) \qquad \frac{\Delta;\Gamma \vdash e : all \; \tau' \quad \Delta \vdash^{\text{CIC}} \tau : \sigma'}{\Delta;\Gamma \vdash e[\tau] : \tau' \; \tau} \quad (17)$$

$$\frac{\Delta \vdash^{\text{CIC}} \sigma : eq \; \tau_1 \; \tau_2 \quad}{\Delta;\Gamma \vdash e : \tau_1} \quad (18) \qquad \frac{\Delta \vdash^{\text{CIC}} \tau_1 : \sigma \quad \Delta \vdash^{\text{CIC}} \tau_2 : \sigma \to Ty}{\Delta \vdash^{\text{CIC}} \sigma : \text{SET} \quad \Delta;\Gamma \vdash e : \tau_2 \; \tau_1} \quad (19)$$

$$\frac{\Delta;\Gamma \vdash e : ex \; \tau \quad \Delta \vdash^{\text{CIC}} \tau' : Ty}{\Delta,\alpha{:}\sigma;\Gamma,x{:}(\tau \; \alpha) \vdash e' : \tau'} \quad (20) \qquad \frac{\Delta;\Gamma \vdash e : \tau \; (mu \; \tau)}{\Delta;\Gamma \vdash \textbf{fold} \, e \; \textbf{as} \; \tau : mu \; \tau} \quad (21)$$

$$\frac{\Delta;\Gamma \vdash e : mu \; \tau}{\Delta;\Gamma \vdash \textbf{unfold} \, e : \tau \; (mu \; \tau)} \quad (22) \qquad \frac{\Delta;\Gamma \vdash e_i : \tau \, \widehat{i} \quad \forall i < n}{\Delta;\Gamma \vdash \langle e_0,...,e_{n-1} \rangle : tup \; \widehat{n} \; \tau} \quad (23)$$

$$\frac{\Delta;\Gamma \vdash e_1 : tup \; \sigma_1 \; \tau_1 \quad \Delta;\Gamma \vdash e_2 : snat \; \sigma_2 \quad \Delta \vdash^{\text{CIC}} \sigma : lt \; \sigma_2 \; \sigma_1}{\Delta;\Gamma \vdash e_1 @ e_2 [\sigma] : \tau_1 \; \sigma_2} \quad (24)$$

$$\frac{\Delta;\Gamma \vdash e_1 : tup \; \sigma_1 \; \tau_1 \quad \Delta;\Gamma \vdash e_2 : snat \; \sigma_2}{\Delta;\Gamma \vdash e_3 : \tau_1 \; \sigma_2 \quad \Delta \vdash^{\text{CIC}} \sigma : lt \; \sigma_2 \; \sigma_1} \quad (25)$$
$$\frac{}{\Delta;\Gamma \vdash e_1 @ e_2 [\sigma] \leftarrow e_3 : tup \; \sigma_1 \; \tau_1}$$

$$\frac{\Delta;\Gamma \vdash e : tup \; \tau_1 \; \tau_2 \quad \Delta;\Gamma \vdash \langle e_1,...,e_n \rangle : tup \; \tau'_1 \; \tau'_2}{\Delta;\Gamma \vdash e;\langle e_1,...,e_n \rangle : tup \; (plus \; \tau_1 \; \tau'_1) \; (append \; \tau_1 \; \tau_2 \; \tau'_2)} \quad (26)$$

$$\frac{\Delta;\Gamma \vdash e_i : \tau_i \quad \wedge \quad \tau \, \widehat{l_i} = Some \; \tau_i \quad \forall i < n}{l \notin l \Rightarrow \tau \, \widehat{l} = None} \quad (27)$$
$$\frac{}{\Delta;\Gamma \vdash \{l_0 = e_0,...,l_{n-1} = e_{n-1}\} : dict \; \tau}$$

$$\frac{\Delta;\Gamma \vdash e : dict \; \tau}{\Delta \vdash^{\text{CIC}} \sigma : eq \; (\tau \, \widehat{l}) \; (Some \; \tau')} \quad (28) \qquad \frac{\Delta;\Gamma \vdash e : \tau \quad \tau =_{\beta\eta\iota} \tau'}{\Delta;\Gamma \vdash e : \tau'} \quad (29)$$
$$\frac{}{\Delta;\Gamma \vdash e \# l [\sigma] : \tau'}$$

4   Typed Compilation of Classes

We now return to the running example, whose Links translation was provided in figure 3. In this section, we will develop the typed encoding of that example in stages, showing additionally how objects are created from classes, and how various implementations of the base class `circle` can be specified.

4.1   Class Representation

Recall that in Links, *CircleBBox* was represented as a function that generates a new class from a given one. The class argument was depicted as a triple $\langle \text{sz}, \text{vt}, \text{dc} \rangle$. We know very little about this (non-manifest) base class: the size and layout of the vtable (vt) are unknown. We just know that the dictionary (dc) contains bindings for the three known methods: center, radius, and area. Moreover, the dictionary maps the method names to offsets that may be applied to the vt to select functions of the correct type. Many different representations of this base class are possible.

The components of the class triple must be typed, so we begin by supposing that sz has type *snat n* (for some *n*), that vt has type *tup n f* (for some *f*), and finally that dc has type *dict g* (for some *g*). These three parameters (n, f, and g) uniquely specify the *representation* of a class:

> **Definition** *Rep* : SET ≡ (*nat* × (*Ty* → *nat* → *Ty*) × (*sym* → *option Ty*)).
> **Definition** *size* ≡ $\lambda r : Rep$. **match** *r* **with** $(n, \_, \_) \Rightarrow n$ **end**.
> **Definition** *tupfn* ≡ $\lambda r : Rep$. **match** *r* **with** $(\_, f, \_) \Rightarrow f$ **end**.
> **Definition** *dictfn* ≡ $\lambda r : Rep$. **match** *r* **with** $(\_, \_, g) \Rightarrow g$ **end**.

We have made one small departure from the description above: the type of the tuple function *f* includes an extra *Ty* argument. This is because the elements of the tuple are methods, or functions over an explicit self parameter. The *Ty* argument is the type of self. This cannot be fixed in one place, but must be a parameter because the method will be reused in derived classes with different types for self. We will demonstrate how this works in section 4.3.

Let us specify two distinct representations of circle, the base class in our example. The methods use floating-point types, which we have not defined formally, but we can suppose that they exist:

> **Parameter** *float* : *Ty*.
> **Definition** *fpoint* : *Ty* ≡ tup_2 *float float*.
> **Definition** *frect* : *Ty* ≡ tup_2 *fpoint fpoint*.

Additionally, *fpoint* is a pair of floats, and *frect* is a pair of points (for the bounds method). Here is the simplest representation, where the three methods appear in order in the vtable, with nothing extra:

> **Definition** *circA_rep* : *Rep* ≡
>   (3, λ *self*. *ith* (*arw self fpoint* :: *arw self float* :: *arw self float* :: *nil*),
>   *lookup* ((*center*, *snat 0*) :: (*radius*, *snat 1*) :: (*area*, *snat 2*) :: *nil*)).

With this representation, we have the following equivalences in CIC:

$$size\ circA\_rep =_{\beta\eta\iota} 3$$
$$dictfn\ circA\_rep\ center =_{\beta\eta\iota} 0$$
$$tupfn\ circA\_rep\ \tau\ 0 =_{\beta\eta\iota} arw\ \tau\ fpoint$$

We can encode a more complex representation, where the methods appear in different slots, and some slots are taken up by unknown values:

> **Definition** *circB_rep* : *Rep* ≡
>   (5, λ *self*. *ith* (*arw self* (*ex snat*) :: *arw self float* :: *arw self fpoint* ::
>   *snat 0* :: *arw self float* :: *nil*),
>   *lookup* ((*radius*, *snat 4*) :: (*area*, *snat 1*) :: (*center*, *snat 2*) :: *nil*)).

Here, slots 0 and 3 are taken up by other values; one of them is not even a function. Still, the *dictfn* tells us where to find the three circle methods.

4.2   Class Specification

Now, how do we ensure that the three *Rep* components (n, f, g) correspond with one another? The constraint, roughly, is that for each method m, there exists some $j : nat$ such that $j < n$ and $g\ m = Some\ (snat\ j)$ and $f\ j = \tau$ where τ is the expected type of the method. We can encode precisely this property in CIC:

Inductive *HasMethod* $(r : Rep)\ (m : sym)\ (t : Ty)$: SET $\equiv$
   method : $\Pi\ i : nat.\ lt\ i\ (size\ r) \rightarrow eq\ (dictfn\ r\ m)\ (Some\ (snat\ i)) \rightarrow$
   $(\Pi\ self.\ eq\ (tupfn\ r\ self\ i)\ (arw\ self\ t)) \rightarrow HasMethod\ r\ m\ t.$

Notice that the offset i is specified in the *method* constructor, but does not appear in the *HasMethod* term itself. This is a form of *dependent pair*, and thanks to the dependent elimination feature of CIC, we can create selectors that mimic the *dot notation* described by Cardelli and Leroy [6]. Here is the term to fetch the offset:

Definition *offset* $\equiv \lambda\ r\ m\ t.\ \lambda\ p : HasMethod\ r\ m\ t.$
   match *p* **with** *method i pf dc tp* $\Rightarrow i$ **end**.

The other selectors have return types that include the *offset* of the parameter itself.

Definition *proof* $\equiv \lambda\ r\ m\ t.\ \lambda\ p : HasMethod\ r\ m\ t.$
   match *p* **as** *q* **return** *lt* (*offset q*) (*size r*) **with** *method i pf dc tp* $\Rightarrow pf$ **end**.
Definition *dicteq* $\equiv \lambda\ r\ m\ t.\ \lambda\ p : HasMethod\ r\ m\ t.$
   match *p* **as** *q* **return** *eq* (*dictfn r m*) (*Some* (*snat* (*offset q*)))
   with *method i pf dc tp* $\Rightarrow dc$ **end**.
Definition *tupeq* $\equiv \lambda\ r\ m\ t.\ \lambda\ p : HasMethod\ r\ m\ t.$
   match *p* **as** *q* **return** $\Pi\ s.\ eq$ (*tupfn r s* (*offset q*)) (*arw s t*)
   with *method i pf dc tp* $\Rightarrow tp$ **end**.

So, if we had some evidence that a representation r has a method *center* returning an *fpoint*, it would be expressed as a term $p : HasMethod\ r\ m\ fpoint$. We can tuple several *HasMethod* terms to create a *signature* for a class:

Definition *circ_signature* $\equiv \lambda\ r.$
   (*HasMethod r center fpoint* $\times$ *HasMethod r radius float* $\times$
   HasMethod r area float).

Now we create a term to use as evidence that *circB_rep* meets the *circ_signature*. It consists of proofs that the indices in the dictionary are less than the tuple size, that the types in the vtable match the signature, and so on.

Definition *self_equal* $\equiv \lambda\ t\ s.\ refl\_equal\ (arw\ s\ t).$
Definition *circB_witness* : *circ_signature circB_rep* $\equiv$
   (*method circB_rep center* (*le_S* (*le_S* (*le_n 3*))) (*refl_equal _*) (*self_equal fpoint*),
   method circB_rep radius (*le_n 5*) (*refl_equal _*) (*self_equal float*),
   method circB_rep area (*le_S* (*le_S* (*le_S* (*le_n 2*)))) (*refl_equal _*) (*self_equal float*)).

Not all of the *method* parameters need to be specified, thanks to Coq's implicit arguments feature. The offset of each method, for example, is inferred from the proof term. The center method appears at offset 2, so we must show that $2 < 5$. The *lt* relation in the Coq library is specified in terms of *le* (less than or equal): $lt\ i\ n \equiv le\ (S\ i)\ n$. The term $le\_n\ 3$ is the proof of $3 \leq 3$, and the two le_S constructors transform that into a proof of $3 \leq 5$ or, equivalently, $2 < 5$. We define projections over *circ_signature* types, to be used later in examples:

> **Definition** *circ_center* : $\Pi\ r.\ circ\_signature\ r \rightarrow HasMethod\ r\ center\ fpoint \equiv$
> $\lambda\ r\ p.$ **match** p **with** $(ce, ra, ar) \Rightarrow ce$ **end**.
> **Definition** *circ_radius* : $\Pi\ r.\ circ\_signature\ r \rightarrow HasMethod\ r\ radius\ float \equiv$
> $\lambda\ r\ p.$ **match** p **with** $(ce, ra, ar) \Rightarrow ra$ **end**.
> **Definition** *circ_area* : $\Pi\ r.\ circ\_signature\ r \rightarrow HasMethod\ r\ area\ float \equiv$
> $\lambda\ r\ p.$ **match** p **with** $(ce, ra, ar) \Rightarrow ar$ **end**.

4.3 Object Types and Method Invocation

Now that we can encode class representations (and constraints on them), we are ready to define the types of objects. In this section, we will represent an object as a pair containing the dictionary and the vtable. We ignore object fields throughout this work, because they are orthogonal. Also, we mentioned before that in Moby and OCaml, where classes can be functor parameters, it is not necessary to package the dictionary with each object. In section 5, we demonstrate an optimized encoding that separates the two components, so that dictionary lookups can be hoisted to the module level. Here is the type of an object pair, given a class representation and the type of self:

> **Definition** *objrep* : $Rep \rightarrow Ty \rightarrow Ty \equiv \lambda\ r\ self.$
> $tup_2\ (dict\ (dictfn\ r))\ (tup\ (size\ r)\ (tupfn\ r\ self))$.

Note the outer type constructor is tup_2 (syntactic sugar for a pair) while the inner one is *tup*, which receives the size of the tuple from the representation r. The self type is resolved with a fixpoint, indicating that the self parameter must be an object of exactly the same type as the object containing the method.

> **Definition** *selfty* : $Rep \rightarrow Ty \equiv \lambda\ r.\ mu\ (objrep\ r)$.

Finally, we must hide the representation type. Two existential quantifiers are used here. The outer one hides the *Rep*, while the inner one hides the evidence that the representation matches some specified signature.

> **Definition** $objty''$: $\Pi\ sig : Rep \rightarrow \text{SET}.\ \Pi\ r.\ sig\ r \rightarrow Ty \equiv \lambda\ sig\ r\ \_.\ selfty\ r$.
> **Definition** $objty'$: $(Rep \rightarrow \text{SET}) \rightarrow Rep \rightarrow Ty \equiv \lambda\ sig\ r.\ ex\ (objty''\ sig\ r)$.
> **Definition** $objty$: $(Rep \rightarrow \text{SET}) \rightarrow Ty \equiv \lambda\ sig.\ ex\ (objty'\ sig)$.

So, the type of a circle object is *objty circ_signature*. In more conventional notation, the object encoding is: $\exists r : Rep.\ \exists p : circ\_signature\ r.\ \mu\alpha : Ty.\ objrep\ r\ \alpha$. (It is not necessary to split the existentials over three Coq definitions, but it allows for shorter annotations in some programs.)

let invoke_radius = λ x : *objty circ_signature*.
   open x **as** $[r, x_1]$ **in open** x_1 **as** $[p, x_2]$ **in let** x_3 = **unfold** x_2 **in**
   let dc = x_3 @ 0 $[lt02]$ **in let** vt = x_3 @ 1 $[lt12]$ **in**
   let j = dc # radius $[dicteq\ (circ\_radius\ p)]$ **in**
   let f = vt @ j $[proof\ (circ\_radius\ p)]$ **in**
   let f = **cast** $[tupeq\ (circ\_radius\ p)\ (selfty\ r)]$ f **in** f x_2

Fig. 5. Code to invoke the radius method on an object x

Now we present a function that invokes the radius method on an object x. In section 2, with untyped terms, this was written simply as $((x\ @\ 1)\ @\ ((x\ @\ 0)\ \#\ radius))\ x$. Figure 5 contains a function that takes x as a parameter, and calls radius. The code is shown in A-normal form [21] for readability, but this is not essential. Apart from the open-open-unfold sequence in the beginning, the burden imposed by the type system includes the proof annotations on tuple selection and dictionary lookup, and the cast expression just before the (virtual) function call. This cast converts the function f from an abstract type to an arrow type, so that it may be applied to a parameter. The terms *lt02* and *lt12* in the select statements refer to these proof constants:

Definition $lt02 : lt\ 0\ 2 \equiv le\_S\ (le\_n\ 1)$.
Definition $lt12 : lt\ 1\ 2 \equiv le\_n\ 2$.

If the objects contained fields, then these proofs would depend on the number of fields in the tuple. To support this, the existential would also need to hide the size of the tuple, m, and a proof of $lt\ 1\ m$ (from which the proof of $lt\ 0\ m$ could be derived).

These type operators and proof annotations buy quite a lot in terms of flexibility and safety. In languages that support non-manifest base classes, the representations of classes and objects have complex invariants that are now enforced by the type system of the intermediate language.

4.4   Class Types and Instantiation

The type of a class is slightly more complex because the vtable in the class plays a different role than the vtable embedded in an object (even though they are the same data structure at run time). Methods must be inheritable. This means that the *self* parameter will have different types at different points in the hierarchy. Therefore, in the class, the vtable must be parameterized by the type of self. The only restriction is that self must have at least the methods defined in the class in which the method is defined. We call this parameterized vtable a *method suite:*

Definition *methsuite″* : Π *sig* : *Rep* $\rightarrow$ SET. *Rep* $\rightarrow$ Π r' : *Rep. sig* r' $\rightarrow$ *Ty* $\equiv$
   λ *sig* r r' _. *tup* (*size* r) (*tupfn* r (*selfty* r')).
Definition *methsuite′* : (*Rep* $\rightarrow$ SET) $\rightarrow$ *Rep* $\rightarrow$ *Rep* $\rightarrow$ *Ty* $\equiv$
   λ *sig* r r'. *all* (*methsuite″* *sig* r r').
Definition *methsuite* : (*Rep* $\rightarrow$ SET) $\rightarrow$ *Rep* $\rightarrow$ *Ty* $\equiv$
   λ *sig* r. *all* (*methsuite′* *sig* r).

Notice the subtle difference in usage between the representations r and r'. The former is the representation of the current class (and determines the methods that appear in

let new_circ = $\lambda\, c_0 : classty\ circ\_signature$.
open c_0 **as** $[r, c_1]$ **in open** c_1 **as** $[p, c_2]$ **in**
let dc = c_2 @ 1 $[lt13]$ **in let** ms = c_2 @ 2 $[lt23]$ **in**
let vt = ms $[r]$ $[p]$ **in let** x = **fold** $\langle$dc, vt$\rangle$ **as** $objrep\ r$ **in**
$[r, [p, \mathsf{x} \triangleright objty''\ circ\_signature\ r] \triangleright objty'\ circ\_signature]$

Fig. 6. Create a new circle object, given a circle class

the tuple), while the latter is the representation of some subclass that is inheriting these methods. Its only impact is on the type of the self parameter.

We noted previously that each class is represented as a triple. Here is the definition of the triple, in terms of the class signature *sig* and representation *r*.

Definition $classtup : (Rep \rightarrow \mathrm{SET}) \rightarrow Rep \rightarrow Ty \equiv$
$\lambda\,sig\ r.\ tup_3\ (snat\ (size\ r))\ (dict\ (dictfn\ r))\ (methsuite\ sig\ r).$

As with object types, we must conceal the representation along with the proof that it meets the specified signature.

Definition $classty'' : \Pi\,sig : Rep \rightarrow \mathrm{SET}.\ \Pi\,r.\,sig\ r \rightarrow Ty \equiv \lambda\,sig\ r\ \_.\ classtup\ sig\ r.$
Definition $classty' : (Rep \rightarrow \mathrm{SET}) \rightarrow Rep \rightarrow Ty \equiv \lambda\,sig\ r.\ ex\ (classty''\ sig\ r).$
Definition $classty : (Rep \rightarrow \mathrm{SET}) \rightarrow Ty \equiv \lambda\,sig.\ ex\ (classty'\ sig).$

This way, both the 'A' and 'B' implementations of the circle class can appear to have the same type: *classty circ_signature*.

Figure 6 contains an implementation of the 'new' operator, that creates a new object from a class. It instantiates the method suite with the representation of the provided class, so that the methods will accept the new object as the self argument. Then, the dictionary and vtable are paired together, folded, and re-packaged. As before, *lt13* and *lt23* stand for constant proof terms.

4.5 Class Declarations

These sophisticated representations of class and object types would be for naught if we are unable to implement a circle class in the first place. In this section, we demonstrate that the type *classty circ_signature* is habitable: see the definition of the 'B' circle class in figure 7. We do not provide complete implementations of the methods: for that, we would need to define floating-point operations and fields.

With this class, we can now connect together the code in the two previous figures like this: *invoke_radius (new_circ circB)*. This creates a new circle from *circB*, invokes

let circB =
  let dc = {radius=4, area=1, center=2} **in**
  let ms = $\Lambda\,r : Rep.\Lambda\,p : circ\_signature\ r.$
          $\langle \lambda\,\mathsf{s} : selfty\ r.$ /* code of type *ex snat* */, $\lambda\,\mathsf{s} : selfty\ r.$ /* code of type *float* */,
          $\lambda\,\mathsf{s} : selfty\ r.$ /* code of type *fpoint* */, 0, $\lambda\,\mathsf{s} : selfty\ r.$ /* code of type *float* */ $\rangle$ **in**
  let c = $\langle 5, dc, ms\rangle$ **in**
  $[circB\_rep, [circB\_witness, \mathsf{c} \triangleright classty''\ circ\_signature\ circB\_rep] \triangleright classty'\ circ\_signature]$

Fig. 7. An implementation of the circle class signature

the radius method of that object, and returns a *float*. We leave it as an exercise to define a different implementation *circA*, using the *circA_rep* defined on page 86.

4.6   Extending an Unknown Base Class

Now we have come to the heart of the whole problem: typed compilation against a non-manifest base class. Our running example extends some unknown class (that matches the circle signature) by overriding area and adding a new method bounds. In CIC, we can define a signature for this derived class, *bbox*:

> **Definition** *bbox_signature* $\equiv \lambda r$.
> (*HasMethod r center fpoint* $\times$ *HasMethod r radius float* $\times$
> *HasMethod r area float* $\times$ *HasMethod r bounds frect*).

The representation of the derived class will of course depend on the layout of its parent. Still, we can define a function to produce a *bbox* representation, given another representation *r* that matches the *circ_signature*:

> **Definition** *bbox_rep* : Πr : *Rep.circ_signature* $r \to Rep \equiv \lambda r p$.
> (*plus 1* (*size r*), λ *self. append* (*size r*) (*tupfn r self*) (*ith* (*arw self frect* :: *nil*)),
> *lookup* ((*center, snat* (*offset* (*circ_center p*))) ::
> (*radius, snat* (*offset* (*circ_radius p*))) :: (*area, snat* (*offset* (*circ_area p*))) ::
> (*bounds, snat* (*size r*)) :: *nil*)).

This works by retrieving the offsets of the inherited methods from the witness *p*, and placing the bounds method in slot *n*—the size of the parent representation. The tuple function uses *append* to join the type of the new method with the types of the parent. With this (parameterized) representation, we have the following:

$$size\ (bbox\_rep\ circB\_witness) =_{\beta\eta\iota} 6$$
$$dictfn\ (bbox\_rep\ circB\_witness)\ center =_{\beta\eta\iota} Some\ (snat\ 2)$$
$$dictfn\ (bbox\_rep\ circB\_witness)\ bounds =_{\beta\eta\iota} Some\ (snat\ 5)$$
$$tupfn\ (bbox\_rep\ circB\_witness)\ \tau\ 5 =_{\beta\eta\iota} arw\ \tau\ frect$$

The next step is to prove that the extended representation matches the *bbox* signature. This is more difficult than it may seem at first. It depends critically on the semantics of *append*. First, extending a tuple with new elements does not alter the types of existing elements. Second, the new elements can be retrieved by adding the size of the original tuple to their offsets. These properties are expressed by the following Coq lemmas:

> **Lemma** *append_semantics*$_1$: $\Pi i n. lt\ i\ n \to \Pi f\ g. eq\ (append\ n\ f\ g\ i)\ (f\ i)$.
> **Lemma** *append_semantics*$_2$: $\Pi k\ n f\ g. eq\ (append\ n\ f\ g\ (plus\ k\ n))\ (g\ k)$.

With these properties, we can prove the following term:

> **Definition** *bbox_witness* : $\Pi r. \Pi p$: *circ_signature r.bbox_signature* (*bbox_rep p*).

As needed, this shows that the extended representation matches the *bbox* signature. (Proofs for these properties appear in a companion technical report [24].)

```
let circle_bbox = λ c : classty circ_signature.
  open c as [r, c] in open c as [p, c] in
  let sz = c @ 0 [lt03] in let dc = c @ 1 [lt13] in let ms = c @ 2 [lt23] in
  let ci = dc # center [dicteq (circ_center p)] in
  let ri = dc # radius [dicteq (circ_radius p)] in
  let ai = dc # area [dicteq (circ_area p)] in
  let dc′ = {center=ci, radius=ri, area=ai, bounds=sz} in
  let ms′ = Λ r″ : Rep.Λ p″ : bbox_signature r″.
    let vt = ms [r″] [bbox2circ p″] in
    let bounds_m = λ s : selfty r″. /* code of type frect */ in
    let area_m = vt @ ai [proof (circ_area p)] in
    let area_m = cast [tupeq (circ_area p) (selfty r″)] area_m in
    let area_m′ = λ s : selfty r″. /* code of type float */ in
    let area_m′ = cast [sym_eq (tupeq (circ_area p) (selfty r″))] area_m′ in
    let vt′ = vt @ ai [proof (circ_area p)] ← area_m′ in
    vt′; ⟨bounds_m⟩ in
  let c′ = ⟨1 + sz, dc′, ms′⟩ in
  let c′ = [bbox_witness p, c′ ▷ classty″ bbox_signature (bbox_rep p)] in
  [bbox_rep p, c′ ▷ classty′ bbox_signature]
```

Fig. 8. Code to extend a non-manifest base class

Just one more definition is needed to extend a non-manifest base class. We instantiate the super class dictionary with the representation of the derived class. This is what permits us to pass *bbox* objects to those *circle* methods. To do this, we must prove that the derived representation still matches the super class signature. Fortunately, this is trivial: just a repackaging of the *HasMethod* properties, to drop the one referring to the bounds method:

Definition *bbox2circ* : $\Pi r. bbox\_signature\ r \rightarrow circ\_signature\ r \equiv$
$\lambda\ r\ p.$ **match** p **with** $(ce, ra, ar, bo) \Rightarrow (ce, ra, ar)$ **end**.

Figure 8 contains the complete code for extending an unknown base class. It corresponds to the OCaml functor given in the introduction, and is a typed version of the Links code in section 2. Most of the non-trivial typing aspects have already been explained. Look for occurrences of *bbox_rep*, *bbox_witness*, and *bbox2circ* in the typing annotations. In our example, the area method included a super call. We omitted the call itself in the figure (along with the rest of the method bodies), but it works very simply. At the point where we define area_m′, we have already selected the area method from vt, the super class vtable. Within the body of area_m′, we would apply area_m to s to call the super-class method.

Also, notice the **cast** applied to the overridden area method before updating the vtable. It is the inverse of the cast used when selecting a method from the vtable. We just defined area_m′, so it has an arrow type to begin with. But the designated slot of the vtable has an opaque type, literally *tupfn* r (*selfty* r″) (*offset* (*circ_area* p)), which cannot be reduced because r is a variable. But we can use (a symmetric version of) the *tupeq* property to cast from the concrete to the opaque, and then update that slot of the vtable.

5   Extensions

5.1   Encoding Subsumption as Type Coercions

Object-oriented languages enjoy *subsumption:* a context expecting an object of type *t* will be satisfied with an object of some *subtype* of *t*. The precise rules about what constitutes a subtype, and where subsumption may be used, differ with each language.

Our intermediate language does not directly support subtyping. Nevertheless, if we examine object types of two classes in a subclass relationship, we notice they differ only in what is known about the (hidden) representation. It is always possible to open and repackage the object with *less* information about its representation. The example in Fig. 9 casts a bbox object to a circle (its super class).

This is done entirely with type coercions, so it has no cost at run time. The *bbox2circ* operator, defined on page 92, coerces the witness from type *bbox_signature r* to type *circ_signature r*, by dropping the information about the bounds method.

This alone is sufficient to support many object-oriented languages, in which subsumption is really just *forgetting* information about some of the methods or fields in the object. This is equivalent to so-called *width* subtyping on records. Some languages (including OCaml) support limited forms of *depth* subtyping, where the types of the fields or methods themselves can change, in a co- or contra-variant manner.

Subtyping can always be encoded using explicit coercions, but that would have a negative impact on the efficiency of our object code—unless the coercions are just type-level operators, like the open and pack in Fig. 9. We believe it would be possible to define a (co-)inductive relation $subtype : Ty \rightarrow Ty \rightarrow$ SET in CIC, whose constructors implement the usual subtyping rules. A term that inhabits $subtype\ \tau_1\ \tau_2$ would thus be equivalent to a meta-logical derivation of $\tau_1 \leq \tau_2$. Our *cast* operator would be extended to accept proofs of $subtype\ \tau_1\ \tau_2$ rather than just $eq\ \tau_1\ \tau_2$. This is reminiscent of the explicit coercion techniques proposed by Crary [15], but formulating the techniques within our framework remains an avenue for future work.

Perhaps surprisingly, it is also possible to encode dynamic casts in this framework. It just requires a way to identify classes at run-time; such an identifier (tag) will be one parameter of the (polymorphic) down-cast operator. League et al. [25] demonstrated one way to do this for Java; we believe the same technique can be adapted to LITL.

let upcast = λ x : *objty bbox_signature*.
open x **as** $[r, x]$ **in open** x **as** $[p, x]$ **in**
$[r, [bbox2circ\ p, x \triangleright objty''\ circ\_signature\ r] \triangleright objty'\ circ\_signature]$

Fig. 9. To upcast a bbox to a circle, we open and repackage the object

5.2   Removing the Dictionary from Object Representations

One of the advantages of Links, as a common IL for object-oriented languages, is its pay-as-you-go efficiency. Languages that do not need dictionaries to find method offsets at run time are not required to use them. For example, if method offsets are known at compile time, they can be hard-coded into the object types, without needing dictionaries or even symbols. Here are updates to some of the definitions from the last section.

Definition *FixedRep* : SET $\equiv$ *(nat* $\times$ *(Ty* $\to$ *nat* $\to$ *Ty))*.
Inductive *FixedMethod (r* : *FixedRep) (i* : *nat) (t* : *Ty)* : SET $\equiv$
   fmethod : *lt i (fst r)* $\to$ *(Π self* : *Ty.eq (snd r self i) (arw self t))* $\to$
   FixedMethod r i t.

We have just removed the dictionary function from the representation. The offset *i* now appears in the *FixedMethod*, rather than remaining hidden. The signature for a circle can be expressed as follows—note the replacement of method names by method offsets:

Definition *circ_fsig* : *FixedRep* $\to$ SET $\equiv$ λ *r*.
   (FixedMethod r 0 fpoint $\times$ *FixedMethod r 1 float* $\times$ *FixedMethod r 2 float)*.

The object type is the same as before, but with offsets now exposed in the bound of one of the existential quantifiers. Supporting link-time (but not run-time) use of dictionaries is more involved. If classes can be module parameters, but modules are not recursive, then all the dictionary lookups ought to be lifted to the top level in each module, outside of any loops. In this case, dictionaries should not be packaged within objects, but should just be module parameters.

5.3 Supporting Mixins and Traits

Bracha and Cook [3] define a mixin as an "abstract subclass; i.e., a subclass definition that may be applied to different super classes to create a related family of modified classes." This seems similar in spirit to the parameterized class we defined. The technical difference is that "mixins properly extend the class that they are applied to" [20]. In our example, base class methods not specified in the CIRCLE signature remain hidden in the derived class. In contrast, a mixin can extend an unknown base class, where any methods unspecified by the mixin are preserved in the interface of the derived class.

   Following our example, a BboxMixin could take any class with center and radius methods, and add a bounds method. Any other super class methods (area, move, enlarge, etc.) would be preserved in the sub class. A mixin thus defines a representation *transformer* that overlays an existing dictionary with some new methods.

   With simple parameterized classes, the signature can be specified as part of the definition. With mixins, this is not so simple. The signature will not be known until the point of instantiation. We do, however, need to know a few things about the transformed representation. First, it must have a bounds method, which returns a pair of points (type *frect*). Second, any methods it previously defined are *preserved*. There is one exception: if it had a bounds method previously, that one is *shadowed* by the newer definition. Thus, we must be able to say that a method label is not equal to bounds:

Definition *noteq* : *sym* $\to$ *sym* $\to$ PROP $\equiv$ λ *m1 m2*.
   Π k : SET. *Π f g* : *k.ifeq m1 m2 f g* = *g*.
Definition *bbmix_sig* : *(Rep* $\to$ TYPE) $\to$ *Rep* $\to$ TYPE $\equiv$ λ *sig r*. *Π r'*.
   (HasMethod r' bounds frect $\to$ *Π m t.noteq m bounds* $\to$
     HasMethod r m t $\to$ *HasMethod r' m t)* $\to$ *sig r'*.

The above definition plays the role of a signature for the mixin, where the *sig* parameter is the ultimate signature, provided when the mixin is applied to a super class; *r* is the super class representation, and *r'* is the subclass representation.

Traits are another, similar mechanism for code reuse [32]. A trait is just a set of named methods, that can depend on some other (specified) methods. "The main difference between mixins and traits is that mixins force a linear order in their composition" [17]. We have not yet determined whether our encoding of mixins extends to traits, but we intend to pursue this as future work.

6 Related Work

There is a long history of encoding objects and classes in typed λ-calculi and other non-object-based representations [5]. Several recent encodings are specifically designed for use in certifying compilers, where run-time efficiency is a concern [9, 16, 22, 25]. They each have their advantages—see [9] or [25] for comparisons—but none of them support separating offset determination from method retrieval.

The encoding presented in this paper is a natural generalization of the one developed by League et al. [25] for Java. They specified tuples as sequences of *rows* [31], where the tail of a sequence could be abstracted by a type variable. An object with a method in slot zero returning τ would have the type: $\exists \rho : Ty \rightarrow R^1 . \mu \alpha : Ty. \langle \alpha \rightarrow \tau ; \rho\ \alpha \rangle$, where the quantified variable ρ conceals the types of any additional methods. Compare that to the encoding introduced in this paper:

$$\exists n : nat. \exists f : Ty \rightarrow nat \rightarrow Ty. \exists p : (0 < n \wedge (\forall \beta : Ty. f\ \beta\ 0 = arw\ \beta\ \tau)).$$
$$\mu \alpha : Ty.\ tup\ n\ (f\ \alpha)$$

This is the 'fixed' representation from section 5.2. In both cases, an existential hides a specification of the elements of the tuple (ρ above, f below), parameterized by the type of the explicit self argument. Both encodings use a recursive type in the same way: to equate the type of the self argument with the type of the object containing the methods. Finally, both encodings reveal (in different ways) the types of known methods in the tuple.

Stone [34] developed a Calculus of Objects and Indices (COI) which has some similarities to our work. Although it is an *object* calculus (method invocation is atomic) Stone says, "it may be possible to use the ideas here to obtain a typed variant [of Links]." Like our language, COI supports dictionaries and first-class indices. Rather than singleton types, indices "have types of the form $\tau \Rightarrow \sigma$; this type classifies offsets that access a component of type σ within an object of type τ."

As specified, COI is not suitable as an intermediate language for compilers, or as a target language for proof-carrying code. It takes objects and object extension as primitive, and encodes classes in terms of objects. The class encoding does not support super calls, though it seems possible to add them. Due to the granularity of the calculus, optimizations like caching method pointers and devirtualization are not expressible.

Pushing COI to a lower level while maintaining soundness may be challenging. As is, its soundness relies on distinguishing between exact and inexact object types. What becomes of these concepts when objects are no longer primitive? Often, decomposing objects into tuples and functions opens up unintended ways of accessing them, leading to unsoundness [26, 8]. It would be very interesting to see the impact of the COI design at a lower level.

A few other works deserve mention. Based on our previous work on Java [25], Vanderwaart [35] designed a typed IL for Loom. Because of the richness of Loom, the encoding resulted in inefficient method dispatch. Fisher and Reppy [18] translate Moby classes into an object calculus, designed for studying the foundations but unsuitable as a compiler IL. Ciaffaglione et al. [10] mechanize the semantics for an imperative object-based calculus, using co-inductive definitions in Coq.

7   Conclusion and Future Directions

We have developed LITL, a sound, low-level intermediate language with dictionaries, tuples, functional update, and tuple extension. Fisher et al. [20] showed that these primitives are useful for compiling various object-oriented languages, with different object models and notions of inheritance. Dictionaries support link-time or run-time determination of method offsets, for languages where the layout of a base class may not be known at compile time.

Following Shao et al. [33], the type system of LITL is embedded in the Calculus of Inductive Constructions [14]. Our reliance on CIC permits flexible reasoning about the offsets of methods, which are now first-class values with singleton types constructed from natural numbers.

We proposed a simple example in OCaml—where a super class is provided as a functor parameter—and showed by example how to encode objects, classes, method dispatch, new, and inheritance from a non-manifest base class. Our technique supports width (but not depth) subtyping using type coercions. Alternative representations are possible, where the dictionary is omitted (because offsets are already known) or passed separately from the object.

In the future, we expect to support depth subtyping, using a technique outlined in section 5.1. Furthermore, we intend to choose a small source language with several of these advanced object-oriented features and specify a complete type-preserving translation.

Bibliography

[1] A. W. Appel. Foundational proof-carrying code. In *Proc. IEEE Symp. on Logic in Computer Science (LICS)*, pages 247–258, June 2001.

[2] H. Barendregt. Typed lambda calculi. In S. Abramsky, D. Gabbay, and T. Maibaum, editors, *Handbook of Logic in Computer Science*, volume 2. Oxford, 1992.

[3] G. Bracha and W. Cook. Mixin-based inheritance. In *Proc. Conf. on Object-Oriented Programming Systems, Languages, and Applications*, pages 303–311, October 1990.

[4] K. B. Bruce, A. Fiech, and L. Petersen. Subtyping is not a good 'Match' for object-oriented languages. In *Proc. European Conf. Object-Oriented Prog.*, volume 1241 of *LNCS*, pages 104–127, Berlin, 1997. Springer-Verlag.

[5] K. B. Bruce, L. Cardelli, and B. C. Pierce. Comparing object encodings. *Information and Computation*, 155(1–2):108–133, 1999.

[6] L. Cardelli and X. Leroy. Abstract types and the dot notation. In *Proc. IFIP Working Conf. on Programming Concepts and Methods*, pages 466–491, Israel, April 1990.

[7] L. Cardelli and J. C. Mitchell. Operations on records. In C. A. Gunter and J. C. Mitchell, editors, *Theoretical Aspects of Object-Oriented Programming*, Foundations of Computing Series. MIT Press, 1994.

[8] B.-Y. E. Chang, A. Chlipala, G. C. Necula, and R. R. Schneck. Type-based verification of assembly language for compiler debugging. In *Proc. ACM Workshop on Types in Language Design and Implementation (TLDI)*, pages 91–102, 2005.

[9] J. Chen and D. Tarditi. A simple typed intermediate language for object-oriented languages. In *Proc. Symp. on Principles of Programming Languages*. ACM, January 2005.

[10] A. Ciaffaglione, L. Liquori, and M. Miculan. Imperative object-based calculi in co-inductive type theories. In *Proc. Conf. on Logic for Programming, Artificial Intelligence, and Reasoning*, volume 2850 of *Lecture Notes in Computer Science*, pages 59–77, 2003.

[11] C. Colby, P. Lee, G. C. Necula, F. Blau, K. Cline, and M. Plesko. A certifying compiler for Java. In *Proc. Conf. on Programming Language Design and Implementation*, Vancouver, June 2000. ACM.

[12] Coq Development Team. *The Coq Proof Assistant Reference Manual*. INRIA, version 8.0 edition, June 2004.

[13] T. Coquand and G. Huet. The calculus of constructions. *Information and Computation*, 76: 95–120, 1988.

[14] T. Coquand and C. Paulin-Mohring. Inductively defined types. In *Proceedings of Colog '88*, volume 417 of *Lecture Notes in Computer Science*. Springer, 1990.

[15] K. Crary. Typed compilation of inclusive subtyping. In *Proc. Int'l Conf. Functional Programming*, September 2000.

[16] K. Crary. Simple, efficient object encoding using intersection types. Technical Report CMU-CS-99-100, Carnegie Mellon University, Pittsburgh, January 1999.

[17] K. Fisher and J. Reppy. A typed calculus for traits. In *Proc. Int'l Workshop on Foundations of Object-Oriented Languages*, January 2004.

[18] K. Fisher and J. Reppy. Foundations for moby classes. Technical report, Bell Labs, December 1998.

[19] K. Fisher and J. Reppy. The design of a class mechanism for Moby. In *Proc. Conf. on Programming Language Design and Implementation*, New York, 1999. ACM.

[20] K. Fisher, J. Reppy, and J. G. Riecke. A calculus for compiling and linking classes. In *Proc. European Symp. on Programming*, pages 135–149, 2000.

[21] C. Flanagan, A. Sabry, B. F. Duba, and M. Felleisen. The essence of compiling with continuations. In *Proc. Conf. on Programming Language Design and Implementation*, pages 237–247, Albuquerque, June 1993.

[22] N. Glew. An efficient class and object encoding. In *Proc. Conf. on Object-Oriented Programming Systems, Languages, and Applications*. ACM, October 2000.

[23] W. A. Howard. The formulae-as-types notion of constructions. In *To H.B. Curry: Essays on Computational Logic, Lambda Calculus, and Formalism*. Academic Press, 1980.

[24] C. League and S. Monnier. Typed compilation against non-manifest base classes. Extended version, available from authors' web sites, December 2005.

[25] C. League, Z. Shao, and V. Trifonov. Type-preserving compilation of Featherweight Java. *ACM Trans. on Programming Languages and Systems*, 24(2):112–152, March 2002.

[26] C. League, Z. Shao, and V. Trifonov. Precision in practice: A type-preserving Java compiler. In G. Hedin, editor, *Proc. Int'l Conf. on Compiler Construction*, volume 2622 of *Lecture Notes in Computer Science*, pages 106–120. Springer, April 2003.

[27] D. A. Moon. Object-oriented programming with Flavors. In *Proc. Conf. on Object-Oriented Programming Systems, Languages, and Applications*, pages 1–8, November 1986.

[28] G. Morrisett, D. Walker, K. Crary, and N. Glew. From System F to typed assembly language. *ACM Trans. on Programming Languages and Systems*, 21(3), May 1999.

[29] G. C. Necula. Proof-carrying code. In *Proc. Symp. on Principles of Programming Languages*, pages 106–119, Paris, January 1997. ACM.

[30] F. Pfenning and C. Elliot. Higher-order abstract syntax. In *Proc. Conf. on Programming Language Design and Implementation*, pages 199–208, 1988.

[31] D. Rémy and J. Vouillon. Objective ML: An effective object-oriented extension to ML. *Theory and Practice of Object Systems*, 4, 1998.

[32] N. Schärli, S. Ducasse, O. Nierstrasz, and A. P. Black. Traits: Composable units of behaviour. In *Proc. European Conf. Object-Oriented Programming*, July 2003.

[33] Z. Shao, V. Trifonov, B. Saha, and N. Papaspyrou. A type system for certified binarios. *ACM Trans. on Programming Languages and Systems*, 27(1):1–45, January 2005.

[34] C. A. Stone. Extensible objects without labels. *ACM Trans. on Programming Languages and Systems*, 26(5):805–835, September 2004.

[35] J. C. Vanderwaart. Typed intermediate representations for compiling object-oriented languages. Williams College Senior Honors Thesis, 1999.

The Design of Application-Tailorable Operating System Product Lines⋆

Daniel Lohmann, Wolfgang Schröder-Preikschat, and Olaf Spinczyk

Friedrich-Alexander University of Erlangen-Nuremberg,
Department of Computer Sciences,
Martensstr. 1, D-91058 Erlangen, Germany
http://www4.cs.fau.de

Abstract. System software for deeply embedded devices has to cope
with a broad variety of requirements and platforms, but especially with
strict resource constraints. To compete against proprietary systems (and
thereby to facilitate reuse), an operating system product line for deeply
embedded systems has to be highly configurable and tailorable. It is
therefore crucial that all selectable and configurable features can be encapsulated into fine-grained, exchangeable and reusable implementation
components. However, the encapsulation of non-functional properties is
often limited, due to their cross-cutting character. Fundamental system
policies, like synchronization or activation points for the scheduler, have
typically to be reflected in many points of the operating system component code. The presented approach is based on feature modeling,
C++ class composition and overcomes the above mentioned problems
by means of aspect-oriented programming (AOP). It facilitates a fine-
grained encapsulation and configuration of even non-functional properties in system software.

1 Introduction

Due to the need for customized solutions, particularly the embedded systems domain calls for a large assortment of specialized operating system components.
Depending on the application case, not only are number and kind (in functional
terms) of the components varying, but also the same single component may appear in highly different versions. This is especially true for the broad field of deeply
embedded systems. Here, the phrase "deeply embedded" refers to systems forced
to operate under extreme constraints in terms of e.g. memory and/or CPU resources, power consumption, and heat dissipation. The market of such systems is
huge and subject to an enormous cost pressure. In year 2000 about eight billion
microprocessors have been manufactured [32]. Only about two percent of them
went into the PC, laptop, workstation or server market, while 98 % were dedicated to embedded systems. About five billions of all were 8-bit microprocessors.
From the point of view of procurement, this "old-fashioned" technology is the best

---

⋆ This work was partly supported by the DFG, grant no. SCHR 603/4.

G. Barthe et al. (Eds.): CASSIS 2005, LNCS 3956, pp. 99–117, 2006.

compromise with respect to functionality and cost. The situation is not that different today, as a look at automotive industry, chipcard technology, or the consumer product market shows. Moreover, it can not be expected to change soon, given that the envisioned scenarios of *smart dust* [20], *ubiquitous computing* [35] and *proactive computing* [32] crucially depend on the bulk availability of very cheap, self-organizing "intelligent" devices. Because of cost pressure—and in many cases also because of misunderstandings about what the notion of "operating system" stands for—one is faced with a situation in which the wheel is getting to be reinvented fairly often. There is a zoo of commercial operating systems available at the embedded systems market. Nevertheless, about 50 % of the embedded systems products come with proprietary solutions [34]. OS-functionality such as threading and interrupt handling is developed from scratch—again and again. The reason is, that is simply impossible to build a "one-fits-all" system that fulfills the requirements of all potential applications, while still being thrifty and economical with system resources. The solution is therefore to tailor down the operating system so it provides exactly the functionality required by the intended application, but nothing more. Understanding an (embedded) operating system as a *software product line* [36] seems to be a promising way to go. Commonalities of and differences between individual members of the operating system family, as well as their interdependencies and conflicting combinations, can be adequately expressed on the basis of *feature models* [12], with the features representing the functional and non-functional system properties. This leads to a family-based [27] design approach. Examples for family-based, configurable operating systems in the domain are e.g. eCos by RedHat Inc. [1], the OSEK standard which is widely used in automotive industry [2], or our PURE operating system product line [5] for the domain of deeply embedded devices. Although the results achieved with these systems motivate the reuse of system software components for a number of reasons, operating system product line development is not yet exercised very well in this market. Another example that underpins the increasing demand of software product line engineering is the automotive domain. Automobile electronics makes up about 80 % of all the innovations in a car. Furthermore, 90 % of these innovations come up with software and not hardware. Thus, software is not only a functional issue of the mechatronics product "automobile", but also an economical one of high strategic importance. On the one hand, there is a strong need to reuse software solutions across the different variants and models of a car. On the other hand, in a large number of cases, highly specialized software solutions need to be built depending on the actual car variant or model. Resolving this contradiction is challenging and calls for highly careful system software designs and implementations. Most crucial in this setting are non-functional properties that are ingredient parts of single components or cross-cut in the extreme case the entire system software. These properties not only limit component reusability but also impair software maintenance in general. Being able to deal with software variability—not only in the realm of operating systems—becomes more and more eminent for embedded systems. For operating systems, this is of particular concern because of their qualified placement between "a rock and a hard place", namely application software at the top and computer hardware at the bottom. Software variability was and is an important issue in operating systems, and it will ever be. Alone relying on object-oriented approaches to cope with the diversity of problems coming up when developing embedded-systems software is not enough. Specialization by means of inheritance, e.g., soon may result in unmaintainable class hierarchies if the combinational complexity increases [26, 18]. Not to mention the risk of performance loss and large memory footprints in the case of an excessive exploitation of interface inheritance and, thus, late binding [14]. Alternative as well as supplementing approaches are required in order to benefit from object orientation if one wants to develop system software that is reusable and tailorable at the same time. *Aspect-oriented programming* (AOP) [21] appears to be a proper paradigm in order to maintain implementations of non-functional properties separate from software components and, thus, improve reusability of the latter. The paper describes principles of the design and development of operating systems aiming at a very high degree of customization not only with respect to lower-level hardware but also higher-level user programs. Discussed are design rules, techniques, and issues of tool support which are applicable not only in the course of developing embedded operating systems from scratch, but also in the process of re-engineering existing system software. Moreover, the approach presented may also be successfully applied in order to develop and maintain extensible as well as contractible application software. Thus, the paper is about a fairly general approach that is not only limited to the design and development of operating systems. Application domain of the described principles is the field of deeply embedded systems. Fundamental concepts and techniques to produce highly reusable operating system components are presented in section 2. Section 3 is about a case study, the *thread abstraction layer* (TAL) of the PURE family of embedded operating systems [5]. In section 4, we will briefly discuss the approach as followed by the PURE successor CiAO [30] to encapsulate non-functional properties and to isolate cross-cutting concerns. Conclusions are drawn in section 5.

2   Operating System Engineering

Most important in the development of operating systems for the embedded systems domain is the postponement of all those design and implementation decisions that will potentially restrict applicability of system functions or components. This includes that, perhaps, certain decisions are never be made in the OS itself, but are rather postponed to the application programmer. References to implementations of some non-functional properties are examples of such design decisions. The following subsections discuss the cornerstones of an operating system development process that supports highly scalable and customizable designs and implementations.

2.1   Incremental System Design

Predominant issue in the development process of deeply embedded operating systems must be understanding the system software as a *program family* [27] and to follow a classical bottom-up approach. Strictly speaking, design decisions are to be met bottom-up, but the design process is to be controlled in a top-down manner. The idea is to design family members that are particularly tailored to support specific application scenarios by sharing as many as possible system abstractions, i.e. reusable components. A highly distinct *functional hierarchy* of "fine-grain sized" components is the outcome. The entire system structure is a logical one in the sense that the design is hierarchical, and not its implementation [17]. Realizing a program family by an object-oriented implementation may result in highly flexible and yet efficient system structures. But this will be true only if both design and implementation follow an incremental approach [11]. Starting point must be a minimal subset of system functions which undergoes a stepwise *functional enrichment* by minimal system extensions. These enrichments can be turned into efficient programs by means of *implementation inheritance.* Note that this does not necessarily hold with interface inheritance. The point of problem is late binding of those methods which are subject to subsequent specialization in derived classes. This concept may result in overhead-prone implementations and entail very large memory footprints, especially in the case of deep class hierarchies. The decision for late binding must be postponed as far as possible in the design and implementation of object-oriented program families. As a consequence, functional enrichment for creating new object-oriented abstractions of a program family favors implementation inheritance over interface inheritance. Interface inheritance is the right choice only when the family-based design requires multiple implementations of the same interface to coexist. In certain cases it is sensible for such kind of requirement to be considered a non-functional property of object-oriented (operating) system software. In order not to limit reusability of a class implementing that kind of interface, the non-functional property of interface inheritance needs to be separated properly.

2.2   Variabilty Management

By consequently following the family-based approach of software development, highly customizable operating systems are feasable. Variant building, however, is only a first step in the development process. Without being able to organize and manage the many possible variants of an operating system family in an adequate and user-friendly manner, this approach will be doomed to failure. Feature modeling appears to be a promising way to tackle the variability management problem. This technique is understood as "the activity of modeling the common and the variable properties of concepts and their interdependencies and organizing them into a coherent model referred to as a *feature model.*" [12] Goal is to come up with directives for and a first structure of a design of a system that meets the requirements and constraints specified by the features. Common is a graphical representation of the feature model in terms of a *feature diagram.* The diagram is of tree-like structure (fig. 1), with the nodes referring to specific feature categories. Four feature categories are defined: *mandatory, optional, alternative,* and *or.* A feature diagram describes the options and constraints that

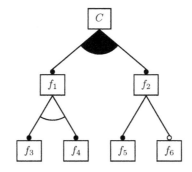

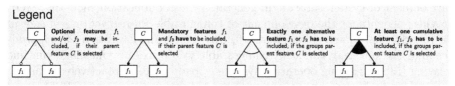

Fig. 1. Example of a Feature Diagram

shall exist within a system. It models the variable and fixed properties of a family of programs which implement that system. The diagram shown in figure 1 describes a specific concept C, e.g. the process management subsystem of an operating system. If concept C gets to be included in the final system configuration, then any non-empty subset of features from the set $\{f_1, f_2\}$ of or-features is also included. The *feature set* with respect to C at this level of abstraction is either $\{f_1\}$, $\{f_2\}$, or $\{f_1, f_2\}$. If feature f_1 is present, one feature from the set $\{f_3, f_4\}$ of alternative features must be included. Thus, the feature set of f_1 consists of either f_3 or f_4. If feature f_2 is selected, mandatory feature f_5 must and optional feature f_6 may be included in the final configuration. For f_2, this leads to the feature set $\{f_5\}$ or $\{f_5, f_6\}$. This technique allows for a compact and precise specification of interdependencies of functional as well as non-functional properties of fairly complex systems [12]. Basing on a tool which aids the construction process of a feature model and supports the mapping of features to implementations, automated generation of highly specialized operating systems becomes possible [6].

2.3   Modularization of Non-functional Properties with AOP

Not in every case is it sensible to follow a development process that solely relies on a universal family-based design and object-oriented implementation as described above. Eminent problematic issues are the cross-cutting concerns given with many non-functional properties. Trying to reflect these concerns in a hierarchical design may lead to an explosion of the resulting functional and/or class hierarchy. For software maintenance reasons, a cross-cutting concern needs to be separated from its points of action and implemented as a single module. When a specific family member is going to be instantiated, all missing cross-cutting concerns will be applied to the relevant software components. Referring to non-functional properties then may become a configuration matter. Automated configuration may take place by having a software transformation tool in charge of interweaving the program module representing a specific cross-cutting concern with all the programs that refer to the corresponding non-funtional property. This kind of final customization of selected software components from a program family can be best achieved using AOP [21]. In this setting, an aspect program implements a specific cross-cutting concern. These programs take care of the manifestation of a particular non-functional property by describing code transformations that need to be applied to selected components. The transformation process is performed by an aspect weaver. AOP turns out to become a powerful paradigm in the design and development of system software in general. Several publication show that AOP provides benefits for the development of configurable *infrastructure software* in the broad sense, namely middleware [10, 9, 37, 19, 28] and databases [28, 33] product lines, as well as dynamically configurable web proxies by means of runtime weaving [13]. Regarding operating systems, Coady et al. retroactively evaluated the evolution of four partly non-functional OS concerns in the FreeBSD kernel using the general-purpose AspectC language [8, 7]. It was shown that an aspect-oriented implementation would have led to significantly better evolvability. Due to missing tool support (namely a weaver), her study did cover only a relatively small part of the kernel code base and no heavily crosscutting concerns such as tracing or kernel diagnostics. Not a general-purpose AOP language, but an AOP-inspired language of temporal logic was used by Åberg et al. to integrate the Bossa scheduler framework into the Linux kernel [3]. C4 uses AOP concepts to implement a "semantic patch system" for the application of kernel patches [15].

3   Case Study of a Thread Abstraction Layer

PURE [5] is a family of operating systems targeted at the highly resource-constrained domain of deeply embedded devices and available for a large number of 8 and 16 bit processor platforms. A branch of the PURE family that provides elementary process management functions is the *thread abstraction layer*(TAL). This layer is a refinement of the original PURE threads package and serves for various experimental purposes related to fine-grain (operating system) software product line development. The following two subsections give a brief overview about the concepts and techniques that were used to make PURE software extensible as well as contractible. First, excerpts from the TAL feature model are discussed to exemplify the concept of variability management having been applied to PURE. Second, the functional hierarchy of TAL is presented to illustrate some of the internals of the design and to give also an idea on what fine-grain operating system software product line development means in PURE.

3.1   Feature Modeling

The TAL feature model aims at describing commonalities of as well as differences between the various possible variants of a system software component commonly

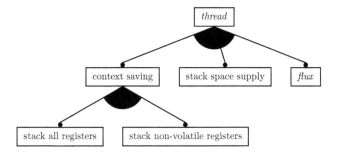

Fig. 2. Thread concept. This TAL feature is made of a hierarchy of or-features covering functions that save/restore a thread context (*context saving*), take care of expansion directions and alignment restrictions of a stack (*stack space supply*), and manage a thread of control of program execution (*flux*).

known as a threads package. Focus was on the deeply embedded systems domain. Above all this means that the system design resulting from the feature model must be minimal in any respect: each level of abstraction introduced need to be a minimal extension to the minimal subset of system functions existing so far. Figure 2 shows the three main subfeatures of the *thread concept*, which are defined as follows:

context saving. Spans functions needed to save and restore a thread context. A stack-based approach is assumed. The feature is constituted by two or-features that differentiate between three combinations of context saving functions. A TAL configuration may encompass functions to stack all and/or only non-volatile CPU registers. The latter are a subset of the former and make thread switching more lightweight (in execution time and memory space).

stack space supply. Provides fundamental stack management functions concerned with allocation, alignment restrictions, and expansion direction (top down or bottom up) of a stack.

flux. covers the functions needed to implement the flow of control represented by a thread and its binding to program text. Figure 3 shows a refinement of this subfeature.

As shown in figure 2, the TAL thread concept consists of three or-features. Thus, an application is provided with seven configuration options at this level, depending on the number of thread subfeatures selected. This is in line with the idea of program families: PURE applications are not forced to go with all TAL functions, but rather is given choices from which they may or may not make their decisions. Heart of TAL is *flux* (fig. 3), which describes a hierarchy of abstractions modeling a thread of control including its binding to program text. The decisive idea is to postpone decisions on how to represent and manage the context of a thread as far as possible. Figure 3 shows a feature hierarchy which corresponds to an implementation that implies functional enrichment of a minimal subset of threading functions. The *flux* subfeatures model the evolution steps from flyweight to lightweight threads. Their meaning is as follows:

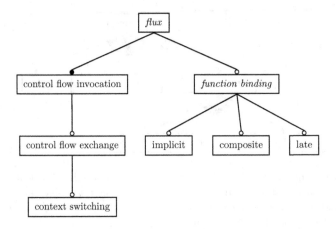

Fig. 3. Flux concept. The feature diagram models functional enrichment of thread abstractions, starting from a simple run-to-completion mode of operation (*control flow invocation*) and an optional binding of user-defined code to a thread (*function binding*).

control flow invocation. Describes the minimal subset of system functions needed to instantiate and terminate a thread. The principle of operation of a thread at this level of abstraction is *run to completion*. The spawning thread inherits the processor state (stored by the working registers) to the spawned thread and implicitly releases CPU control. Upon termination, the spawning thread takes over the processor state again and receives back CPU control.

control flow exchange. A minimal system extension that allows for thread switching in a coroutine-like fashion. Thus, run to completion is no longer the only principle of operation provided at this level of abstraction. Both threads, i.e. spawner and spawnee, may resume each other by sharing the processor state except the contents of the stack pointer register.

context switching. Another minimal system extension which adds functions to save and restore the processor state of a thread. This abstraction requires the *context saving* feature shown in figure 2. The key idea is that every thread is responsible to manage its processor state on its own: the state needs to be saved before resuming execution of another thread and will have to be restored after having been resumed execution by some other thread. Thus, no thread needs to know about the size and organization of the processor state of another thread.

function binding. This *flux* subfeature models different ways of how to bind user-defined functions to a thread. By default, the code executed by a thread always is in-line with the basic block or scope that instantiated the thread. However, if *function binding* is selected, the code to be executed by a thread may be subject to (1) *implicit* binding using a default function, (2) *composite* binding using a template function, or (3) *late* binding using a virtual function.

If *flux* is going to be selected, TAL comes at least with *control flow invocation*. All other *flux* subfeatures are optional so that no application program of TAL

```
slot = label();          // remember current thread of control
split(flux);             // spawn additional thread of control
if (slot != label()) {   // did a control flow switch occur?
  ...                    // yes, spawnee takes on execution
  latch(slot);           // spawnee finishes and resumes spawner
}                        // spawnee never returns to here
  ...                    // no, spawner continues execution
```

Fig. 4. Flyweight thread instantiation (C-like). A new thread is spawned using `split()`, which returns twice. In order to determine whether the spawner or the spawnee returns, `label()` is used: the spawnee returns when `label()` after `split()` delivers a value different from `label()` before `split()`. The spawnee returns first and passes back CPU control to its spawner using `latch()`.

will be forced to pay for functions that it does not need. In addition, the features are organized in such a manner that the resulting implementations will follow the incremental system design approach and, thus, appear as minimal system extensions. To get an idea of how the minimal subset of TAL functions can be used to instantiate threads that will operate according to run to completion, see figure 4. Functions `label()`, `split()`, and `latch()` basically implement the *control flow invocation* feature. The resulting assembly-level code generated from this C fragment is shown in figure 5. TAL functions are implemented as **inline** functions, mostly. The code sequence shown in figure 5 is semantically equivalent to the code sequence of figure 4: it is the result of the compilation process using the GNU C/C++ compiler. The two examples demonstrate what family-based design of PURE actually implied, namely coming up with a large number of tiny system functions. The motivation to start out with a minimal subset of threading functions (as shown in figures 4 and 5) that only save/restore a very minimal

```
    leal  -4(%esp),%edx    # slot = label()
    pushl $1f              # split(flux)
    movl  flux,%esp        #     "     activate spawnee
1:                         # spawner resumes execution
    leal  -4(%esp),%eax    # <aux> = label()
    cmpl  %eax,%edx        # if (slot == <aux>)
    je    2f               # goto 2
    ...                    # spawnee takes on execution
    movl  %edx,%esp        # latch(slot)
    ret                    #     "     goto 1
2: ...                     # spawner continues execution
```

Fig. 5. Flyweight thread instantiation (x86-like). The example shows how run to completion is actually realized for the spawned thread: the spawner transforms into the spawnee by assigning `flux` to the stack pointer register. The spawnee terminates by (1) assigning the spawners stack pointer (`slot`) to the stack pointer register and (2) restoring the spawners program counter (`ret`).

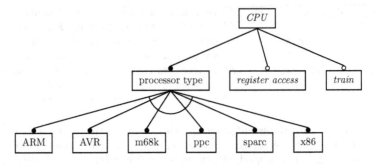

Fig. 6. CPU concept (excerpt). Mandatory feature *processor type* specifies the CPU architecture that can be supported by a PURE family member. Optional feature *register access* is root of a bunch of subfeatures related to processor state management. Support for trap/interrupt handling is modeled by the optional feature *train*.

processor state consisting of program counter and stack pointer registers was to have a compiler in charge of context switching. A compiler exactly knows about the non-volatile processor state of a thread and that state may differ from thread to thread. The idea was to be able to take advantage of compiler pragmas that specify the size of the processor state to be saved/restored upon thread switches in dependence on the actual scope where the thread switch takes place.

Another important issue of TAL (and the encompassing operating system kernel) is CPU management. Figure 6 shows an excerpt of the feature model describing the CPU concept. Mandatory feature is the *processor type*, which

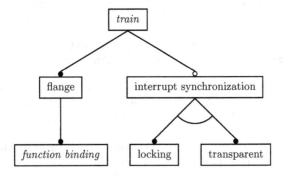

Fig. 7. Train concept (excerpt). Mandatory feature *flange* models the binding technique used to make trap/interrupt handlers physically known to the CPU. Basically, this feature directly maps to the *function binding* feature of *flux* (fig. 3). Optional feature *interrupt synchronization* describes the alternatives for the coordination of event-triggered activities in PURE. Either "hard synchronization" using interrupt locking or interrupt transparent non-blocking "soft synchronization" (without relying on dedicated CPU instructions) is supported.

in turn consists of a number of alternative features. Each of these alternatives stands for the processor platform that is supported by TAL. Usually, for a given system configuration, only one target platform will be supported. The optional feature *register access* describes abstractions provided to read and write the registers of the CPU indicated by *processor type*. Register access functions are implemented by means of operator overloading using a C++ class instance for each of the registers provided by a particular CPU. An overloaded assignment operator performs write access, while the overloaded type cast operator performs read access. The operators are implemented as inline assembly functions. They are used, e.g., to implement thread context management already in a high-level and problem-oriented programming language such as C++. The third subfeature of concept *CPU* models the art of trap/interrupt (*train*) handling for a selected *processor type*. A refined feature model of *train* is shown in figure 7. In that subtree, mandatory feature *flange* describes the kind of *function binding* in order to make problem-oriented trap/interrupt handlers known to the CPU. This is realized by letting *train* logically share the same binding techniques with concept *flux* (see also fig. 3). A major part of *train* is made of *interrupt synchronization*, which is an optional feature: not in every use case will interrupts raise race conditions and, thus, need to be synchronized for coordination purposes. Two alternatives are given:

1. Interrupt locking, i.e., interrupts are disabled and (re-) enabled to secure critical code sections. This is the traditional case of coping with concurrency issues due to hardware interrupts and is fairly easy to implement. However, blocking of interrupts comes with the risk of loosing hardware events and, thus, turns out not to be a good choice especially for embedded real-time systems with high interrupt frequency.
2. Interrupt transparent synchronization [29], i.e., interrupts are never disabled by an operating system kernel. This feature corresponds to a set of synchronization abstractions that allow for interrupts at any time. Coordination is achieved using a variant of non-blocking synchronization.

Interrupt transparent synchronization can be done with and without specific (e.g. CAS-like) CPU instructions. As a consequence, the alternative feature *transparent* consists of an ensemble of or-features, with each of these subfeatures describing a specific synchronization technique.

Developing feature models to aid the design process of a family of operating systems and for documentation purposes is one aspect. Using these models to support the configuration and generation process of operating systems is another aspect. With pure::variants [4] a feature-based configuration tool has been developed that supports the workflow from the creation of a feature model up to the automatic generation of user-customized operating systems for very specific problem domains. The tool not only allows for creation but also verification of feature models such that logically consistent system configurations will be the outcome of the generation process.

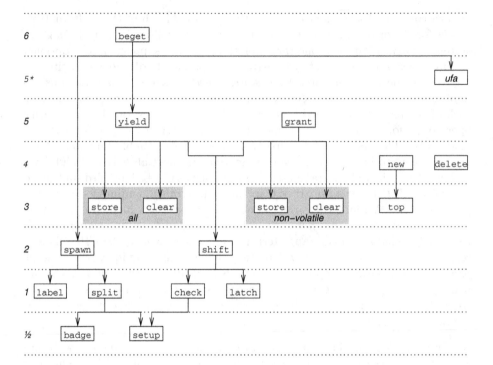

Fig. 8. Functional hierarchy of TAL. The levels serve the following purposes: 1 *control flow invocation*, 2 *control flow exchange*, 3 *context saving* and *stack space supply*, 4 *stack space supply*, 5 *context switching*, 5∗ *function binding*, 6 thread instantiation. Level $\frac{1}{2}$ supports level 1 only: its functions came into existence with the design of **check()**, which showed commonalities with the already existing **split()**. These commonalities then became subject to factorization which led to **badge()** and **setup()**.

3.2 Functional Hierarchy and Component View

The TAL feature model is turned into an implementation using a very fine-grain incremental system design approach. Result of this process is a functional hierarchy (fig. 8). Figure 8 makes explicit the levels of abstraction a TAL function is assigned to. Level 5∗ is not really part of TAL, but rather of the application program using TAL. This level stands for some *user function abstraction* (UFA) that corresponds to the *function binding* feature of *flux* (fig. 3). In addition, level $\frac{1}{2}$ stands for a level of abstraction that resulted from a refinement step in the design process: when level 2 was designed, one figured out commonalities in the implementation of **split()** and **check()**, which then where factorized out and led to the additional level. Level 2 takes care of *control flow exchange*, levels 3 and 5 cover *context saving* and *switching* issues, while level 4 and function **top()** of level 3 turn the feature *stack space supply* into implementation. Level 6 is responsible for thread instantiation. TAL offers a very high degree of customization at the cost of a fairly complex internal structure. The structural complexity becomes manageable for an expert using e.g. feature-modeling and

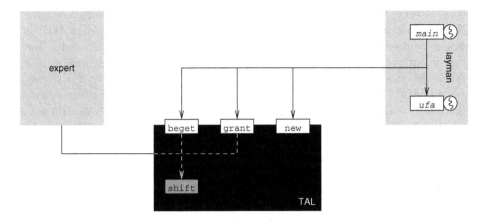

Fig. 9. Component view of TAL

configuration tools such as **pure::variants**. Nevertheless, a layman will be lost for all the many puzzle bricks offered by TAL. For these sorts of customers, TAL appears to be a black box that comes with a minimal export interface. Figure 9 shows this component view in some more detail. Actually, there are only three "fallback functions" making up TAL to an easy to use threads package. These functions are **new()** to allocate stack space for a thread, **beget()** to instantiate a thread, and **grant()** to pass control between threads while maintaing the processor state invariant for inactive threads. The user-defined code to be executed by a thread (on behalf of **beget()**) comes with the UFA instance as provided by the user itself. In fact, TAL is an *open component* [16] that provides a basis for operating system product line development in the small, in particular for a process management subsystem. For the large case, TAL becomes a component whose export interface hides the internal complexity from the user. This way, a high degree of reusability is achieved not only for the expert but also for the layman. Since the export interface is made of customizable system functions, even the layman is given some options for specialization.

4   Aspect Orientation of Operating Systems

The approach discussed so far is not only suited to model functional relationships between abstractions or members of operating system families, but also non-functional ones. Being able to model non-functional interdependencies, however, is only one issue, another issue is to implement them in a modular way to generally improve software maintenance [23, 25]. PURE proved that it must not be a contradiction to come up with a highly modular operating system design and implementation and at the same time keeping the many building blocks manageable. Key to success was family-based design, feature modeling, and aspect-oriented programming, as well as tool support. However, AOP came into play at a fairly late point in time of the PURE development. It mainly served re-engineering purposes of selected pieces of the entire PURE software base. PURE is not an aspect-oriented operating system, but benefits from AOP in various respects. PURE re-engineering in terms of AOP was considered a first experiment and showed that it would pay to consider aspect orientation as a central design issue being followed from the very beginning. With the PURE successor CiAO[1] [24, 25], we are now developing a new family of operating systems that aims to achieve an even higher level of configurability. CiAO focuses on non-functional properties of operating systems whereby these properties technically appear as cross-cutting concerns which impair maintainability of a reasonable large fraction of the system software. Emphasis is on the configuration of *architectural features*, i.e. to consider the duality of operating system structures [22] as a non-functional system property.

4.1   Non-functional Properties Considered Harmful

Traditionally, operating system development is a field in which non-functional properties are of fundamental relevance and imply a number of design decisions. Examples of such properties are synchronization, protection, isolation, sharing, and interaction. In general, these properties are fairly independent from the actual application domain. They are *domain unspecific* and typical, e.g., for general-purpose operating systems. Especially for embedded operating systems, additional *domain specific* non-functional properties are of importance such as energy, timeliness, and dependability. The term "non-functional" sometimes implies fairly complex implementations in order to provide and enforce a certain property. But this is not really the problem. Dependability is an example of highly elaborated designs and implementations, while synchronization may result in very simple solutions (e.g., in case of interrupt locks). The problems with non-functional properties are the possibly many (explicit/implicit) references to their implementations spread across the software of the intrinsic functions of a specific (sub-) system. It is a problem of program fragments repeatedly being closely related to functional code for reflecting certain configuration decisions. When being intermixed with the intrinsic functional implementation, these *cross-cutting concerns* impair reusability to a vast extent. They link implementations to applications, although the pure functional code may be highly independent therefrom. Most non-functional properties are *emergent properties*. They are neither visible in the code nor structure of single components, but "suddenly" emerge from the orchestration of many components into a complete system. Properties that manifest in the integrated system only are indeed cross-cutting, as they result from certain (unknown) characteristics of every single component. Due to their inherent emergence it is, however, not possible to tackle them by decomposition techniques. They need to be understood holistically, that is, on the global scope of software development. One could say they need to be addressed by "*holistic aspects*", meaning that the realization of non-functional concerns does not cross-cut (just) the code, but the whole process of software development. In a number of cases, program fragments representing the non-functional

---

[1] CiAO is Aspect-Oriented

properties are as simple as conditional expressions or they solely wrap around the respective function. In other cases, tons of such software prevents one from realizing the gist of the matter. A first step in order to lessen the problems is to cleanly separate non-functional properties by design: *separation of concerns* need to be a must. Ideally, as a following step the code implementing or referencing these concerns should be automatically generated and inserted at the respective places of the system software. Thus, at a fairly late point in time the implementation of an intrinsic function gets adjusted for a specific configuration.

4.2   Separation of Cross-Cutting Concerns

Central topic of CiAO is to consequently isolate cross-cutting non-funtional properties both by design as well as by means of language support. CiAO strongly follows an aspect-oriented design and is implemented in AspectC++ [31], an aspect-oriented extension to C++. As an idea sketch of AspectC++, a synchronization aspect is being considered in the following. In CiAO, as was in PURE (and is in almost any other operating system), synchronization is a typical cross-cutting concern. Its implementation is separated from the functional code by means of the AspectC++ *pointcut* concept. A pointcut is a set of points in the code (so called *join points*), which are affected by the same cross-cutting concern. In AspectC++ these sets can be defined in a very flexible way by using a declarative language consisting of predefined pointcut functions, wildcards for matching names, and algebraic operations to combine pointcuts. The pointcut definition shown in figure 10 enumerates the (non-preemptive) scheduling functions `block()`, `ready (Thread*)`, and `yield()`, each of which representing a critical section when being reused in order to support preemptive mode of operation. Calls to these functions need to be synchronized. In addition to the pointcut definitions, actions need to be defined that are to be executed when any of the join points in the pointcut is reached at run time. Any of these actions is called an *advice*. Figure 10 shows the definition of the two actions needed to take care of synchronization of the cricial scheduling functions. The first advice definition means that *before* the body of any function described by `critical()` is executed, entrance to the critical section is requested by calling `enter()`. Similarily the second advice causes the call on

```
pointcut critical() =  execution("void block()") ||
                       execution("void ready(Thread*)") ||
                       execution("void yield()");
aspect Synchronization {
    advice critical(): before() { enter(); }
    advice critical(): after()  { leave(); }
};
```

Fig. 10. Modularization of a non-functional property "synchronization" in the AOP language AspectC++. The AspectC++ aspect weaver translates `aspect` into a C++ `class`. In addition, it looks for `critical()` join points in a given source code and, once matched, inserts the `advice` code before/after them, accordingly.

Table 1. Memory footprint (in bytes, x86) of members of the PURE nucleus family

	text	data	bss	total
exclusive processor usage	434	0	0	434
interruptive mode of operation	812	64	392	1268
cooperative scheduling	1620	0	28	1648
non-preemptive scheduling	1671	0	28	1699
coordinative interrupt propagation	1882	8	416	2306
preemptive scheduling	3642	8	428	4062

leave() *after* the critical section is left. Both advice definitions are encapsulated in a named modular unit, which is an *aspect*. Besides the advice definitions, aspects can (similar to classes) store and manage state information, which is also accessible by the advice code bodies. The AspectC++ compiler (resp. aspect weaver) expands the advice code at the specified join points, it interweaves component code and code that manifests a certain non-functional property. The two advice functions enter() and leave() implement the *interrupt synchronization* feature shown in figure 7, either by means of interrupt locking or in an interrupt transparent manner. Moreover, by using pure::variants, the synchronization aspect will be implicitly applied when that feature is going to be selected during the configuration process of the system software. That is to say, pure::variants automatically calls the AspectC++ compiler with the synchronization aspect as additional input when interrupt synchronization needs to be a feature of the resulting system. The AOP approach was motivated by experiences having been made with PURE. By turning the design of the PURE family into an object-oriented implementation using C++ and by enforcing domain-specific configuration decisions with AOP on the basis of AspectC++, a highly efficient software product line was the outcome. Table 1 shows some of the results, giving the memory footprints of individual products of the *nucleus family* of PURE. In this example, the nucleus member providing preemptive scheduling has been automatically generated by (1) reusing the two branches "non-preemptive scheduling" and "coordinative interrupt propagation" and (2) applying the synchronization aspect to that mixing. Thus, a new family member was generated automatically from an already existing system software product line by using AOP techniques. Non-preemptive scheduling functions which are critical in a preemptive environment remain fully reusable. Every single point of invocation of these functions is considered a join point where synchronization code is automatically inserted in order to make preemptive scheduling work.

5   Conclusion

Developing and maintaining software product lines of (embedded) operating systems largely benefits from aspect-oriented programming. By relying on an aspect language such as AspectC++, many non-functional properties can be expressed as aspects and, thus, separated from functional code. This significantly improves reusability of that code. Typical cases of domain unspecific non-functional properties of an operating system are synchronization, protection, isolation, and sharing. For the domain of embedded systems, non-functional properties such as energy, timeliness, and dependability additionally need to be taken into account. An aspect weaver will take care of interweaving aspect code with functional code. Application of such a tool depends on configuration decisions related to the specific problem domain for which a specialized system software solution is going to be created. By considering the aspect weaver an ingredient part of an operating system workbench that supports feature-based configuration (e.g., by means of tools such as `pure::variants`), giving functional code non-functional properties becomes an automated process. The PURE development shows that design and implementation of highly reusable and yet specialized operating system abstractions or functions must not be a contradiction in terms. Key to success was to understand an operating system as a software product line. The outcome was a solution that scales with the demands of many embedded systems. As indicated by the TAL case study, PURE demonstrates that feature-based development of an operating system family is a very promising approach in order to master the increasing functional complexity of embedded systems in spite of utmost resource scarceness. AspectC++ evolved as a logical consequence from the PURE development and mainly was applied to selected PURE components in the course of re-engineering. With CiAO, the PURE successor, an aspect-oriented operating system is being developed now in which aspect orientation (and in particular AspectC++) plays the central role from the very beginning. Goal is to come up with an aspect-oriented operating system that, on the one hand, fulfills the many very specific requirements of deeply embedded systems and, on the other hand, improves reusability as well as maintainability of the respective system software better than PURE was able to do.

References

1. eCos homepage. http://ecos.sourceware.org/.
2. OSEK/VDX standard. http://www.osek-vdx.org/.
3. R. A. Åberg, J. L. Lawall, M. Südholt, G. Muller, and A.-F. L. Meur. On the automatic evolution of an os kernel using temporal logic and aop. In *18th IEEE Int. Conf. on Automated Software Engineering (ASE '03)*, pages 196–204, Montreal, Canada, Mar. 2003. IEEE.
4. D. Beuche. Variant management with pure::variants. Technical report, pure-systems GmbH, 2003. http://www.pure-systems.com/.
5. D. Beuche, A. Guerrouat, H. Papajewski, W. Schröder-Preikschat, O. Spinczyk, and U. Spinczyk. The PURE family of object-oriented operating systems for deeply embedded systems. In *2nd IEEE Int. Symp. on OO Real-Time Distributed Computing (ISORC '99)*, pages 45–53, St Malo, France, May 1999.
6. D. Beuche, O. Spinczyk, and W. Schröder-Preikschat. Fine-grained application-specific customization for embedded software. In *Proceedings of the International IFIP TC10 Workshop on Distributed and Parallel Embedded Systems (DIPES 2002)*, pages 141–151, Montreal, Canada, Aug. 2002. Kluwer Academic Publishers, ISBN 0-140207156-6.

7. Y. Coady and G. Kiczales. Back to the future: A retroactive study of aspect evolution in operating system code. In M. Akşit, editor, *2nd Int. Conf. on Aspect-Oriented Software Development (AOSD '03)*, pages 50–59, Boston, MA, USA, Mar. 2003. ACM.

8. Y. Coady, G. Kiczales, M. Feeley, and G. Smolyn. Using AspectC to improve the modularity of path-specific customization in operating system code. In *ESEC/FSE '01*, 2001.

9. A. Colyer and A. Clement. Large-scale AOSD for middleware. In K. Lieberherr, editor, *3rd Int. Conf. on Aspect-Oriented Software Development (AOSD '04)*, pages 56–65, Lancaster, UK, Mar. 2004. ACM.

10. A. Colyer, A. Clement, R. Bodkin, and J. Hugunin. Using AspectJ for component integration in middleware. In *18th ACM Conf. on OOP, Systems, Languages, and Applications (OOPSLA '03)*, pages 339–344, New York, NY, USA, 2003. ACM.

11. J. Cordsen and W. Schröder-Preikschat. Object-Oriented Operating System Design and the Revival of Program Families. In *2nd Int. W'shop on Object Orientation in Operating Systems (I-WOOOS '91)*, pages 24–28, Palo Alto, CA, October 17–18, 1991.

12. K. Czarnecki and U. W. Eisenecker. *Generative Programming. Methods, Tools and Applications*. AW, May 2000.

13. M. Devillechaise, J. Menaud, G. Muller, and J. Lawall. Web cache prefetching as an aspect: Towards a dynamic-weaving based solution. In M. Akşit, editor, *2nd Int. Conf. on Aspect-Oriented Software Development (AOSD '03)*, pages 110–119, Boston, MA, USA, Mar. 2003. ACM.

14. K. Driesen and U. Hölzle. The direct cost of virtual function calls in C++. In *11th ACM Conf. on OOP, Systems, Languages, and Applications (OOPSLA '96)*, Oct. 1996.

15. M. Fiuczynski, R. Grimm, Y. Coady, and D. Walker. patch (1) considered harmful. In *10th W'shop on Hot Topics in Operating Systems (HotOS '05)*. USENIX, 2005.

16. A. Gal, W. Schröder-Preikschat, and O. Spinczyk. Open components. In *Proceedings of the First OOPSLA Workshop on Language Mechanisms for Programming Software Components*, pages 75–78, Tampa, Florida, Oct. 2001.

17. A. N. Habermann, L. Flon, and L. Cooprider. Modularization and Hierarchy in a Family of Operating Systems. *CACM*, 19(5):266–272, 1976.

18. W. Harrison and H. Ossher. Subject-oriented programming—a critique of pure objects. In *8th ACM Conf. on OOP, Systems, Languages, and Applications (OOPSLA '93)*, pages 411–428, Sept. 1993.

19. F. Hunleth and R. Cytron. Footprint and feature management using aspect-oriented programming techniques. In *2002 Joint LCTES & SCOPES Conferences (LCTES/SCOPES '02)*, pages 38–45, Berlin, Germany, June 2002. ACM.

20. J. M. Kahn, R. H. Katz, and K. S. J. Pister. Next century challenges: Mobile networking for "smart dust". In *International Conference on Mobile Computing and Networking (MOBICOM '99)*, pages 271–278, 1999.

21. G. Kiczales, J. Lamping, A. Mendhekar, C. Maeda, C. Lopes, J.-M. Loingtier, and J. Irwin. Aspect-oriented programming. In M. Aksit and S. Matsuoka, editors, *11th Eur. Conf. on OOP (ECOOP '97)*, volume 1241 of *LNCS*, pages 220–242. Springer, June 1997.

22. H. C. Lauer and R. M. Needham. On the duality of operating system structures. *ACM OSR*, 13(2):3–19, Apr. 1979.

23. D. Lohmann, W. Schröder-Preikschat, and O. Spinczyk. Functional and non-functional properties in a family of embedded operating systems. In *10th IEEE Int. W'shop on Object-oriented Real-time Dependable Systems (WORDS '05)*, pages 413–420, Sedona, AZ, USA, Feb. 2005.

24. D. Lohmann and O. Spinczyk. Architecture-Neutral Operating System Components. *23rd ACM Symp. on OS Principles (SOSP '03)*, Oct. 2003. WiP presentation.
25. D. Lohmann, O. Spinczyk, and W. Schröder-Preikschat. On the configuration of non-functional properties in operating system product lines. In *4th AOSD W'shop on Aspects, Components and Patterns for Infrastructure Software (AOSD-ACP4IS '05)*, pages 19–25, Chicago, IL, USA, Mar. 2005. Northeastern University, Boston (NU-CCIS-05-03).
26. S. Matsuoka and A. Yonezawa. *Analysis of inheritance anomaly in object-oriented concurrent programming languages*. MIT Press, Cambridge, MA, USA, 1993.
27. D. L. Parnas. On the design and development of program families. *IEEE TOSE*, SE-2(1):1–9, Mar. 1976.
28. A. Rashid and N. Leidenfrost. Supporting flexible object database evolution with aspects. In G. Karsai and E. Visser, editors, *3rd Int. Conf. on Generative Programming and Component Engineering (GPCE '04)*, volume 3286 of *LNCS*, pages 75–94. Springer, Oct. 2004.
29. F. Schön, W. Schröder-Preikschat, O. Spinczyk, and U. Spinczyk. On interrupt-transparent synchronization in an embedded object-oriented operating system. In *3rd IEEE Int. Symp. on OO Real-Time Distributed Computing (ISORC '00)*, pages 270–277, Newport Beach, CA, USA, Mar. 2000.
30. O. Spinczyk and D. Lohmann. Using AOP to develop architecture-neutral operating system components. In *11th SIGOPS European W'shop*, pages 188–192, Leuven, Belgium, Sept. 2004. ACM.
31. O. Spinczyk, D. Lohmann, and M. Urban. Advances in AOP with AspectC++. In H. Fujita and M. Mejri, editors, *New Trends in Software Methodologies, Tools and Techniques (SoMeT '05)*, number 129 in Frontiers in Artificial Intelligence and Applications, pages 33–53, Tokyo, Japan, Sept. 2005. IOS Press.
32. D. Tennenhouse. Proactive computing. *CACM*, pages 43–45, May 2000.
33. A. Tešanović, K. Sheng, and J. Hansson. Application-tailored database systems: a case of aspects in an embedded database. In *8th Int. Database Engineering and Applications Symp. (IDEAS '04)*, Coimbra, Portugal, July 2004. IEEE.
34. C. Walls. The Perfect RTOS, 2004. embedded world 2004.
35. M. Weiser. The computer for the 21st centrury. *Scientific American*, 265(3):94–104, 1991.
36. D. M. Weiss and C. T. R. Lai. *Software Product-Line Engineering: A Family-Based Software Development Process*. Addison-Wesley, 1999.
37. C. Zhang and H.-A. Jacobsen. Quantifying aspects in middleware platforms. In *2nd Int. Conf. on Aspect-Oriented Software Development (AOSD '03)*, pages 130–139, New York, NY, USA, 2003. ACM Press.

Bringing Ease and Adaptability to MPSoC Software Design: A Component-Based Approach

Ali Erdem Özcan[1], Sébastien Jean[2], and Jean-Bernard Stefani[2]

[1] Advanced Technology Lab. STMicroelectronics
Ali-Erdem.Ozcan@st.com
[2] SARDES Project, INRIA Rhône-Alpes
Name.Surname@inrialpes.fr

Abstract. Multi-Processor Systems-on-Chips (MPSoCs) gather multiple processors and hardware accelerators in a single chip to meet the performance and energy consumption requirements of mobile devices. To follow the rapid evolution of such applications, the MPSoC community need flexible and programmable platforms intended to be diverted to many use cases, and hence consider definitely the software as one of the main aspects of the system design. To deal with an ever growing complexity when designing for such heterogeneous and evolving platforms, software developers have to adopt a novel software design methodology that encourages the software customization through modularity, reuse and module assembly to build systems and applications. Component-based Software Engineering (CBSE), enabling software customization by adding, removing and substituting components seems to be adequate to reach that goal. We investigate this area while developing Think, a lightweight implementation of the Fractal component model, which applies CBSE principles down to the lowest software layer: the operating system. Think allows various kinds of communication semantics from simple method invocations to RPC, recursive component composition, and comes with retargetable configuration and specification tools. In this paper, we show how Think can make flexible and customizable the operating system and application design for MPSoC a reality.

1 Introduction

In the late sixties, Gordon Moore predicted that integrated circuits complexity would grow exponentially while circuits size would be reduced similarly [1]. The evolution of semi-conductors technology has turned this prediction into a law, and it is nowadays possible to integrate hundreds of millions of transistor on a single chip. Circuits known as Multi-Processor System-on-Chips (MPSoCs) now embed entire applications like multimedia codecs, data cyphering, ... The word *system* is in this case justified by the fact that such circuits gather several interacting components like processing units, memories, I/O peripherals, ... In a not so distant future, the 50 nm lithography technology should allow in early 2010 to integrate billions of transistors working at a frequency approaching tens

G. Barthe et al. (Eds.): CASSIS 2005, LNCS 3956, pp. 118–137, 2006.
© Springer-Verlag Berlin Heidelberg 2006

of GHz. However, reaching this performance level will increase design complexity. As the conception of a new MPSoC is long and costly, today's best practice tends to the design of long-life multi-purpose platforms that can be reused for several applications. Such generic platforms give a more important place to software than before in order to increase customizability and reuse. In this context, using component-based software engineering techniques seems to be one of the best ways for rapid application development.

In this paper, we demonstrate the benefits of using component-based technology to design MPSoC software. We provide software to designers a methodology and associated tools to easily develop (and retarget if needed) both operating system and applications for such platforms. Our approach is based on Fractal component model, and one of its implementation called Think that focuses on operating system design. We show how Fractal features fulfill most MPSoCs software customization and configuration requirements. We also present how Think has been extended in order to make it suitable for MPSoCs software design, particularly to support parallel programming.

Section 2 replaces our work within its context by presenting MPSoCs technology, applications and design challenges. Section 3 follows with a presentation of component-based software engineering principles as well as a relevant state-of-the-art of its application to operating system design, and finishes by underlining the shape of the appropriate component technology. Then, Section 4 gives an in-depth view of the component model on which we based our work. Section 5 presents how this technology can be used to efficiently design MPSoCs software, focusing on the way a C implementation called Think has been extended in order to take into account the constraints of MPSoCs. Section 6 is dedicated to evaluations while Section 7 concludes and introduces future work.

2   MPSoCs Technology, Applications and Software Design Challenges

In this section, we first present some basic design issues related to MPSoCs, focusing on architecture and applications, to finally point out the software design challenges for these platforms.

2.1   Technology and Applications

Digital convergence, bringing multimedia and communications to end-users, has lead to a new generation of integrated circuits able to satisfy the constraints of modern home entertainment and mobile applications. Home appliances and mobile multimedia devices need important computational power for intensive use of multimedia codecs, digital transmission, cryptography, and so on, combined with low energy budget and integration cost constraints. Circuit designers answered to this need with System-on-Chips (SoCs). In this solution, the computational power comes from customized hardware (*Application Specific Integrated Circuits*), single chip integration brings low energy consumption while low fabrication cost becomes possible with mass production (even if SoC design is highly costly).

Vis-a-vis the increasing number of applications that must be supported, SoCs became more and more programmable by integrating multiple-processors instead of specific hardware accelerators which resulted the emergence of Multi-Processor Systems-on-Chips (MPSoCs). MPSoCs can be seen as reusable multi-purpose programmable platforms where on-chip resources are optimized for a generic kind of application but many of its features are handled by additional software. Hence, MPSoCs are no longer completely designed by hardware designers but also by software designers who are in charge of customizing generic platforms according to the applications that are going to be hosted.

Basically, MPSoCs are characterized by the gathering on a single silicon die of several processors and hardware accelerators (usually about ten) interacting via advanced communication links. Embedded processing units, from Digital Signal Processor (DSP) to Very Large Instruction Word (VLIW) parallel processor, are highly heterogeneous. They can manage their own memory or cache (coherently shared among units or stand-alone) and usually share an external memory. MPSoCs also embed various I/O peripherals like wireless communication devices, network interfaces and so on. To make all these units work together efficiently, different communication paradigms can be deployed from classical buses to packet-switched communication mediums, mostly called *Network-on-Chip* (NoC).

2.2   Software Design Challenges

Since their birth, MPSoCs have been used to host applications that need efficiency in terms of computation, energy consumption and space footprint. Today, MPSoC designers face challenges related to four crucial factors: diversity, time-to-market, cost and computation performance.

The Evolution Factor. Today's markets have become highly fragmented and often unpredictable. Furthermore, the multiple standards that rule multimedia and communications do not keep evolving. Figure 1 gives an example of short-term evolutions that should occur in communication and multimedia areas.

The Time-to-Market Factor. The traditional MPSoC design cycle typically requires two years between freezing the product's specification and starting

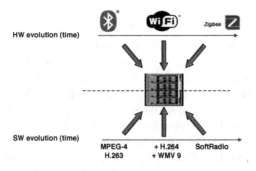

Fig. 1. Hardware/software short-term evolution examples for MPSoC platforms

the volume production, while the equipment manufacturers face increasing pressures from their own markets to introduce new models every year or even more frequently. It is thus necessary, particularly considering the evolution factor, that silicon manufacturers reduce as most as possible the time-to-market.

The Cost Factor. On one hand, porting an existing chip design from one technology generation to the next, without making any other change, costs around a million dollars. On the other hand, designing a new chip or enhancing a previous design can require huger expenses. Even if silicon manufacturers succeed in facing the time-to-market factor, it does not seem reasonable to switch to a new chip design at every standard evolution.

The Computational Performance Factor. The last key challenge consists at using as efficiently as possible the computational capacities of MPSoCs. As the number of processing units increases according to Moore's law, it becomes necessary to find ways to also increase the level of parallelism when running applications. This leads to consider MPSoCs as almost traditional distributed systems.

Above mentioned challenges influence naturally the ongoing efforts that are centered around the design of adequate operating systems which would let application designers use as efficiently as possible the underlying hardware while supporting several application evolutions. Beside their classical role which is the reliable and efficient management of hardware resources for hosted applications, the embedded operating systems for MPSoC must offer three main capabilities: customizability, reconfigurability and distribution-awareness.

Customizability. The operating system must be tailored respecting the application needs to provide high efficiency. For example, if an application does not need multi-threading nor networking, these features should be removed from the operating system in order to increase the performance.

Reconfigurability. Because these general-purpose platforms are designed to host various applications during their life-cycle, the underlying operating system must be reconfigurable for adapting its services to application needs.

Distribution-awareness. Vis-a-vis the increasing number of processing elements embedded into MPSoCs, application distribution will become an important bottleneck in the future. This means that MPSoC operating systems should be designed as distributed systems, allowing various parallelism paradigms (Symmetrical Multi-Processor, distributed memory pipelining, and so on).

Beside these features, one must have a larger view of software design for MPSoCs. It is indeed necessary to have customizable and reconfigurable distributed operating systems, it is also much more convenient to have a methodology that allows to design both operating systems and applications in the same way and to easily port the whole set from one platform to another.

In the following, we present the basis of our approach to ease MPSoCs software design. This approach relies on component-based software engineering principles and offers to software designers a development methodology and an adequate toolset for building customized and reconfigurable operating systems and applications.

3   Component-Based Software Engineering for Operating System Design

This Section reminds component-based software engineering principles, and shows how they can help facing the software design challenges for MPSoCs.

3.1   Component-Based Software Engineering Principles

Components can be considered as a step beyond objects principles, while ever questing for more reusability. As Szyperski stated in [2], components can be seen as software bricks with well defined frontiers which let third parties to compose applications respecting their own needs.

From the outside, a component is only seen as a black box through the set of interfaces that it exposes (which are expressing a contract). A component is an independent unit of software that incarnates the grain of deployment and composition: a component-based application is made of an assembly of components where each one is deployed independently from each other. In addition to objects that specifies the services that they provide through interfaces, components specifies also by the same way the services that they require. Thus, components can provide and require multiple interfaces. Components need to be connected for interacting. Such a communication link that connects the client interface of a component to a server interface of another is usually called a binding or a connector. Since components hide their implementation through interfaces, they can easily be substituted by other components that provide the same services, even at runtime. Components are often related to the *separation of concerns* principle, which argues that functional aspects (application logic) must be defined and managed independently of non-functional ones (security, persistency, transactions, ...).

Component-based software engineering aims at providing a methodology and tools to take benefits of component technology. First, component models define component's structures, lifecycles, interaction methods and composition rules. Several component models are proposed by academic and industrial actors to satisfy different application needs. Among them, the most known ones are CCM [4] or EJB [5], and Microsoft's COM component model. Component models can also be characterized by their recursive or reflective behavior. A recursive component model (in opposition to a flat one) is able to consider component assemblies as components, allowing to hide their fine/coarse grain while managing them in the same way. Finally, a reflective component model is able to have its self-vision, and to act on it. Reflectivity is an intrinsic requirement for reconfiguration.

Second, implementation frameworks let programmers to build software that is conform to a given component model using a given implementation language. For example, Fractal component model [3] has two main implementations which are Julia [15] (for Java) and Think [16] (for C/Assembly).

Finally, some component composition tools such as Architecture Description Languages goes with some models for providing to programmers the architectural view of component-based softwares. ADLs, whose [8] presents a survey, are not only powerful tools to express the software structure (what set of components makes the application, how components are bound), but also deployment and configuration elements where components are instantiated and the packages can be found.

3.2 Component-Based Software Engineering Applied to MPSoCs Software Design

In the last ten years, many academic and industrial research efforts have been concentrated on applying component-based software engineering principles to operating system design [9]. We present below the most significants of them.

Choices. [10] is an object-oriented, customizable operating system whose main goal is to allow users to easily optimize and adapt the system for specific application behaviors and workloads. Its design consists in a hierarchy of frameworks made of classes representing the system entities that can be configured to perform different roles. Customization is achieved by subclassing and by overriding methods. Regarding the configurability and composition, Choices provides an interactive graphical tool, OS View, which allows both system and user-level services to be dynamically reconfigured, customized, and evaluated. Reconfiguration is here limited to the loading of new operating system classes.

OS-Kit. [11] is a domain-specific set of software components intended to facilitate the construction of standalone systems on Intel x86 hardware. To provide usability, OS-Kit adopted a subset of COM as the basic framework allowing components to interact with each other efficiently (but without any protection) through well-defined interfaces. Composition is left solely to the kernel developer; there is no tool to help with. The OS-Kit is essentially a collection of code segments that must be integrated and connected manually by a third party. This system does not focus on embedded systems neither supports reconfiguration.

Pure. [12] was developed to offer an operating system tailored to the application, in the context of deeply embedded systems. Components are herein arranged in a structure made of a nucleus and an extension. The nucleus is responsible for the implementation of a minimal subset of system functions for the scheduling of interrupts and threads. Features that represent some kind of extension, called minimal system extensions, are added to the system in the nucleus extension. PURE comes with tools that let users specify their needs and requirements for the customized system, using an annotation language to provide the necessary informations such as dependency and attributes and to help the generation tool to evaluate and choose the right building units for combination. The result of the configuration process is a kind of *makefile* that produces the desired system. Pure does not support reconfiguration.

Pebble. [13] is designed to be an efficient application-specific operating system and to support component-based applications. As an operating system, it adopts a microkernel architecture with a minimal privileged mode nucleus that is only responsible for switching between protection domains ensuring the code safety. The functionality of the operating system is provided by user-level operating system components (servers) that can be dynamically replaced, augmented, or layered. The programming model is client/server; client components (applications) request services from system components (servers). Based on a system description, Pebble includes no composition tool to provide the construction of the system. The Pebble kernel has a small footprint (nearly 560 kB of memory usage) which turns it appropriate for various embedded systems. However, like Choices, Pebble provides reconfiguration only through the loading of new services.

All these previous examples of component-based operating systems have certain limitations with regards to requirements stated for MPSoCs. First, they all need core runtime functions in order to execute components, mainly an hardware abstraction layer and some convenient abstractions like processes, protection and communication mechanisms. MPSoC software needs, much more than elsewhere, a high level of customizability. There is no place for classical software abstraction levels that are imposed to programmers. Second, few of these operating systems provide dynamic reconfiguration support, and none allows the substitution/removal of components neither supports distribution. Finally, none of these propositions offers a homogeneous development methodology that can respond to both operating system and application programming.

We present below our vision on the key challenges and required features of component technology to satisfy the needs of software design for MPSoCs such as we identified in section 2.

Software customization. One of the main elements for customization is a development methodology that enables the component assembly. This feature can be enhanced by an ADL and adequate code generation tools.

Reconfiguration. In a component based system, (re)configuration units are components. Reflexivity is a key concept for the dynamic reconfiguration since it provides the possibility to introspect and to intercept the system on-the-fly. Another key mechanism is flexible bindings whose boundaries can be dynamically changed in order to substitute a component by another. All of these mechanisms can be enforced with a high-level description tool such as a dynamic ADL.

Distributed Multi-Processor System. Components are also the units of distribution and deployment. Flexible bindings are the key aspect of a distribution framework for supporting remote interface invocations transparently to both client and server sides. Finally, high level distribution constructs can be supported by the ADL and its code generation tool chain to be able to specify distributed systems.

In the following, we present our approach for MPSoCs software design. We first introduce the component model we have adopted, called Fractal. Fractal encloses most of the properties that are required to reach our goal: reflexivity, flexible bindings, ADL-based configurability. We then show how this component model can be implemented in the context of MPSoCs and what tools can be provided to alleviate software designers' burden.

4 Fractal Component Model Principles

We based our work on Fractal [14], a last generation and very flexible component model which has been defined for building highly configurable systems and applications. It is founded on a reduced set of concepts: *components, interfaces* and *bindings*. In Fractal, components are runtime entities that incarnate encapsulation, configuration and composition units. Components interact with other components via their *client* and *server* interfaces. *Server interfaces* give access to functionalities provided by components while *client interfaces* enable components to invoke required services on other components. Since the interfaces are the unique access points of components, *bindings* are needed to link them. In Fractal, *bindings* can implement arbitrary communication protocols.

Fractal reveals many original aspects in comparison to other component models. First, Fractal is neutral against programming languages and can thus lead to a very large number of implementations targeting different application contexts. Second, in opposition to mostly well-known component-based environments, Fractal does not rely on any system nor runtime services for executing components. Hence, it is possible to use Fractal components at the lowest software level, even within the operating system. We enumerate below some significant novelties of Fractal.

4.1 Recursive Composition and Component Sharing

As illustrated on Figure 2, Fractal distinguishes two kinds of components which are *primitive* and *composite* components. *Primitive components* encapsulate functional code. *Composite components* are created by the composition of other components, either primitives or composites. Every Fractal system results in a top-level component composed by an arbitrary number of subcomponents. Since subcomponents themselves can be composite components, a recursive composition feature is enabled. This recursion ends with primitive components. By this way, arbitrary levels can be achieved to model hierarchical levels of abstraction, reuse, control, composition and so on.

In Fractal, a component instance can be shared by multiple composite components. As a result, all these composites' subcomponents can be directly bound to the shared component, without any indirection. This original feature is very useful to model shared resources such as a memory allocator of an operating system.

4.2 Separation of Concerns

Fractal defines two kinds of interfaces for distinguishing the control and functional concerns of components. (*i*) *Functional interfaces* are used to expose the

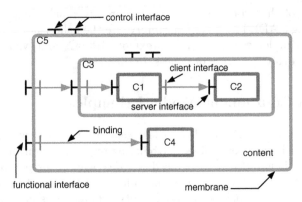

Fig. 2. Fractal components

services provided by a component (server interfaces) or to invoke required operations (client interfaces) on other components. On the other hand, (*ii*) *control interfaces* embody the control behavior of a component. This separation of interface natures results into the division of component structure into two parts. While the *content* of a component implements the functional interfaces, the *membrane* implements the control interfaces. The membrane is in charge of providing arbitrary control actions through control interfaces providing introspection and/or modification of the internal structure and the behavior of components. One can notice that, in the case of composite components, the *content* is implemented by a set of other components. Both primitive and composite components have *membranes* that can implement an arbitrary number of control interfaces with generic or specific behaviors.

Fractal support runtime reflection in the sense that components can provide some controller interfaces that give information and manipulation access on their structural and behavioral features. Fractal specifies an extensible and also reducible set of control interfaces. These interfaces are :

Binding controller: If a component needs dynamic bindings and unbindings (i.e. case of reconfiguration) of some server interfaces to its client interfaces, it provides the *Binding Controller* interface. The implementation of this interface can vary with regards to components' needs. For instance, one can set up a counter when a binding occurs in order to trace further clients' invocations.

Content controller: Composite components can provide the *Content Controller* interface for listing, adding and removing subcomponents in their contents. This interface is particularly required for dynamic reconfiguration support since it provides introspection and possibility of manipulation of the internal structure of a component.

Lifecycle controller: A component can provide via the *Lifecycle Controller* interface some control over its lifecycle phases (starting/holding/stopping components). This interface is also useful for capturing a quiescent state of components that are subject of reconfiguration.

Attribute controller: A component can give access to its attributes via `getter` and `setter` operations via the *Attribute Controller* interface.

4.3   Flexible Bindings

Fractal does not make any assumption on communication protocols for component interactions. Thanks to this flexibility, any interaction semantics can be implemented within bindings. In its simplest form, a *binding* can be implemented as a memory pointer that refers to the server interface (in this case, the interaction is achieved by a simple function invocation). Bindings can also encompass more complex communication semantics such as RPC or system call or even data streaming. In these cases, bindings are also modeled with components (primitive or composite).

4.4   Architecture Description Language Support

Fractal allows to capture the architectural view of software through the use of an extensible architecture description language. This ADL offers high-level constructs for specifying the components in terms of their content, interfaces, attributes and interconnections. As the Fractal ADL is extensible, software designers can add new constructs into component descriptions to satisfy specific needs.

5   MPSoCs Software Design with Think

Fractal is neutral with regards to programming language in which it is implemented. Among its several implementations, Think is the one that allows Fractal programming in C. Even if it is originally designed for building component-based operating systems, we believe that it has good foundations to also be used for application programming especially in the context of highly specialized embedded software. Think framework is made of three main elements: a programming model mapped on standard C language, a complete compilation tool-chain based on the use of both IDL and ADL, and finally, a library of components that can be used to build multi-processor system and application software.

The work that we describe in this paper is an extension of the open source repository of Think project [16] that contains additional features for MPSoC software programming. Between others, we contributed to Think with a novel programming guide that eases component implementation and gives some optimization perspectives. We also extended the compilation chain and the component library for building distributed operating systems and applications.

5.1   Think Programming Environment

Think's programming environment involves the use of three different languages, dedicated to define components interfaces (Think IDL), to give their implementation (ANSI C + guidelines), and to assemble them (Think ADL) in order to build an entire application. We describe hereafter, using the simple example of an "hello world" kernel[1], how these elements are jointly used to easily produce an ad'hoc kernel and application from scratch.

Interface Description Language. In order to describe interfaces, Think provides an IDL whose syntax is closer to the one used to define Java's interfaces (with few types and keywords restrictions). Think IDL considers basic types of Java (e.g. *int, short, char*), enables the construction of complex types as others interfaces and has package support.

The benefit of using such an IDL is first to have a neutral language for enabling multiple back-end implementation languages. Second, such a strongly typed language enables some type-based verifications at compile-time that C language does not allow. Finally, well-defined interfaces allow automatic generation of interaction adapters, such as stubs and skeletons for remote communications between components.

The following code sample illustrates the description of our example's *Console* interface. This interface makes part of the *video.api* package and provides two methods that respectively display a character or a string on the console media.

```
package video.api ;
public interface Console {
  void putC(char c) ;
  void putString(string C) ;
}
```

Architecture Description. A little bit differentiated from Fractal ADL which is XML-based, this language adopts a Java-like syntax and supports most of the issues that are specified by Fractal.

As illustrated in Figure 3, Think ADL provides two component declaration constructs for primitive and composite components. As mentioned in section 4.1 both types of components have an arbitrary number of provided (server) and required (client) interfaces. Each interface is declared by a reference to its type and the assignment of a name. In the case of a primitive component (Figure 3.a), the implementation is done in C language, thus the implementation file should be referred. In the case of composite components (Figure 3.c, 3.d), the content is constituted by subcomponents. Hence, the composite construct allows subcomponent declarations that associate a name to each instance of subcomponent. For convenience reasons, programmers have choice between referring a component type or a real component when they declare subcomponents (Figure 3.c).

The "=" operator is used to refer a real component declaration while the ":" operator is used to refer a component type (Figure 3.b). In the case of a component type reference, one must overload this reference by a real component declaration at another level of description (Figure 3.d). The kind of subcomponent declaration is very useful for creating reusable composite declarations that will be used for example to describe later some platform specific declarations. By this way, the concrete implementation of the component can differ according to target hardware platform's characteristics.

---

[1] A kernel dedicated to display the "hello world" string on console.

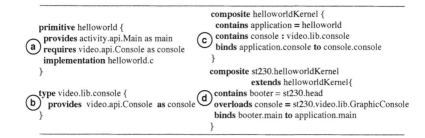

Fig. 3. ADL code example that describes a basic *Hello World* kernel for ST230 platform

Composite components allow also *binding* constructs for specifying the connections between their subcomponents and/or their *server* and *client* interfaces. Finally, components can extend other components for overloading or adding some subcomponents and/or giving some more precisions about their internal structures such as creating new bindings or also assigning some attributes.

Think Programming Guide for C. Once interfaces and application architecture have been defined, implementations of primitive components remain to be written. For that purpose, programmers should use a programming guide which is mapped on C language. Theses guidelines are defined through macros that will be used by standard C compilers. This feature is crucial for the portability and the reusability of the implementation code. Programmers are also free to not use these guidelines if this does not answer their specific needs. In this case, they are supposed to respect some naming and binary interface conventions for enabling the interactions with other components. The binary interface of Think components are detailed in [6].

The mentioned programming guide provides five macros for enabling component programming in C.

- `DECLARE_DATA{<variable>*}`, to declare components instances' private instance data.
- `METHOD(<interface>, <method>)`, to declare provided interfaces methods.
- `REQUIRED.<interface>`, to access to a required interface
- `DATA.<variable>`, to access to components instances' data.
- `ATTRIBUTE.<variable>`, to access to an attribute of the component.
- `CALL(<interface>, <method> [, <argn>]*)`, to invoke operations on a required interface

We give hereafter a source code example for the **helloworld** client component in order to illustrate the implementation of a simple component. Each instance owns a private attribute called **counter** which is incremented, when calling the **main** method, before calling the **putString** method on the **console** required interface.

```
DECLARE_DATA
{int counter ;}
void METHOD(mItf, main)(void *_this, int argc, char **argv) {
  DATA.counter ++ ;
  CALL(REQUIRED.console, putString, "Helloworld") ;
}
```

The value of these macros are obviously specific to each component. The specialization of these macros is done by our compilation chain. In fact, an encapsulation file is generated for each component with regards of the information given in ADL and IDL description of components. This generated file first defines each of these macros and a set of data structures that are necessary for the implementation of a given component and then includes the implementation file that is written by the programmer. By this way, these macros are resolved into specific values for each component during the classical C pre-compilation phase.

5.2   Compilation Chain

The Think framework is completed with a compilation chain supporting the above programming environment. This chain takes as input a set of IDL, ADL and C implementation files and gives as output a set of ANSI C files that are compiled and linked with the target platforms' specific C compilers. By this way, Think programs are easily portable to different platforms. Figure 4 details the different compilation steps:

1. IDL files are compiled into C implementation and header files. In its simplest way, an interface is translated into a binary interface that conforms to the one specified in [6]. If more complex communication adapters are needed (such as RPC stubs and skeletons), they are also generated at this step.
2. ADL files are compiled into C files. For primitive components, encapsulation files are generated as described previously. For composite components, the entire implementation code is generated according to the ADL description (the concrete implementation is given in subcomponents).
3. Once all input files are translated into C (or eventually assembly) files, they are compiled into object files using the target platforms C compiler. After this step, a set of binary object files are produced.

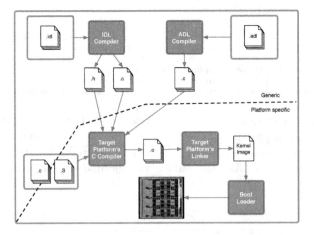

Fig. 4. Think compilation chain. The top part contains target independent code and tools while the bottom part includes the target specific ones.

4. Finally, the set of object files are linked into a kernel image that can be deployed on the hardware device.

5.3   Kortex

Kortex is a library, gathering a set of Think components dedicated to embedded operating system and application design, that aims at enhancing the component reuse. In this subsection, we describe its content. One must remind that these components are given for convenience and do not necessarily make part of a kernel if they are not needed. However, except for the HAL ones, all included components are entirely reusable and help rapid kernel development.

Hardware Abstraction Layer (HAL). HAL components are hardware-specific, and thus vary from a platform to another. This set of components usually includes booters, trap handlers, low-level memory drivers (MMU, TLB, cache, etc.) and some device drivers such as frame-buffers, storage and human-machine interface drivers. Think supports many HAL libraries from general purpose platforms such as PowerPC to specific embedded platforms such as ARM and ST2XX processors.

Operating System Services. Kortex also includes many components implementing operating system services. These ones include dynamic memory managers, thread and scheduler implementations, network stack components, file system components and so on. Using this library, system architects can assemble any kind of kernels from exokernels to general purpose kernels.

Multi-processor Support Services. To ease the development of multi-processor systems and applications, we enhanced Kortex with several communication and synchronization components. Among these ones, we can cite synchronous and asynchronous message passing components, distributed semaphores, . . . One of the major extensions we have made consists in a loop distribution component that eases the distribution of complex computations on multiple nodes with Single Instruction Multiple Data (SIMD) parallelization.

Performance Monitoring Services. Finally, we extended Kortex with many performance monitors such as time and cycle counters that can be used for evaluating timing properties of software written in Think.

5.4   Construction of Distributed Operating Systems for MPSoCs

Fractal offers a unique abstraction for any kind of software which is component. Following this philosophy, an operating system is captured as a component in Think framework. We adapted this idea to distributed operating systems by providing a specific composite component controller that provides control over multiple operating system instances that are hosted on different nodes of an MPSoC. This controller which is quite different than the classical ones acts only during the compilation step, and is in charge of creating and deploying the required stubs and skeletons for inter-processor communication according to the system topology. It also acts on the linker tool to create the kernel images with regards to the memory mappings of the systems for each processor.

One must remark that our approach is not the one adopted by the platform-based design community. In particular, we do not intend to generate the HAL components regarding a platform specification, but assemble automatically a set of existing communication components (hand-written or generated using interface compilers) regarding the architectural specification given in ADL. By this way, the complexity of the communication protocol which depends on the underlying interconnect is embedded into assembled communication components, and hence the purpose and the capacity of the compilation chain remains orthogonal beside the complexity of the underlying platform topology and specificities.

6   Evaluation

With regards to the challenges that we underlined in Section 2, we present below some evaluations of Think framework within the MPSoCs software development context.

6.1   Porting Facility

In opposition to the general purpose computer market which is dominated by few platform architectures and processors, MPSoCs integrate a variety of processors with very different characteristics and instruction sets as well as several different hardware accelerators and I/O sensors. In this context, porting a software to different execution platforms is unavoidable. We believe that the component based approach addresses this issue in two points. First, since this approach produces more modular software, it is easier to find which modules will be affected by the porting process. Second, as components encapsulate code through well-defined interfaces, what remains to do is often just to replace the HAL components by others in most cases.

As explained in the previous section, Think's Kortex library makes an explicit distinction between generic system components and platform-dependent ones. In addition, Think's compilation chain intends to be completely portable since it only generates ANSI C code and integrates any C compiler for back-end binary generation. Thanks to these two features, systems written using Think components can be quickly adapted to any kind of hardware platform.

Think has been ported to many platforms from Macintosh Power-PC to embedded devices such as ST2XX and ARM processors. We estimate that only a little part of the system software (about 25% of a minimalist operating system) has to be rewritten. This part essentially consists on boot components, trap handlers, low-level memory managers and required device drivers. Once these HAL components are written, the rest can be reused from Kortex library to build-up complete systems. For example, when we ported Think on ST230 platform, we adapted the compilation tool chain in about 30 minutes, we had the first boot of a "blank" kernel in about one hour and we rewrote all the Kortex's target depending components in few days.

6.2   Multi-processor System/Application Co-design

One of the relevant experimentations that we have done to evaluate the effectiveness of our framework for MPSoC system and application software co-design consists at rewriting in Think a realistic multimedia decoder application and to deploy it in different execution scenarios from single-thread to multiple processors. We give below a survey of this experimentation which was detailed in [17] in order to illustrate how the component-based approach helps the design and the implementation of such software in the context of MPSoCs.

H.264 Decoder Written in Fine-Grained Components. The base of the decoder code used for our experiments comes from the JM 9.6 H.264 reference software [18] which provides a complete decoder written by several academic and industrial contributors. This decoder is originally written in C language and contains no assumptions nor optimizations for a given hardware platform. It is relatively huge in terms of lines of source code (26KLOC).

The good news is that using Think does not imply rewriting such a code, it comes in particular with a relatively well-defined and robust methodology for creating components from monolithic C code. This methodology is detailed in [17], we only recall here that this procedure is incremental, and that the program can be compiled and run to fix introduced defects after each introduction of new component. From the code writer's point of view, the translation task consists at revisiting the function declarations and the implementations that will be embedded into interfaces to be exposed to other components, by introducing the macros which were described in subsection 5.1. From the software architect's point of view, the task is a bit more complex: the global variables have to be embedded into components and have to be exposed to others through the interfaces, reusable interfaces should be defined and component cut-outs must be defined to obtain really modular software.

At the end of the *componentization* process, we obtained 35 functional components which identify different input (RTP, file, etc.) and output methods (display, file, network streaming, etc.) that use the same interface and some internal decoder modules that correspond to different entropy coding methods (CAVLC,

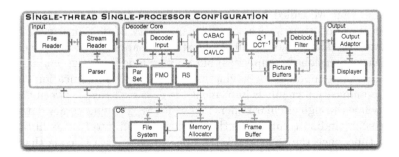

Fig. 5. Component-based architecture of JM H.264 decoder hosted by an operating system that implements exclusively the required services

CABAC). As illustrated at the top part of Figure 5, we basically grouped together these functional components into three composites which depict a logical division of the treatment pipeline: the input, the decoder core and the output.

Single-Threaded Single-Processor Architecture. Having created a component library that contains above mentioned decoder modules, we built different decoder instances adapted to different execution contexts. The first and the most intuitive one adopts a single-thread architecture and is functionally equivalent to the original JM-96 decoder. We compared this configuration to the original code in order to evaluate the cost of having a modular implementation. We measured an execution time overhead of 1.5%. This is encouraging because this reasonable gap is mainly due to the use of virtual function tables that enable dynamic bindings of component interfaces. On the other hand, the memory overhead is about 7%. Beside the data structures used to maintain the meta data of components, this overhead is also due to the informations related to component identification and other reflexivity support. This overhead remains open to optimizations since many informations that are denoted with strings can be replaced by more compact data structures such as hash codes.

The advantages of modular software with explicit required interfaces is felt when it is question to customize the application or the system software. We experimented this issue by customizing the operating system which is in charge of hosting the above decoder application. Since all system service dependencies are explicitly expressed in ADL, the operating system customization consists at assembling the needed system components using the ADL. With about 225 lines of ADL code, we describe a system that contains a dynamic memory allocator, a file system and necessary device drivers to display graphics on screen. The resulting decoder-specific kernel has a footprint of 35kB which is closely comparable to standalone runtime systems provided for bare embedded systems and far less than the size of micro kernels and general purpose operating systems. We believe that execution time results are not an issue since they reveal much more the algorithms used in the system if we consider as constant the above presented overhead which is intrinsic to our component binary interfaces invocations.

Multi-threaded Multi-processor Architecture. In another incarnation of the decoder that we called MTMP, we distributed the three main composites described above on three processors. The specificity of this incarnation is that we achieved the distribution without changing the application components (i.e. the content of mentioned composites) but only by modifying the binding semantics of these three modules for having inter-processor communication channels. These communication channels implement the data exchange between the nodes of the pipeline through circular buffers and hence avoids unnecessary data copies. Creating such binding components that we had to add into Kortex library took very few time since the code written is approximatively a C code that implements a circular buffer FIFO and its ADL description. This binding is platform independent since its heap and synchronization mechanisms are externalized using client interfaces. The implementation of these interfaces makes naturally

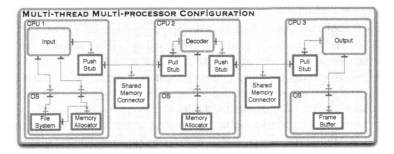

Fig. 6. Three stages pipelined MTMP decoder architecture

part of HAL components. We also customized the operating systems running on each node according to the system dependencies of the stage that it hosts. As illustrated in Figure 6, the OS1 supports a dynamic memory allocator, a file system and optionally a TCP-UDP/IP network stack for the input module, the OS2 only provides a memory allocator for the decoder core and the OS3 simply provides a frame-buffer driver to display the output. The description of such a multi-processor system enlarged the lines of code written in ADL since the components that appears in Figure 6 but not in Figure 5 are added. The creation of this multi-processor kernel image running on the multi-processor shared memory platform that integrates ST2xx processors is handled by our extension described in 5.4.

7   Conclusion and Future Work

Multi-Processor System-on-Chips have become a cornerstone of multimedia and communications for mobile embedded devices. Vis-a-vis the rapid standard and application evolutions, MPSoC software designers must now find new ways to turn their platforms as customizable as possible, for enabling them to be configured with regards to end-users' needs.

In this paper, we have described how component-based software engineering principles could help to reach that goal. We have presented and illustrated by example how Think framework could ease MPSoCs software designers task by providing them a unified methodology and tools to quickly define and customize their software for such platforms. We have also argued around the evaluations of our approach and demonstrated the benefits once again in terms of reusability but also in terms of porting.

Nevertheless, some improvements can be made and are subject to future work. First of all, execution time and memory usage overhead are two key parameters that must be tuned. As presented in the evaluation, if runtime overhead is not significant, memory overhead still remains important and has to be reduced. We are currently working on the binary interfaces of components for improving method invocation latency. The memory overhead is mainly due to strings denoted in components' binary structures for reflexivity support. These relevant informations could be denoted using more compact data structures (like hash tables) and this could lead to a footprint reduction. We also scheduled a revision of the compilation chain for supporting ADL extensions to denote some hardware-specific informations, for instance in order to take into account platforms where coexist not only heterogeneous processing units (homogeneous processors and accelerators) but also heterogeneous processors. As several implementations of Fractal component model exist (C++, Java and C), another project is to unify these implementations under a unified architecture in order to enhance programmability. Finally, we are working on dynamic reconfiguration in order to support structural and architectural modifications of software on-the-fly with efficient mechanisms for quiescent state capture and state transfer issues.

References

[1] Moore, G.: Cramming More Components into Integrated Circuits. Electronics, Vol. 38, Num. 8, April 1965.

[2] Szyperski, C.: Component Software. Addison-Wesley Prfessional; 2nd Edition, November 2002. ISBN 0201745720.

[3] Bruneton E., Coupaye T. and Stefani J.B.: Recursive and Dynamic Software Composition with Sharing. In Proceedings of 7th International Workshop on Component-Oriented Programming (WCOP02), ECOOP 2002, Spain, June 2002.

[4] Object Management Group: CORBA Component Model (CCM), http://www.omg.org/technology/documents/formal/components.htm

[5] Sun Microsystems: EJB Specification, http://java.sun.com/products/ejb/

[6] J-P. Fassino et al.: THINK: A Software Framework for Component-based Operating System Kernels, USENIX Annual Technical Conference, 2002.

[7] Bruneton E., Coupaye T., Leclercq M., Quéma V. and Stefani J.B.: An Open Component Model and its Support in Java. In Proceedings of the International Symposium on Component-based Software Engineering, Scotland, may 2004.

[8] Medvidovic, N. and Taylor, R. N.: A Classification and Comparison Framework for Software Architecture Description Languages. IEEE Transactions on Software Engineering, Vol. 26, Num. 1, 2000.

[9] Friedrich L.F., Stankovic J., Humphrey M., Marley M. and Haskins J.: A Survey of Configurable, Component-Based Operating Systems for Embedded Applications. IEEE Micro, Vol. 21, Num. 3, May 2001.

[10] Campbell R. et al.: Designing and Implementing Choices: An Object-Oriented System in C++. Communications of the ACM, Vol. 36, Num. 9, September 1993.

[11] Ford B. et al.: The Flux OSKit: A Substrate for Kernel and Language Research. In Proceedings of 16th ACM Symposium on Operating Systems Principles (SOSP), ACM Press, New York, 1997.

[12] Beuche D. et al.: The PURE Family of Object-Oriented Operating Systems for Deeply Embedded Systems. In Proceedings 2nd IEEE International Symposium on Object-Oriented Real-Time Distributed Computing, Piscataway, 1999.

[13] Gabber E. et al.: The Pebble Component-Based Operating System. In Proceedings of USENIX Annual Technical Conference, USENIX Association, 1999.

[14] Bruneton E., Coupaye T. and Stefani J.B.: The Fractal Specification, version 2.0.3, February 2004. http://fractal.objectweb.org/specification/index.html.

[15] Fractal web site, http://fractal.objectweb.org.

[16] THINK web site, http://think.objectweb.org.

[17] Layaïda O., Özcan A.E. and Stefani J.B.: A Component-based Approach for MP-SoC SW Design: Experience with OS Customization for H.264 Decoding. In Proceedings of 3rd ESTIMEDIA Workshop under CODES+ISSS, September 2005, New York, USA.

[18] JVT Software Page, JM/TML Software Coordination. http://bs.hhi.de/suehring/tml/.

Modular Proof Principles for Parameterised Concretizations

David Pichardie

IRISA/ENS Cachan (Bretagne),
IRISA, Campus de Beaulieu,
F-35042 Rennes, France
david.pichardie@irisa.fr

Abstract. Abstract interpretation is a particularly well-suited methodology to build modular correctness proof of static analysers. Proof modularity becomes essential when correctness proof is machine checked for realistic languages To deal with complex concrete and abstract domains, the notion of parameterised concretization has been proposed to allow a structural decomposition of the abstract domain and its concretization. In this paper we develop proof principles for such concretizations, based on the theoretical notion of concretization functor, with the aim of obtaining modular correctness proofs. Our technique has been tested on a machine-checked correctness proof of a static analysis for a Java-like bytecode language.

1 Introduction

Machine-assisted deductive methods improve the reliability of analysers, by providing machine-checked correctness proofs from which implementations of analysers are automatically *extracted*. The feasibility of the approach was demonstrated in a previous paper [3], but the human cost of such a work remains a major drawback to develop a large number of such *certified* static analysers. In [3], a first basis of a generic framework for proving and extracting static analysers in the Coq [5] proof assistant was proposed but this reusable part was mainly dedicated to the specification of the analysis and the extraction of the analyser. The correctness proof of the abstract semantic with respect to the standard semantics was done in an *ad hoc* fashion due to a lack of methodology. This paper aims at improving this point by proposing proof techniques that allow to modularise such proofs. The technical concept underlying these techniques is that of *parameterised concretization functions*.

Abstract interpretation proposes a rich mathematical framework for conducting such correctness proofs of static analysers. It is particularly well-suited to propose modular and generic construction usable for several analyses and programming languages. It is then a very promising tool when dealing with machine checked proof. In this context proof are done *in-extenso* with a high level of detail. The global architecture of the proof becomes then a critical point, specially when dealing with static analysis of "real" languages.

G. Barthe et al. (Eds.): CASSIS 2005, LNCS 3956, pp. 138–154, 2006.
© Springer-Verlag Berlin Heidelberg 2006

A simple example of modular technique is the abstraction product. To abstract a concrete domain of the form $\mathcal{P}(C \times D)$ a simple modular approach is to split the proof into two distinct parts : an abstract domain $C^\sharp$ to abstract $\mathcal{P}(C)$ (using a monotone concretization function $\gamma^C \in C^\sharp \to \mathcal{P}(C)$) and an abstract domain $D^\sharp$ to abstract $\mathcal{P}(D)$ (using $\gamma^D \in D^\sharp \to \mathcal{P}(D)$). Each abstraction can then be developed and proved correct forgetting the other. Global abstraction is then done on the product domain $C^\sharp \times D^\sharp$ with a concretization $\gamma \in C^\sharp \times D^\sharp \to \mathcal{P}(C \times D)$ defined by

$$\forall (c^\sharp, d^\sharp) \in C^\sharp \times D^\sharp, \; \gamma \left(c^\sharp, d^\sharp \right) = \left\{ (c,d) \; \middle| \; \begin{array}{l} c \in \gamma^C(c^\sharp) \\ d \in \gamma^D(d^\sharp) \end{array} \right\}$$

This technique is particularly tempting for a real language like Java bytecode whose memory space looks like:

Heap $\times$ Static Heap $\times$ Operand Stack $\times$ Local Variable

In this setting, this technique allows to split the proof effort into four independent parts. Unfortunately this modular technique restricts enormously the power of the abstraction usable because it necessarily forgets any relation on $C \times D$. On the other side, full relational abstractions compute properties on $C \times D$ but are difficult to modularize. In this paper we study a restricted class of relational abstraction, called *parameterised*, where a concretization function can be parameterised by a concrete element. For example, for the analysis of heap structure, the concretization for reference sometimes only makes sense in the context of a concrete heap. At the global abstraction level, the concretization is then of the form

$$\forall (c^\sharp, d^\sharp) \in C^\sharp \times D^\sharp, \; \gamma \left(c^\sharp, d^\sharp \right) = \left\{ (c,d) \; \middle| \; \begin{array}{l} c \in \gamma^C(c^\sharp) \\ d \in \gamma_c^D(d^\sharp) \end{array} \right\}$$

As we will see in Section 4, this dependence of γ^D with respect to C is one obstacle for proof modularity. The main contribution of this paper is to propose a modular proof technique compatible with parameterised concretization. This proof technique is based on a natural notion of concretization functor. The technique requires some restriction on the used abstraction but we have nevertheless been able to experiment it on a realistic representation of bytecode language with two non-trivial abstractions dynamical allocated values: abstraction by class and abstraction by creation site. The whole proof of a generic static analysis has been machine-checked using this technique. The Coq source of development are available on-line at http://www.irisa.fr/lande/pichardie/CarmelCoq/Cassis05/main.html.

Plan of the paper. Our machine-checked proof concerns a language similar to the Java byte code, named Carmel, presented in Section 2. In Section 3, we present classic modular constructions which appear to be difficult to use with concretization functions (presented in Section 4). We then propose a notion of concretization functor in Section 5 and shows it modularity capabilities. The machine-checked proof is briefly described in Section 6. Section 7 presents the relative work and Section 8 concludes.

Notations and prerequisites. We write :: for the list concatenation symbol, A^+ represents the set of non empty sequences of elements in a set A, $\to_m$ denotes the monotone functions constructor and $\to$ the partial function constructor. The pointed notation on order symbol ($\dot{\sqsubseteq}$) represents the associated point-wise extension of the order ($f_1 \dot{\sqsubseteq} f_2 \overset{\text{def}}{\Longleftrightarrow} \forall x, f_1(x) \sqsubseteq f_2(x)$). We assume basic knowledge of abstract interpretation [8] concepts such as concretization function and partial trace semantics.

2   Target Case Study

The notion of parameterised concretization functions is not linked to a particular programming language or abstraction, but we have chosen to present our results in the concrete setting of a representative subset of the Carmel language [10, 3]. The language is a bytecode for a stack-oriented machine, much like the Java Card bytecode. We concentrate here on the intraprocedural fragment with instructions about stack operations, numeric operations, conditionals, object creation and modification. We leave out method calls which are not needed to explain our results and which would only complicate the presentation. Thus, the role of objects are reduced to dynamically allocated records. Nevertheless, the semantic domain includes a heap and an environment and is sufficiently complex to test our proof modularization technique. In this setting, a program is composed of a list of class declaration and a list of bytecode attached to program points.

$$
\begin{aligned}
\text{Val} &= \mathbb{N} + \text{Reference} + \{\text{null}\} \\
\text{LocalVar} &= \text{Var} \to \text{Val} \qquad\qquad\qquad \text{Stack} = \text{Val}^* \\
\text{Object} &= \text{ClassName} \times (\text{FieldName} \to \text{Val}) \qquad \text{Heap} = \text{Reference} \to \text{Object} \\
\text{State} &= \text{ProgPoint} \times \text{Heap} \times \text{LocalVar} \times \text{Stack}
\end{aligned}
$$

Fig. 1. Carmel semantic domains

The language is given a small-step operational semantics manipulating states of the form $\langle\!\langle pc, h, l, s \rangle\!\rangle$, where pc is a program point, h a heap of objects, l a set of local variables, and s a local operand stack (see [15] or [4] for details). Formal definitions of the semantic domains are given in Figure 1 and the different semantic rules are presented in Figure 2. We write $s_1 \to_i s_2$ if s_2 is the new state resulting from the execution of instruction i in state s_1. The values we manipulate are either integers or memory references. We let n ranges over integers and loc over references. The instruction numop is parameterised by an operator name op (addition, multiplication, ...) whose semantics is given by $[op]$. The value stored in the local variable x is represented by $l[x]$ (see instruction load). $l[x \mapsto v]$ assigns the variable x to the value v and leaves the others values in l unchanged (similar notations are used for heaps and objects). Two rules define

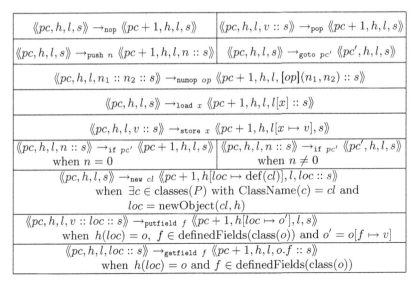

Fig. 2. Operational semantic rules of Carmel

the `if` instruction behavior according to the first value of the current operand stack. The last three instructions deal with object manipulation. The function newObject computes, for a class name cl and a heap h, a new memory reference loc where a new object $def(cl)$ of class cl will be stored. The notation $o.f$ represents the access to a field f in the class instance o (f should be a declared field of the class of o, see condition $f \in$ definedFields(class(o))).

The *partial trace semantics* $[P]$ of a Carmel program P is defined as the set of reachable partial traces:

$$[P] = \left\{ s_0 s_1 \cdots s_n \in \text{State}^+ \;\middle|\; \begin{array}{l} s_0 \in S_{init} \; \wedge \\ \forall k < n, \; \exists i, \; s_k \rightarrow_i s_{k+1} \end{array} \right\} \in \mathcal{P}(\text{State}^+)$$

where S_{init} is the set of initial states.

The goal of the analysis is to compute an approximation of $[P]$ for any given program P. The approximation lives in an abstract domain $\mathcal{D}^\sharp$ with a poset structure $(\mathcal{D}^\sharp, \sqsubseteq)$. The correctness[1] of the approximation is specified by a monotone concretization function γ belonging to $(\mathcal{D}^\sharp, \sqsubseteq) \rightarrow_m (\mathcal{P}(\mathcal{D}), \subseteq)$. All these elements form what we called a *connection* (in reference to Galois connections whose abstraction function is nevertheless not explicitly used in this paper). We note such a connection $(\mathcal{P}(\mathcal{D}), \subseteq) \xleftarrow{\gamma} (\mathcal{D}^\sharp, \sqsubseteq)$.

For simplicity, the example taken in Section 3, 4 and 5 will not be directly related to Carmel. They will nevertheless be inspired by the analysis effectively proved in Coq and presented in Section 6.

---

[1] The result $[P]^\sharp$ of the analysis is then said correct if its concretisation is a consequence of the property $[P]$: $[P] \subseteq \gamma([P]^\sharp)$.

3 Modular Construction of Connection

The theory of abstract interpretation explains how to compose connections in order to build new connections from old. A classical example of such a construction is the abstraction of variable environments (partial maps from variable names to value designed here by the set Env) which can be constructed for any abstraction of values.

Definition 1 (*Generic environment connection*). *A* generic environment connection *is a functional which maps a connection* $(\mathcal{P}(\mathit{Val}), \subseteq) \xleftarrow{\;\gamma^{\mathit{Val}}\;} (\mathit{Val}^{\sharp}, \sqsubseteq_{\mathit{Val}^{\sharp}})$ *to a 5-tuple* $(\mathit{Env}^{\sharp}, \sqsubseteq_{\mathit{Env}^{\sharp}}, \gamma^{\mathit{Env}}, \mathrm{get}^{\sharp}, \mathrm{subst}^{\sharp})$ *with*

- $(\mathit{Env}^{\sharp}, \sqsubseteq_{\mathit{Env}^{\sharp}})$ *is a partially ordered set,*
- $\gamma^{\mathit{Env}} \in (\mathit{Env}^{\sharp}, \sqsubseteq_{\mathit{Env}^{\sharp}}) \to_m (\mathcal{P}(\mathit{Env}), \subseteq)$ *is a monotone concretization function between* $\mathit{Env}^{\sharp}$ *and the set of environments,*
- $\mathrm{get}^{\sharp} \in \mathit{Env}^{\sharp} \times \mathit{Var} \to \mathit{Val}^{\sharp}$ *is a correct approximation of the function giving the value attached with each variable*

$$\forall \rho^{\sharp} \in \mathit{Env}^{\sharp},\ \forall x \in \mathit{Var}, \quad \{\rho(x) \mid \rho \in \gamma^{\mathit{Env}}(\rho^{\sharp})\} \subseteq \gamma^{\mathit{Val}}(\mathrm{get}^{\sharp}(\rho^{\sharp}, x))$$

- $\mathrm{subst}^{\sharp} \in \mathit{Env}^{\sharp} \times \mathit{Var} \times \mathit{Val}^{\sharp} \to \mathit{Env}^{\sharp}$ *is a correct approximation of the function which substitutes a value with an other one in a variable*

$$\forall \rho^{\sharp} \in \mathit{Env}^{\sharp},\ \forall x \in \mathit{Var},\ \forall v^{\sharp} \in \mathit{Val}^{\sharp},$$
$$\left\{ \rho[x \mapsto v] \ \middle|\ \begin{matrix} \rho \in \gamma^{\mathit{Env}}(\rho^{\sharp}) \\ v \in \gamma^{\mathit{Val}}(v^{\sharp}) \end{matrix} \right\} \subseteq \gamma^{\mathit{Env}}(\mathrm{subst}^{\sharp}(\rho^{\sharp}, x, v^{\sharp}))$$

Hence a generic environment connection constructs an abstract domain, a concretization function and two correct approximations of the primitive function for manipulating environments, given a connection for abstracting values.

An example of such connection constructor is given by the classical non-relational abstraction.

Lemma 1. *The functional which associates with all connection* $(\mathcal{P}(\mathit{Val}), \subseteq) \xleftarrow{\;\gamma^{\mathit{Val}}\;}$ $\left(\mathit{Val}^{\sharp}, \sqsubseteq_{\mathit{Val}^{\sharp}}\right)$ *the 5-upplet* $\left(\mathit{Env}^{\sharp}, \sqsubseteq_{\mathit{Env}^{\sharp}}, \gamma^{\mathit{Env}}, \mathrm{get}^{\sharp}, \mathrm{subst}^{\sharp}\right)$ *with*

- $\mathit{Env}^{\sharp} = \mathit{Var} \to \mathit{Val}^{\sharp}$
- $\sqsubseteq_{\mathit{Env}^{\sharp}} = \dot{\sqsubseteq}_{\mathit{Val}}$
- $\forall \rho^{\sharp} \in \mathit{Env}^{\sharp},\ \gamma^{\mathit{Env}}(\rho^{\sharp}) = \{\rho \mid \forall x \in \mathit{Var},\ \rho(x) \in \gamma^{\mathit{Val}}(\rho^{\sharp}(x))\}$
- $\forall \rho^{\sharp} \in \mathit{Env}^{\sharp},\ \forall x \in \mathit{Var},\ \mathrm{get}^{\sharp}(\rho^{\sharp}, x) = \rho^{\sharp}(x)$
- $\forall \rho^{\sharp} \in \mathit{Env}^{\sharp},\ \forall x \in \mathit{Var},\ \forall v^{\sharp} \in \mathit{Val}^{\sharp},\ \mathrm{subst}^{\sharp}(\rho^{\sharp}, x, v^{\sharp}) = \rho^{\sharp}[x \mapsto v^{\sharp}]$

is a generic environment connection.

This lemma expresses that the non-relational abstraction of environments can be constructed for any abstraction of values. Hence, several value abstractions can be used without having to redo any proof about abstract environments. This is a crucial point for the proof effort required by a proof assistant. Generic connections have an additional advantage when working with a proof assistant: during construction, the value abstraction is opaque and hence the proof is simpler, only focusing on environment manipulations. It is thus particularly convenient to use such generic constructors in machine-checked proofs. Unfortunately they are difficult to use for more sophisticated value abtractions. In particular, analyses of the *heap* structure (or the memory) of dynamically allocated data structures (references, cells, objects, ...) can require other form of connections.

Example 1. If all values in the language are references on dynamically allocated object in a heap, an abstraction of these references by the set of class names of the associated objects only makes sense in the context of a concrete heap.

$$\forall s \in \mathcal{P}(\text{Class}),$$
$$\gamma(s) = \big\{(h, \text{loc}) \mid \text{loc} \in \text{dom}(h) \ \wedge \ \text{class}(h(\text{loc})) \in s \big\} \subseteq \text{Heap} \times \text{Val}$$

with Heap and Object defined as for Carmel semantic domains.

This kind of concretization is generally written in a nicer, parameterised form

$$\forall h \in \text{Heap}, \ \forall s \in \mathcal{P}(\text{Class}),$$
$$\gamma_h(s) = \big\{\text{loc} \mid \text{loc} \in \text{dom}(h) \ \wedge \ \text{class}(h(\text{loc})) \in s \big\} \subseteq \text{Val}$$

We will now formally define this kind of concretization and show how we can use them during correctness proofs.

4   Parameterised Concretization

The concretization function we study here depends on a context. Each abstract value is concretized into a relation between a concrete value and a context element, where the context element is necessary to give a non-trivial concretization of the abstract element. We are hence interested in connections of the following form

$$(\mathcal{P}(C \times D), \subseteq) \xleftarrow{\gamma} (D^\sharp, \sqsubseteq)$$

with C the *context domain*. Some examples:

Example 2. The same kind of concretization as in example 1 can be used to abstract references by the super-class of all objects they refer (this is the abstraction taken in the Java bytecode verifier).

$$\forall \tau \in \text{Class},$$
$$\gamma(\tau) = \big\{(h, \text{loc}) \mid \text{loc} \in \text{dom}(h) \ \wedge \ \text{class}(h(\text{loc})) \prec_P \tau \big\} \subseteq \text{Heap} \times \text{Val}$$

where $\prec_P$ is the subtyping relation associated with the class hierarchy of program P.

Example 3. A more precise abstraction than abstraction by set of class names can be obtained by abstracting with set of creation points [14]. The formal definition of the concretization function is then relative to a partial execution trace.

As in Carmel semantics, partial trace are a non-empty sequences $< pc_0, m_0 >::$ $\cdots ::< pc_n, m_n >$ of states, each state containing a program point pc_i (taken in a set ProgPoint) and a memory m_i. If the instruction found at a program point pc is an object creation with class cl (event noted $\text{instr}(pc) = \textbf{new } cl$), a new address newObject(cl, m) is allocated in the memory m to stock an object of class cl inside.

The associated concretization is

$\forall s \in \mathcal{P}(\text{ProgPoint})$,

$$\gamma(s) = \left\{ \left(< pc_0, m_0 >:: \cdots ::< pc_n, m_n >, \text{loc} \right) \left| \begin{array}{l} \exists k \in \{0, \ldots, n\}, \\ pc_k \in s \\ \text{instr}(pc_k) = \textbf{new } cl \\ \text{newObject}(cl, m_k) = \text{loc} \end{array} \right. \right\}$$

End of examples.

This kind of concretization can be represented under an equivalent **parameterised** form. We will note γ^{param} the function of $C \rightarrow D^\sharp \rightarrow \mathcal{P}(D)$ defined by

$$\forall c \in C, \ \forall d^\sharp \in D^\sharp, \ \gamma_c^{\text{param}}(d^\sharp) = \{d \mid (c, d) \in \gamma(d^\sharp)\}$$

Most of the time, we will omit the $.^{\text{param}}$ notation because the context will allow us to do it without ambiguity.

4.1   Using Generic Connections with Parameterised Concretization

When fixing an element $c \in C$ in the context, we can treat γ_c as a concretization in $(D^\sharp, \sqsubseteq) \rightarrow_m (\mathcal{P}(D), \subseteq)$, forgetting the relational view. We are then back to the application framework of the modular construction exposed in the previous section: a parameterised concretization $(\mathcal{P}(\text{Val}), \subseteq) \xleftarrow{\gamma_c^{\text{Val}}} \left(\text{Val}^\sharp, \sqsubseteq_{\text{Val}^\sharp} \right)$ (with c a fixed element in C) can be used to instantiate any generic environment connection. We obtain a collection of 5-tuple $\left(\text{Env}^\sharp, \sqsubseteq_{\text{Env}^\sharp}, \gamma_c^{\text{Env}}, \text{get}^\sharp, \text{subst}^\sharp \right)_{c \in C}$ with $\text{get}^\sharp$ for example verifying

$$\forall c \in C, \ \forall \rho^\sharp \in \text{Env}^\sharp, \ \forall x \in \text{Var}, \quad \{\rho(x) \mid \rho \in \gamma_c^{\text{Env}}(\rho^\sharp)\} \subseteq \gamma_c^{\text{Val}}(\text{get}^\sharp(\rho^\sharp, x))$$

A generic environment connection is then able to use a parameterised value concretization to produce a parameterised environment concretization with its correct basic operators. Nevertheless, note that the correctness property assured by these operators are relative to the same context c. As we will see now this will be a major limitation when proving correctness of abstract transfer functions.

4.2   Proving Correctness of Abstract Transfer Functions

The difficulties with parameterised concretizations become apparent when we consider proving the correctness of transfer functions (the abstract interpretation of each byte code). For example, in a language with variables and dynamic allocations the memory state is of the form Mem $\stackrel{\text{def}}{=}$ Heap $\times$ Env with Heap $\stackrel{\text{def}}{=}$ Val $\rightharpoonup$ Object, Env $\stackrel{\text{def}}{=}$ Var $\rightharpoonup$ Val and Val the domain value, reduced here at addresses in the heap.

Because the memory is split into two different structures, it is natural to abstract it with two distinct abstract elements. Given a heap connection

$$(\mathcal{P}(\text{Heap}), \subseteq) \xleftarrow{\gamma^{\text{Heap}}} (\text{Heap}^\sharp, \sqsubseteq_{\text{Heap}})$$

and let suppose, for the variable environments, the value abstraction has required a heap parametrization (as in example 1): the abstraction is hence of the form

$$\left((\mathcal{P}(\text{Env}), \subseteq) \xleftarrow{\gamma_h^{\text{Env}}} (\text{Env}^\sharp, \sqsubseteq_{\text{Env}}) \right)_{h \in \text{Heap}}$$

The concretization of a couple $(h^\sharp, \rho^\sharp)$ of abstract elements will be

$$\gamma\left(h^\sharp, \rho^\sharp\right) = \left\{ (h, \rho) \;\middle|\; \begin{array}{l} h \in \gamma^{\text{Heap}}(h^\sharp) \\ \rho \in \gamma_h^{\text{Env}}(\rho^\sharp) \end{array} \right\} \subseteq \text{Heap} \times \text{Env}$$

Each transfer function will be of the form

$$\begin{aligned} \mathcal{F} : \text{Heap} \times \text{Env} &\rightarrow \quad \text{Heap} \times \text{Env} \\ (h, \rho) &\mapsto (f(h, \rho), g(h, \rho)) \end{aligned}$$

To correctly abstract a transfer function, we have to propose a function $\mathcal{F}^\sharp$ of the form

$$\begin{aligned} \mathcal{F}^\sharp : \text{Heap}^\sharp \times \text{Env}^\sharp &\rightarrow \quad \text{Heap}^\sharp \times \text{Env}^\sharp \\ (h^\sharp, \rho^\sharp) &\mapsto \left(f^\sharp(h^\sharp, \rho^\sharp), g^\sharp(h^\sharp, \rho^\sharp)\right) \end{aligned}$$

and verifying the following "classical" correctness criterion

$$\forall (h^\sharp, \rho^\sharp) \in \text{Heap}^\sharp \times \text{Env}^\sharp,$$
$$\left\{ (f(h, \rho), g(h, \rho)) \;\middle|\; \begin{array}{l} h \in \gamma^{\text{Heap}}(h^\sharp) \\ \rho \in \gamma_h^{\text{Env}}(\rho^\sharp) \end{array} \right\} \subseteq \left\{ (h', \rho') \;\middle|\; \begin{array}{l} h' \in \gamma^{\text{Heap}}(f^\sharp(h^\sharp, \rho^\sharp)) \\ \rho' \in \gamma_{h'}^{\text{Env}}(g^\sharp(h^\sharp, \rho^\sharp)) \end{array} \right\}$$

This criterion can be equivalently reduced to the conjunction of two criteria

$$\begin{aligned} &\forall (h^\sharp, \rho^\sharp) \in \text{Heap}^\sharp \times \text{Env}^\sharp, \\ &\forall (h, \rho) \in \gamma^{\text{Heap}}(h^\sharp) \times \gamma_h^{\text{Env}}(\rho^\sharp), \quad f(h, \rho) \in \gamma^{\text{Heap}}(f^\sharp(h^\sharp, \rho^\sharp)) \end{aligned} \tag{1}$$

$$\begin{aligned} &\forall (h^\sharp, \rho^\sharp) \in \text{Heap}^\sharp \times \text{Env}^\sharp, \\ &\forall (h, \rho) \in \gamma^{\text{Heap}}(h^\sharp) \times \gamma_h^{\text{Env}}(\rho^\sharp), \quad g(h, \rho) \in \gamma_{f(h,\rho)}^{\text{Env}}(g^\sharp(h^\sharp, \rho^\sharp)) \end{aligned} \tag{2}$$

Contrary to the criterion (1), the criterion (2) is problematic because it contains two distinct instances γ_h^{Env} and $\gamma_{f(h,\rho)}^{\text{Env}}$. As we have seen previously, properties produced by combining generic connections and parameterised concretizations only contain a single context element. So we can not prove (2) by only combining this kind of properties.

We can however, reduce the proof of (2) into two sufficient (but not necessary) conditions, one dealing with f, the other with g:

$$\forall (h^\sharp, \rho^\sharp) \in \mathrm{Heap}^\sharp \times \mathrm{Env}^\sharp,$$
$$\forall (h, \rho) \in \gamma^{\mathrm{Heap}}(h^\sharp) \times \gamma_h^{\mathrm{Env}}(\rho^\sharp), \quad g(h, \rho) \in \gamma_h^{\mathrm{Env}}(g^\sharp(h^\sharp, \rho^\sharp)) \tag{3}$$

$$\forall (h, \rho) \in \mathrm{Heap} \times \mathrm{Env}, \quad \gamma_h^{\mathrm{Env}} \mathrel{\dot{\subseteq}} \gamma_{f(h,\rho)}^{\mathrm{Env}} \tag{4}$$

The criterion (3) now only contains a single instance γ_h^{Env} of the environment concretization (contrary to (2)) and is well-suited to be proved by combining properties given by some generic connection constructors.

The criterion (4) remains nevertheless problematic because like in (2), several instance of γ^{Env} appear. The next section will be dedicated to this criteria. We will propose a slight change in the generic environment connection definition which will allow us to prove (4) in a modular way without making appear a notion of context in the definition.

5   Concretization Functors

The improvement we will make in generic connection definition will be based on *concretization functionals* : operators which transform concretizations into other concretizations.

5.1   Example and Definition

An example of such operator has already been seen in lemma 1.

$$\Gamma : \left(\left(\mathrm{Val}^\sharp, \sqsubseteq_{\mathrm{Val}^\sharp} \right) \xrightarrow{\gamma^{\mathrm{Val}}}_m (\mathcal{P}(\mathrm{Val}), \subseteq) \right) \longrightarrow \left(\left(\mathrm{Env}^\sharp, \sqsubseteq_{\mathrm{Env}^\sharp} \right) \rightarrow_m (\mathcal{P}(\mathrm{Env}), \subseteq) \right)$$
$$\mapsto \rho^\sharp \mapsto \left\{ \rho \mid \forall x \in \mathrm{Var}, \ \rho(x) \in \gamma(\rho^\sharp(x)) \right\}$$

This kind of operator is under-lying in many generic construction found in the abstract interpretation literature. A natural condition we could impose on such operator is *monotonie*, hence obtaining *concretization functors*.

Definition 2 (*Concretization functor*). *Given four partially ordered sets* $(A, \sqsubseteq_A)$, $(A^\sharp, \sqsubseteq_{A^\sharp})$, $(B, \sqsubseteq_B)$ *and* $(B^\sharp, \sqsubseteq_{B^\sharp})$, *a concretization functor is an operator* Γ *taken in* $\left((A^\sharp, \sqsubseteq_{A^\sharp}) \rightarrow_m (A, \sqsubseteq_A) \right) \rightarrow \left((B^\sharp, \sqsubseteq_{B^\sharp}) \rightarrow_m (B, \sqsubseteq_B) \right)$ *which verifies the monotonicity property:*

$$\forall \gamma_1, \gamma_2 \in \left((A^\sharp, \sqsubseteq_{A^\sharp}) \rightarrow_m (A, \sqsubseteq_A) \right), \quad \gamma_1 \mathrel{\dot{\sqsubseteq}_A} \gamma_2 \quad \Rightarrow \quad \Gamma(\gamma_1) \mathrel{\dot{\sqsubseteq}_B} \Gamma(\gamma_2)$$

A concretization functor is hence preserving relative precision between concretizations. This monotony property appears to be very natural and satisfied by many concretization operators found in the literature (see the generic construction of weak relational environment in [11] for a good example). As far a we know this property has never been explicitly used or noticed.

This notion will now be integrated in a new definition of generic environment connection.

Definition 3 (Revisited *generic environment connection*). *A generic environment connection is a functional which associates to any partially ordered set* $\left(Val^\sharp, \sqsubseteq_{Val^\sharp} \right)$ *a 5-tuple* $\left(Env^\sharp, \sqsubseteq_{Env^\sharp}, \Gamma^{Env}, \mathrm{get}^\sharp, \mathrm{subst}^\sharp \right)$ *where*

- $\left(Env^\sharp, \sqsubseteq_{Env^\sharp} \right)$ *is a partially ordered set,*
- $\Gamma \in \left((Val^\sharp, \sqsubseteq_{Val^\sharp}) \to_m (\mathcal{P}(Val), \subseteq) \right) \to$
$$\left((Env^\sharp, \sqsubseteq_{Env^\sharp}) \to_m (\mathcal{P}(Var \to Val), \subseteq) \right)$$
  is a concretization functor,
- $\mathrm{get}^\sharp \in Env^\sharp \times Var \to Val^\sharp$ *is a correct approximation of the function giving the value attached with each variable*

$$\forall \gamma \in \left(Val^\sharp, \sqsubseteq_{Val^\sharp} \right) \to_m (\mathcal{P}(Val), \subseteq),$$
$$\forall \rho^\sharp \in Env^\sharp, \ \forall x \in Var, \quad \{\rho(x) \mid \rho \in \Gamma^{Env}(\gamma)(\rho^\sharp)\} \ \subseteq \ \gamma(\mathrm{get}^\sharp(\rho^\sharp, x))$$

- $\mathrm{subst}^\sharp \in Env^\sharp \times Var \times Val^\sharp \to Env^\sharp$ *is a correct approximation of the function which substitute a value with an other one in a variable*

$$\forall \gamma \in \left(Val^\sharp, \sqsubseteq_{Val^\sharp} \right) \to_m (\mathcal{P}(Val), \subseteq),$$
$$\forall \rho^\sharp \in \rho^\sharp, \ \forall x \in Var, \ \forall v^\sharp \in Val^\sharp,$$
$$\left\{ \rho[x \mapsto v] \ \middle| \ \begin{array}{l} \rho \in \Gamma^{Env}(\gamma)(\rho^\sharp) \\ v \in \gamma(v^\sharp) \end{array} \right\} \ \subseteq \ \Gamma^{Env}(\gamma)(\mathrm{subst}^\sharp(\rho^\sharp, x, v^\sharp))$$

The modification used here is made at the level of the concretization function which is no more fixed but now parameterised by any value concretization. Concerning primitive abstract operators $\mathrm{get}^\sharp$ and $\mathrm{subst}^\sharp$, the quantification made on all value concretization does not require more proofs than in the previous definition because γ_{Val} was already anonymous (*ie.* its definition was not necessary to build the proof). We can hence affirm that this new definition is not more restrictive or specialized than the previous: only the monotonicity property of Γ has been added and it is a very natural property which do not restrict the generic construction we can use.

We will now explain why these generic connections enable us to prove (4) in a modular fashion.

5.2   Using the Functorial Property in Proof

With our new definition of generic environment connection, the concretization γ^{Env} used in the example of Section 4 is now of the form

$$\gamma^{Env} = \Gamma^{Env}\left(\gamma^{Val}\right)$$

Hence the criterion (4) can now be reduced to a property on γ^{Val}.

Lemma 2. *If* $\gamma^{Env} = \Gamma^{Env}\left(\gamma^{Val}\right)$ *with* Γ^{Env} *a concretization functor, then the criterion*

$$\forall (h, \rho) \in Heap \times Env, \ \gamma_h^{Val} \ \dot{\subseteq} \ \gamma_{f(h,\rho)}^{Val} \tag{5}$$

implies

$$\forall (h, \rho) \in Heap \times Env, \ \gamma_h^{Env} \ \dot{\subseteq} \ \gamma_{f(h,\rho)}^{Env}$$

Proof. It is a direct consequence of the monotony property of $\varGamma^{Env}$.

The remaining proof condition (5) is thus structurally smaller: it now deals with value abstraction. It can be seen has a *conservative* requirement. The concretization associated with the transformation of the heap h should contain all the properties of the original one. It is a strong property but the generic connection definition allow us to move it at the level of the value connection without sacrificing the genericity of the environment connection.

It remains us to explain how such proof can be managed at the level of the value abstraction.

5.3   Establishing the Conservative Requirement

In the context of a full correctness proof there will be as many proof condition like (5) as functions f encountered in the different transfer functions of the language. We propose to factorize these proofs by cutting such conditions into two new conditions. This cut is done by introducing a well-chosen pre-order on the context domain.

We will need to introduce a notion of *monotone parameterised concretization*.

Definition 4 (monotone parameterised concretization). *Given a pre-order relation $\preceq_C \subseteq C \times C$ on a set C, a parameterised concretization $\gamma \in C \to D^\sharp \to \mathcal{P}(D)$ is monotonously parameterised with respect to $\preceq_C$ if*

$$\forall (c_1, c_2) \in C^2, \ c_1 \preceq_C c_2 \ \Rightarrow \ \gamma_{c_1} \ \dot{\subseteq} \ \gamma_{c_2}$$

Lemma 3. *Let $S \subseteq (Heap \times Env) \to Heap$ be a set of function. Let γ^{Val} be a parameterised value concretization and $\preceq_{Heap}$ a pre-order on Heap. If*

$$\gamma^{Val} \ \text{is monotone with respect to } \ \preceq_{Heap} \tag{6}$$

and

$$\forall f \in S, \ \forall (h, \rho) \in Heap \times Env, \ h \preceq_{Heap} f(h, \rho) \tag{7}$$

then

$$\forall f \in S, \ \forall (h, \rho) \in Heap \times Env, \ \gamma_h^{Val} \ \dot{\subseteq} \ \gamma_{f(h,\rho)}^{Val}$$

As we explained before, this proof method is not applicable for all parameterised value concretization. The main restriction is on the existence of a well-suited pre-order on context domain.

This existence is nevertheless ensured in all the non trivial examples we gave previously in Section 3 and 4:

– For example 1, we can take

$$\preceq_{\mathrm{Heap}} = \left\{ (h_1, h_2) \; \middle| \; \begin{array}{l} \mathrm{dom}(h_1) \subseteq \mathrm{dom}(h_2) \\ \forall \mathrm{loc} \in \mathrm{dom}(h_1), \; \mathrm{class}(h_1(\mathrm{loc})) = \mathrm{class}(h_2(\mathrm{loc})) \end{array} \right\}$$

The value concretization chosen in this example is then monotone with respect to this pre-order because if h_1 and h_2 are heap verifying $h_1 \preceq_{\mathrm{Heap}} h_2$, if loc belongs to $\gamma_{h_1}(s)$ then loc $\in \mathrm{dom}(h_1)$ and $\mathrm{class}(h_1(\mathrm{loc})) \in s$. But $\mathrm{dom}(h_1) \subseteq \mathrm{dom}(h_2)$, so loc $\in \mathrm{dom}(h_2)$ and because $\mathrm{class}(h_1(\mathrm{loc})) = \mathrm{class}(h_2(\mathrm{loc}))$, we can affirm that $\mathrm{class}(h_2(\mathrm{loc})) \in s$. We then have demonstrated that loc $\in \gamma_{h_2}(s)$.

The property 7 will be verified by any transfer function which does not remove objects in the heap, neither modify their class. It is effectively the case for all transfer function of programming language like Java or bytecode Java without dealing with garbage collector[2].
– The same pre-order as before can be used to deal with example 2.
– For example 3, the context is no more a heap but a partial trace. The relation $\preceq_{\mathrm{Trace}}$ is thus sufficient :

$$\preceq_{\mathrm{Trace}} = \{ (tr_1, tr_2) \mid tr_1 \text{ is a prefix of } tr_2 \}$$

Indeed, if tr_1 is a partial trace prefix of a partial trace tr_2, all allocations made in tr_1 appear in tr_2. Thus the monotonicity of γ^{Val} with respect to $\preceq_{\mathrm{Trace}}$ is proved.

For the criterion 7, we only have to verify that all transfer function only put new states on previous partial trace, which is indeed the case.

5.4   Summarizing the Proof Method

We now summarize our proof method for establishing the correctness of the function $\mathcal{F}^{\sharp}$ with respect to $\mathcal{F}$ (example taken in Subsection 4.2)

– The correctness criterion is split into two equivalent criteria (1) and (2). (1) leads to modular proofs because it relies on the same parameterised concretization, but (2) is not.
– The criterion (2) is then split into two sufficient criteria (3) and (4). (3) is provable using generic connection constructions.
– To establish (4) we introduce a notion of concretization functor and a well chosen pre-order. (4) is hence split into criteria (6) and (7). (6) only deal with the abstraction made on values. (7) is a proof about the semantic of the language.

---

[2] Dealing with garbage collection could be done by restricting value to accessible values from the variable in the environment. It would certainly complicate the proof and we have not yet explored this eventuality.

6   Modular Machine Checked Proof of a Bytecode Analyser

This proof technique has been experimented for proving the correctness of a generic Carmel static analyser. This analysis computes a state invariant for each program point. The abstract state is thus of the form

$$\text{State}^\sharp = \text{ProgPoint} \rightarrow \left(\text{Heap}^\sharp \times \text{LocalVar}^\sharp \times \text{Stack}^\sharp \right)$$

with $\text{Heap}^\sharp$, $\text{LocalVar}^\sharp$ and $\text{Stack}^\sharp$ generic abstract domains for heap, local variables and operand stack abstraction.

The generic static analyser is parameterised by five generic connections (for values, operand stacks, local variables, objects and heaps) and two base abstractions (a parameterised one for locations and a classical simple one for integers). Figure 3 shows the Coq interface definition for the operand stack. The interface is parameterised by a lattice structure PV on a set V (the lattice of abstract values). The interface contains 12 elements. First, the set t of abstract stacks, the lattice structure Pos on t, and the concretization functor gamma which takes concretization between $\mathcal{P}(\text{Val})$ and PV and returns a concretization between $\mathcal{P}(\text{Stack})$ and Pos. The monotonicity property of gamma is required by the field gamma_monotone. At last, nil_ab, pop_ab, top_ab and push_ab are four basic abstract operators of the stack domain with their corresponding correctness properties. (Post pop_op) represents the post operator applied on the relation pop_op.

Record OperandStackConnection (V:Set) (PV:Lattice V) :
Type := {
  t : Set;
  Pos : Lattice t;
  gamma : Gamma (PowPoset Value) PV → Gamma (PowPoset OperandStack) Pos;
  gamma_monotone : ∀g1 g2,
    orderGamma g1 g2 → orderGamma (gamma g1) (gamma g2);

  nil_ab : t;
  nil_ab_correct : ∀g, (λs. s = nil) ⊆ (gamma g nil_ab);

  pop_ab : t → t;
  pop_ab_correct : ∀g s, ((Post pop_op) (gamma g s)) ⊆ (gamma g (pop_ab s));

  top_ab : t → V;
  top_ab_correct : ∀g s, ((Post top_op) (gamma g s)) ⊆ (g (top_ab s));

  push_ab : V → t → t;
  push_ab_correct : ∀g v s, ((Post2 push_op) (g v) (gamma g s)) ⊆ (gamma g (push_ab v s))
}.

Fig. 3. Operand Stack connection interface

This interface and the others (for local variables, objects, ...) are collected in the file AlgebraType available on-line for the interested reader.

The correctness of the analysis is established for any correct integer, reference, value, operand stack, local variables, object and heap connection. We have implemented various instanciations of the different interfaces

- integers : abstraction by type (only one element in the abstract domain) and constant abstraction (using Kildall's lattice),
- references : abstraction by class (example 1) and abstraction by creation point (example 2),
- values : abstraction by sum of the reference and the numeric abstraction with two possibilities for the representation of the null constant (represented by the bottom element or by a specific abstract object)
- stacks, local variables, objects : structural abstraction (structure is preserved) or one abstract value to abstract all the elements of the data
- heaps : only one instantiation parameterised by any object abstraction and reference abstraction (with some restriction on the lattice used for references)

Compared with the previous proof done in [3], we have made two important improvements. First, the proof is now modular and abstractions on semantic subdomains can be changed without redoing all the global proof : this is important for incremental development and maintaining of the proof. Second, each subdomain abstraction is generic and independent from the others abstractions, which helps considerably during the proof development by splitting the global proof into several simpler proofs.

7   Related Works

In a previous paper [3], we have shown how to formalise a constraint-based data flow analysis in the specification language of the Coq proof assistant. We proposed a library of lattice functors for modular construction of complex abstract domains. Constraints were expressed in an intermediate representation that allowed for both efficient constraint resolution and correctness proof of the analysis with respect to an operational semantics. The proof of existence of a correct, minimal solution to the constraints was constructive which means that the extraction mechanism of Coq provided a provably correct data flow analyser in Ocaml[12]. The library of lattices together with the intermediate representation of constraints were defined in an analysis-independent fashion that provides a basis for a generic framework for proving and extracting static analysers in Coq. Nevertheless, no specific methodology was proposed to handle the correctness proof of the abstract semantic with respect to the standard semantics.

The majority of mechanical verifications of program analyses have dealt with the Java byte code verifier. Bertot [2] used the Coq system to extract a certified bytecode analyser specialized for object initialization. Barthe et al. [1] have shown how to formalise the Java Card byte code verification in the proof assistant Coq by isolating the byte code verification in an executable semantics of the language. Klein and Nipkow [9] have proved the correctness of a Java byte code verifier using the proof assistant Isabelle/HOL. All these works do not rely on a general theory of static analysis like abstract interpretation, and are oriented towards type verification.

The notion of parameterised concretization function has been implicit in several works and was made explicit in the thesis of Isabelle Pollet [13]. In this work, abstract interpretation of Java program are presented with the help of parameterised concretization functions which are used to relate concrete and abstract values with respect to a relation between locations. However, to the best of our knowledge, no one has identified the *functor property* presented here which is essential for the modularization and mechanization of the proofs.

Concerning proof modularity, only a few works propose a modular approach similar to us. The main reason is that research papers rarely deal with a deep hierarchy of semantic domains. In our context, splitting the proof development following the semantic hierarchy was useful, especially to machine-checked the proof. Much works are dedicated to propose one single powerful construction of abstract domain parameterised by some base domain, see for example works of Miné [11] or Cortesi *and al* [6]. But base abstractions are not parameterised (because the target analyses do not need this notion) and thus they did not encounter the same technical problem as us. In [13] several generic connection constructors are given to analyse heap structure and a common interface is proposed. Nevertheless this interface makes an explicit use of the parameter : what we try to avoid with our notion of concretization functor. But the proposed constructor allow more powerful analyses than those we implement in Coq. A last interesting related work can be found in the course note of Patrick Cousot [7] where the abstract interpreter construction is modularized following each semantic sub-domain. But once again, no parameterised abstraction is used then our functor notion is not required.

8   Conclusion

Mechanised correctness proofs of static analyses for realistic programming languages requires proof principles for simplifying the proof development. Like in other software engineering activities, modular correctness proofs are desirable because they are easier to develop and to maintain. We observe that one obstacle to modularity is the complexity of concrete states chich are built from many apparently inter-related components. The abstract domain has to reflect these relations but using a full-fledged abstract domain with standard (relational) concretizations leads to proofs with poor modular structure. In this paper we have shown how parameterised concretization functions forms a basis for proof principles that allow to capture the necessary relational information while using concretization functions as if we were working with non-relational domains.

To arrive at these proof principles, we have extended the theory of parameterised concretizations with the key notion of concretization functors that make explicit the compositional way in which concretization functions for complex domains are constructed from concretization of their simpler constituents. We have formulated and proved an important property of concretization functors that shows how a properly chosen pre-order on the concrete domains can greatly simplify the correctness proof for a large class of transfer functions.

The motivation for these theoretical developments came from a mechanised correctness proof for a generic static analysis for stack-based byte code language with memory allocation (similar to Java Card). As argued in Section 6 the proof principles have demonstrated their practical value by reducing the proof effort considerably. We tested this genericity by instantiating the abstract domain for memory references with two well-known abstractions while keeping the rest of the abstract state fixed. This was a non-trivial task because these reference abstraction use distinct parameterisations.

We now dispose of a proof technique which allows to certify complex static analysis for real languages in a reasonable time. A further work could be to achieve such an analysis for a byte code languages with all the features of the Java Card languages (exception, array, virtual calls). Propose certified analyser implementation without loosing efficiency require still works when dealing with complex abstraction.

References

1. Gilles Barthe, Guillaume Dufay, Line Jakubiec, Bernard Serpette, and Simão Melo de Sousa. A Formal Executable Semantics of the JavaCard Platform. In *Proc. ESOP'01*, number 2028 in Lecture Notes in Computer Science. Springer-Verlag, 2001.
2. Yves Bertot. Formalizing a JVML Verifier for Initialization in a Theorem Prover. In *Proc. CAV'01*, number 2102 in Lecture Notes in Computer Science. Springer-Verlag, 2001.
3. David Cachera, Thomas Jensen, David Pichardie, and Vlad Rusu. Extracting a Data Flow Analyser in Constructive Logic. In *Proc. ESOP'04*, number 2986 in Lecture Notes in Computer Science, pages 385–400. Springer-Verlag, 2004.
4. David Cachera, Thomas Jensen, David Pichardie, and Vlad Rusu. Extracting a Data Flow Analyser in Constructive Logic. *Theoretical Computer Science*, 342(1):56–78, September 2005. Extended version of [3].
5. The Coq Proof Assistant. http://coq.inria.fr/.
6. Agostino Cortesi, Baudouin Le Charlier, and Pascal Van Hentenryck. Combinations of abstract domains for logic programming. In *POPL*, pages 227–239, 1994.
7. P. Cousot. The calculational design of a generic abstract interpreter. In M. Broy and R. Steinbrüggen, editors, *Calculational System Design*. NATO ASI Series F. IOS Press, Amsterdam, 1999.
8. Patrick Cousot and Radhia Cousot. Abstract interpretation frameworks. *Journal of Logic and Computation*, 2(4):511–547, 1992.
9. Gerwin Klein and Tobias Nipkow. Verified Bytecode Verifiers. *Theoretical Computer Science*, 298(3):583–626, 2002.
10. Renaud Marlet. Syntax of the JCVM language to be studied in the SecSafe project. Technical Report SECSAFE-TL-005, Trusted Logic SA, May 2001.
11. A. Miné. A few graph-based relational numerical abstract domains. In *SAS'02*, volume 2477 of *LNCS*, pages 117–132. Springer-Verlag, 2002.

12. The Objective Caml language. `http://caml.inria.fr/`.
13. Isabelle Pollet. *Towards a generic framework for the abstract interpretation of Java*. PhD thesis, Université catholique de Louvain, Belgium, 2004.
14. Atanas Rountev, Ana Milanova, and Barbara G. Ryder. Points-to analysis for Java using cnnoted constraints. In *OOPSLA*, pages 43–55, 2001.
15. Igor Siveroni. Operational semantics of the Java Card Virtual Machine. *J. Logic and Automated Reasoning*, 2004. To appear.

Formalisation and Verification of the GlobalPlatform Card Specification Using the B Method

Santiago Zanella Béguelin

INRIA Sophia Antipolis,
2004 Route des Lucioles, 06902 Sophia Antipolis, France
Santiago.Zanella@inria.fr

Abstract. We give an overview of an application of the B method to the formalisation and verification of the GlobalPlatform Card Specification. Although there exists a semi-formal specification and some effort has been put into providing formalisations of particular features of smart card platforms, this is, as far as we know, the very first attempt to provide a complete formalisation. We describe the process followed to synthesise a mathematical model of the platform in the B language, starting from requirements stated in natural language. The model consistency has been thoroughly verified using formal techniques supported by the B method. We also discuss how the smart card industry might benefit from exploiting this formal specification and outline directions for future work.

1 Introduction

1.1 Smart Cards

Smart cards [1] are small portable devices, usually the size of a credit card, embedded with either only a memory chip or with both a microprocessor and a memory chip. They are capable of communicating with an external network terminal through a card reader and a contact or contact-less interface by exchanging Application Protocol Data Unit (APDU) messages. Smart cards are broadly used in a significant number of applications, ranging from telecommunications, transport and access control to electronic purses and e-government. Most popular applications include debit cards, prepaid phone cards, and the Subscriber Identity Module (SIM) cards used in mobile phones to hold subscriber's personal information and settings.

Early smart card applications were written for a specific combination of operating system and hardware and designed to run as the sole application in a card. This scheme forced card issuers to commit to a particular implementation without any possibility for post-issuance modification and at the same time compelled users to carry a different card for each application they wished to use. The need to overcome these difficulties lead to the concept of multi-application smart cards, capable of hosting multiple applications and allowing applications

G. Barthe et al. (Eds.): CASSIS 2005, LNCS 3956, pp. 155–173, 2006.

to be loaded, upgraded and unloaded after issuance. Multi-application smart cards became a reality thanks to the increase in the computational power and memory capacity of the cards and the development of general purpose card operating systems in the last decade, including *Java Card*, *MultOS*, *Windows for Smart Cards* and *BasicCard*. Each of these operating systems provides a common development framework and standard programming interfaces that improve the portability of developed applications across different card implementations and enable multiple applications to coexist on a single card sharing services and data. This increased flexibility, unfortunately, does not come for free, since it brings up new security concerns that need to be addressed.

In spite of all its benefits, the adoption of multi-application smart cards had been slowed down due to the absence of standards for the security and application management aspects of smart card platforms until the GlobalPlatform consortium published their specifications, currently accepted as de facto industry standards. However, because GlobalPlatform specifications are expressed in natural language using a semi-formal notation, they are subject to misinterpretations and their consistency cannot be formally verified. The following excerpt from [2, Sect. 6.9.1.1] describing the state transitions of the Cardholder Verification Method (CVM), might help in understanding the level of detail of the natural language specification:

> "At the end of a Card Session the CVM state shall transition back to AC-TIVE, except if the CVM state transitioned to the CVM state BLOCKED during the Card Session".

What should happen if the CVM state transitions to BLOCKED, but is later unblocked and then transitions to another state like VALIDATED (meaning successful cardholder authentication) during the same card session? Common sense dictates that the CVM state should nevertheless be reset to ACTIVE. A careless reader may understand exactly the opposite.

1.2   GlobalPlatform

GlobalPlatform (GP) is a nonprofit organisation established in 1999 by leading companies from the industry, the government sector and vendor community whose goal is to establish and drive the adoption of standards to enable an open and interoperable infrastructure for smart cards, devices and systems that simplifies and accelerates the development, deployment and management of applications across industries.

The main assets of GlobalPlatform are their specifications, available royalty-free and downloadable from their website [3]. GlobalPlatform specifications cover the card itself as well as their associated devices and systems and are applicable to both single and multi-application scenarios. By providing these specifications on a royalty-free basis GlobalPlatform succeeded in promoting their acceptance as standards and in accelerating the adoption of smart card technology. An increasing number of card vendors and application developers are adopting GlobalPlatform specifications as the standard upon which to base their smart card infrastructures. Present estimates indicate that the number of GlobalPlatform compliant smart cards in circulation exceeds 670 million (600 million of which are SIM cards).

1.3 Paper Overview

This work gives an overview of a formal specification of the GlobalPlatform security and application management architecture using the B method. This formal model provides an abstract reference specification expressed using a formal mathematical language that has the potential for eliminating any ambiguity that may remain in the existing semi-formal documentation expressed in natural language. The model also provides a general framework from which other participants may build up and share their contributions.

The remainder of the paper is structured as follows: Section 2 gives a general overview of the B method, Sect. 3 introduces the semi-formal specification provided by GlobalPlatform while Sect. 4 describes its formalisation. Section 5 shows using an example how the formalisation should be interpreted, Sect. 6 describes the formal proof process and finally, Sect. 7 concludes presenting related research on the subject and future work.

2   The B Method

2.1 Overview

The B method is a model-oriented formal method for engineering software systems developed by Abrial [4]. It is not only a notation for specifying systems, it is a comprehensive formal method that covers the entire software development cycle: from requirements specification to code generation. The method is based on the mathematical principles of set theory and predicate calculus while its semantics is given using a variant of Dijkstra's weakest precondition calculus [5].

A B specification is composed of a hierarchy of components that are described using the Abstract Machine Notation (AMN). AMN greatly resembles the notation used in high-level imperative programming languages and provides the representation and manipulation of mathematical objects such as natural numbers, sets and functions. The notation supports typical logical and set-theoretical operators as well as some other useful operators that simplify the manipulation of complex mathematical objects such as functions and relations (see Table 1 for a description of the most common operators).

Each component in a specification represents nothing but a state machine: a set of variables defines its state and a set of operations – state transitions – forms an interface used to query and modify that state. Variable types and additional constraints on the variables are introduced as invariants of a machine. State transitions in AMN are specified by means of *generalised substitutions*. A generalised substitution is a construct built up from basic substitutions, such as $x := e$, corresponding to simple assignments to state variables. The simultaneous substitution $(S_1 || S_2)$, the bounded non-deterministic choice (**CHOICE** S_1 **OR** S_2 **END**),

Table 1. Commonly used B operators

Notation	Semantics
$\mathcal{P}(X)$	Set of all subsets of X
$X \times Y$	Cartesian product of the sets X and Y
$X \leftrightarrow Y$	Set of relations of X to Y, or equivalently $\mathcal{P}(X \times Y)$
$X \nrightarrow Y$	Set of partial functions from X to Y
$X \rightarrow Y$	Set of total functions from X to Y
$X \rightarrowtail\!\!\!\!\rightarrow Y$	Set of partial injective functions from X to Y
$\mathsf{Id}(X)$	Identity relation on X
R^{-1}	Inverse relation of R
$\mathsf{dom}(R)$	Domain of the relation R
$\mathsf{ran}(R)$	Range of the relation R
$R[X]$	Relational image of X under the relation R
$X \triangleleft R$	Binary relation R restricted to pairs with first component in X
$X \triangleleft\!\!\!- R$	Binary relation R restricted to pairs with first component not in X
$R \triangleright X$	Binary relation R restricted to pairs with second component in X
$R \triangleleft\!\!+ S$	Relation R overridden by S. Equivalent to $(\mathsf{dom}(S) \triangleleft\!\!\!- R) \cup S$
$R \otimes S$	Direct product. Defined as $\{x, (y, z) \mid x, y \in R \wedge x, z \in S\}$

and the sequential composition $(S_1; S_2)$ are examples of constructors used to build up generalised substitutions from simpler ones. There exist three different types of components:

Abstract Machines. Top-level components in specifications that describe state machines in an abstract way, perhaps using non-deterministic state transitions. They do not need to be directly implementable. Figure 1 shows the typical structure of an Abstract Machine.

Refinements. Enriched versions of either an Abstract Machine or another Refinement. They must preserve the interface and behaviour but may otherwise reformulate the data and operations of the original machine. The variables in the original machine may be either preserved or refined in terms of new variables. The relationship between the original and the refined variables is stated as an invariant of the Refinement.

Implementations. Ultimate step in the refinement of an Abstract Machine, both data and operations need to be implementable in a high-level programming language. As a consequence, non-deterministic substitutions or abstract variables (e.g. relations, functions) are not allowed in Implementations. An Implementation may rely on the operations and data imported from Abstract Machines.

Operations are made up of a header and a body. The header of an operation is an identifier, designating its name, optionally followed by a parenthesised

```
MACHINE M
SEES
 Constituents of Abstract Machines referred to here can be accessed in a read-only
 fashion
SETS
 Given sets. A given set is introduced by its name and an optional enumeration
 of its values and may be used to type variables and constants
CONSTANTS
 Constants that can be referred to in a read-only way
PROPERTIES
 Properties of given sets and constants. Constants must be typed here
VARIABLES
 State variables
INVARIANT
 Variable typing and additional constraints on the machine variables
INITIALISATION
 Assignment of initial values to the machine variables
OPERATIONS
 Definition of machine operations
END
```

Fig. 1. General structure of an Abstract Machine. A short description follows each clause.

comma-separated list of input formal parameters. A list of output parameters may be specified preceding the name of the operation. The body of an operation is a generalised substitution. An operation that has input parameters is written using a precondition substitution (**PRE** P **THEN** S **END**) that types its input parameters and may express other properties that shall hold at the time the operation is executed.

A B model can be mechanically syntax and type checked. Thanks to the mathematical semantics of the method, a B model may also be subject to formal proof to verify its consistency (including the preservation of invariants) and the correctness of all refinement steps.

2.2 Tool Support and Industrial Applications

There are currently two commercially available toolkits that support the complete development of systems using the method, *Atelier B* from ClearSy, and *B-Toolkit* from B-Core. During the development of this specification we opted to use the Atelier B toolkit which allows to automatically type check and verify the syntax of a specification as well as generate the proof obligations that once discharged guarantee its consistency. To discharge these proof obligations Atelier B provides a theorem prover which can be run either in automatic or interactive mode. A survey of available tools based on the B method can be found in [6].

The B method is particularly suited to support the development of safety-critical systems. It has been successfully applied in large industrial projects as the Meteor automated subway in Paris [7] and the IBM Customer Information

Control System (CICS) [8]. It is also commonly accepted in the smart card field as a suitable method for formalising and verifying applications [9, 10] or particular aspects of smart card platforms [11, 12, 13]. For further details on the method, the reader is encouraged to refer to textbooks such as [4] or [14].

3   GlobalPlatform Semi-formal Specification

The functional and security related requirements for GlobalPlatform cards are specified in a semi-formal way in [2] and [15]. In some aspects both specifications overlap, and this is source of inconsistencies. The functional requirements of GlobalPlatform compliant cards, including all card content management functions (e.g. application installation and deletion) and their runtime behaviour, are described in [2] by means of natural language and conceptual diagrams, while [15] describes in detail, using a semi-formal notation, the security requirements of the platform, including requirements for the underlying Runtime Environment (RTE), Operating System and Integrated Circuit. These requirements are expressed in terms of a number of *Security Features* (SF) which are themselves specified in terms of one or more tables.

The header of a SF table (its first row) states the precondition that triggers its activation. Each following row except the last one describes the rules by which a user is permitted to perform some operation on some object in the card. For example, the unique row in the body of Table 2 describes the conditions that an incoming command in the APDU buffer must meet in order to be accepted for processing. The last row of the table states its postcondition – the actions to be taken in response to the operations.

SF tables are linked together by their preconditions and postconditions as shown in Fig. 2. A glance at the figure should suffice to justify the need to specify

Table 2. A SF table adapted from [15] describing the validation of incoming APDU commands

Precondition:	The Platform Code has control. AN APDU message is received.		
Short Form:	OP_alive	Link(s) back:	Table 5–34: The Supervisor Security Feature (Invocation of security mechanisms)

Operation	Object(s)	Security Attribute(s)	Rule(s)
Any APDU command	APDU Buffer [Command]	Command[CLA] Command[INS] Command[Parameters] GP Registry[Selected App]	(if the GP Registry[Selected App] is the ISD[AID] or any other SD[AID]) or (if the Command is Select[Any App]) then ((the Command[CLA] and Command[INS] shall be included in the card configuration) and (the Command[Parameters] shall not be illegal, missing, unexpected, out of range or have out of range lengths))

Result (rule evaluates to true):	The command is accepted for processing. This Table links to Table 5–37: The Supervisor Security Feature (Command dispatch) to dispatch the command.
Result (rule evaluates to false):	An appropriate GPCS error APDU response message is returned to the off–card entity.

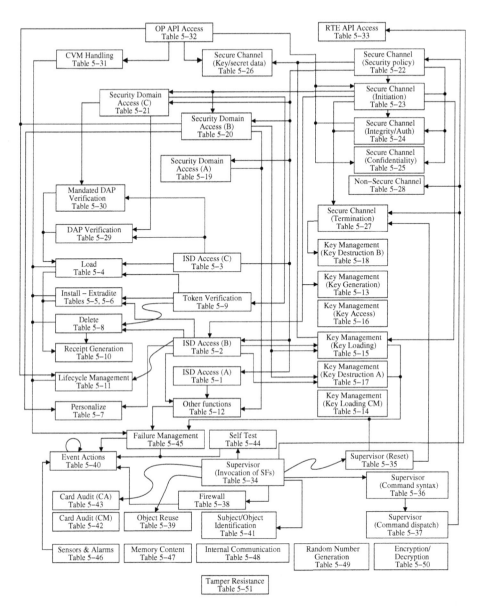

Fig. 2. Pre- and postcondition links between SF tables as appearing in [15]. The postcondition of each table at the tail of an arrow establishes the precondition of the table at the head of the arrow. Tables without incoming arrows are called *Function Tables* and are *activated* on demand.

in a precise manner the interrelationships between tables. The number of tables and the greatly tangled dependencies among them makes a natural language specification error-prone.

A particular SF, the Supervisor SF acts as the starting point for all card operations. The execution of a card operation may be interpreted as follows:

1. The Supervisor SF table is invoked, its postcondition links to another table depending on the operation type;
2. In the new table, the rule field in the row corresponding to the operation is evaluated. According to the result, the table postcondition may link to another table or may terminate the execution of the operation;
3. The previous step is repeated until the execution terminates. Any changes in the card state are committed upon completion of the execution.

4   Formalisation of the GlobalPlatform Specification

A standard specification for such critical functions as the security and card management architecture of a card platform must be carefully designed, validated and verified in order to obtain a maximal level of confidence in its implementations. Stating and structuring the specification in natural language, by means of tables or diagrams is a good starting point. However, natural language specifications are error-prone, subject to misinterpretations and cannot be formally verified. The obvious step to achieve a higher level of reliability is to derive a formal specification and apply formal techniques to verify its consistency and desirable properties. The application of formal methods is also a must for developers seeking the highest Common Criteria evaluations assurance levels (i.e. those from EAL5 to EAL7).

In the rest of this section we describe the formalisation of the GlobalPlatform specification. A royalty-free complete and commented version of the formal model may be obtained from the GlobalPlatform website [3].

4.1   Specification Architecture

Figure 3 shows a view of the specification architecture where arrows represent composition links and boxes represent components. The specification is organised in four layers of increasing detail according to their model of the card state. Each layer except the lowest one is represented by an Abstract Machine and its Implementation and each Implementation relies in turn on the Abstract Machine in the next lower layer in the hierarchy. This hierarchical model facilitates the construction of the specification and its formal verification. A short description of each Abstract Machine is as follows:

Shared_Data. Definitions of sets and constants shared among different components of the specification. Some of these sets and constants are used as types (e.g. *AID*, the set of valid application identifiers), some are used as configuration parameters for the card (e.g. *ISD*, the Issuer Security Domain AID) and others as abstract functions (e.g. *select_aid*, that extracts the AID of the application to be selected from a SELECT APDU command).

Interface. Outlines the execution of APDU commands and the behaviour upon Card Reset with respect to the set of currently open logical channels.

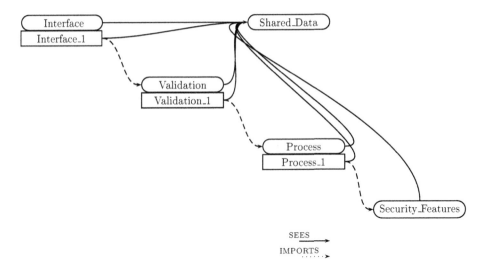

Fig. 3. Overall specification architecture. An arrow pointing from component M to component N should be read as M **SEES|IMPORTS** N. Ovals represent Abstract Machines, boxes Implementations.

Validation. Models the validation, dispatching and processing of APDU commands as well as the behaviour upon Card Reset or Power up. Each operation deals with a different type of interaction, a Card Reset, a Power Up event or a specific type of APDU command. The card state is extended to include the currently selected application and all applications in the GP Registry.

Process. Security Features that deal with the validation, dispatching and security processing of APDU commands as well as GP API methods are first introduced in this machine. The card state is extended to represent most of the card features including registered load files, the CVM and cryptographic keys. The actual processing of APDU commands is specified in detail.

Security_Features. Security Features as defined in [15] are represented as operations in this component. Operations in the *Process* machine make use of this component to ensure conformance to the selected security policies.

The Security Features are described in [15, Chapter 5] in terms of attempted operations performed on objects. The outcome, i.e. whether the attempt succeeds or fails, is decided by a set of rules which are expressed in terms of security attributes. Objects and security attributes identified in [15] are represented by the variables and constants of the machine specifications. The execution of an APDU command is sketched in the *Interface* machine. The state of the card in this machine is only represented by the set of currently open Logical Channels and so there is no need to distinguish among the different types of APDU commands at this stage. In the *Validation* machine the card state is extended to include information about the registered applications and security domains, their life cycle and the currently selected application. The *Interface_1* Implementation describes how the operations in the *Interface* machine are implemented using the operations in the *Validation* Abstract Machine.

The level of detail in each stage depends on how abstract is the representation of the card state: how many and which variables are used to represent it. As the card state is extended in the lower layers, the specification becomes richer and more detailed. Ultimately, all operations are implemented on operations in the *Security_Features* Abstract Machine, meaning – once the specification is proved correct – that the functional requirements of the platform are implementable in terms of the Security Features and satisfy the security policies enforced on the platform.

5   An Example: Installing a New Application

Smart cards employ APDU messages for carrying out the communication with card terminals. An APDU contains either a command message (Table 3) sent from the terminal to the card, or a response message sent from the card to the terminal. The communication is half-duplex and follows a master-slave model. The smart card waits for APDU commands from the terminal in its interface. Once a command is received, the card executes it and sends back a response APDU message.

Navigation through the execution of an APDU command can be accomplished by following in the specification the implementation path from the *Interface* machine to the *Security_Features* machine. If the process is stopped somewhere in between, the result would be an abstract specification of the command behaviour. We illustrate how to obtain a specification of the execution of an INSTALL[FOR INSTALL AND MAKE SELECTABLE] command issued by the Card Administrator in a simplified scenario. The command requests the installation of an application from an executable module and sets its life cycle state to SELECTABLE, enabling the application to be selected and receive commands from off-card entities. The executable module from where the application is instantiated must be present within and executable load file in the card. The structure of a correctly formatted INSTALL[FOR INSTALL AND MAKE SELECTABLE] command is shown in Table 4.

Table 3. APDU command message structure

Field	Description	Length
CLA	Class Byte	1 byte
INS	Instruction Byte	1 byte
P1	Reference Control Parameter P1	1 byte
P2	Reference Control Parameter P2	1 byte
Lc	Data Length	1 byte
Data	Command Data	Variable
Le	Length of Expected Data	1 byte

Table 4. INSTALL[FOR INSTALL AND MAKE SELECTABLE] command content

Field	Content
CLA	CLA_PROPRIETARY/CLA_SPROPRIETARY
INS	INS_INSTALL
P1	P1_INSTALL_SELECTABLE
P2	NULL
Lc	Data Length
Data	Executable Load File AID, Executable Module AID, Application AID, and Application Privileges
Le	NULL

$sw \leftarrow$ **APDU**($CLA,INS,P1,P2,Data,Le$) =
PRE
  $CLA \in$ BYTE $\land$ $INS \in$ BYTE $\land$ $P1 \in$ BYTE $\land$
  $P2 \in$ BYTE $\land$ $Data \in$ DATA $\land$ $Le \in$ BYTE
THEN
  IF $channel(CLA) \notin open\_channels$ **THEN**
   $sw :=$ SW_ERROR
  ELSE
   $sw :\in$ STATUS_WORD ||
   $open\_channels :(open\_channels \subseteq$ LOGICAL_CHANNEL $\land 0 \in open\_channels$)
  END
END

Fig. 4. APDU operation in the *Interface* machine. The notation $v : (P)$ should be read as 'v *becomes such that P holds*'. $v :\in S$ assigns to v any value in the set S.

The reception of an APDU command is represented by the execution of the **APDU** operation in *Interface* (Fig. 4), the input parameters being the command fields. Supposing the channel information contained in the CLA byte of the command corresponds to a currently open logical channel, the specification mandates some status word to be returned and allows the set of open logical channels to be modified. Considering that the card state in this machine is restricted to the set of open logical channels, this is a complete specification of the APDU outcome with respect to this representation.

The implementation of the **APDU** operation in *Interface_1* (Fig. 5) discriminates between different commands, and delegates the processing of the command to the **Install_For_Install** operation in the *Validation* machine (Fig. 6).

Assuming that the command syntax is correct, the card life cycle is not TERMINATED ($app\_life\_cycle(ISD) \neq TERMINATED$), the command data is valid and the off-card entity is authenticated (AUTHENTICATED $\in sl$), the **Install_For_Install** operation restricts the modification of the card state, but does not determine exactly how the state is modified. Up to this point, we have obtained an abstract description of the functional and security requirements for the command.

```
sw ← APDU (CLA,INS,P1,P2,Data,Le) =
 VAR ch,bb IN
  ch := channel(CLA);
  bb ← IsOpen(ch);
  IF bb = FALSE THEN
   sw := SW_ERROR
  ELSE
   sd ← IsSDSelected(ch);
   IF sd = TRUE THEN
    CASE CLA OF
     EITHER CLA_PROPRIETARY,CLA_SPROPRIETARY THEN
      CASE INS OF
       EITHER INS_INSTALL THEN
        CASE P1 OF
         EITHER P1_INSTALL_SELECTABLE THEN
          sw ← Install_For_Install(ch,CLA,INS,P1,P2,Data,Le)
          ...
```

Fig. 5. Implementation of the **APDU** operation in *Interface_1*

```
sw ← Install_For_Install(ch,CLA,INS,P1,P2,Data,Le) =
 PRE
  ch ∈ open_channels ∧
  CLA ∈ {CLA_PROPRIETARY, CLA_SPROPRIETARY} ∧
  INS = INS_INSTALL ∧ P1 = P1_INSTALL_SELECTABLE ∧ P2 ∈ BYTE ∧
  Data ∈ DATA ∧ Le ∈ BYTE ∧ selected(ch) ∈ security_domains
 THEN
  IF
   P2 = NULL ∧ Le = NULL ∧ app_life_cycle(ISD) ≠ TERMINATED ∧
   data ∈ VALID_INSTALL_FOR_INSTALL_DATA ∧ AUTHENTICATED ∈ sl
  THEN
   sw :∈ STATUS_WORD ||
   applications, security_domains, app_life_cycle, default_selected :(
    applications ⊆ AID ∧ applications$0 ⊆ applications ∧
    security_domains ⊆ applications ∧ security_domains$0 ⊆ security_domains ∧
    app_life_cycle : applications ⇸ LIFE_CYCLE ∧
    app_life_cycle$0 ⊆ app_life_cycle ∧
    default_selected ∈ applications)
  ELSE
   sw := SW_ERROR
  END
END
```

Fig. 6. Install_For_Install operation in *Validation*. Observe how modifications to the card state are restricted using the *becomes such that* substitution. The value of a variable prior to the substitution is referenced by appending $0 to its name.

The implementation of the **Install_For_Install** operation makes use of the **Install_For_Install_1** operation in *Process* (Fig. 7) to describe the actual processing of the command. If the card is not locked, the executable module

```
sw ← Install_For_Install_1(ch,CLA,INS, P1,P2,Data,Le) =
PRE
   ch ∈ open_channels ∧
   AUTHENTICATED ∈ security_level(ch) ∧
   app_life_cycle(ISD) ≠ TERMINATED ∧
   ...
THEN
 IF
   app_life_cycle(ISD) ≠ CARD_LOCKED ∧
   mod_aid(Data) ∈ executable_modules ∧
   app_aid(Data) ∉ applications ∧ app_aid(Data) ∉ executable_load_files ∧
   (pr_default_selected ∈ privileges(Data) ⇒
   default_selected = ISD ∧ app_life_cycle(ISD) ≠ OP_READY)
 THEN
   sw := SW_OK ||
   applications := applications ∪ {app_aid(Data)} ||
   app_sd(app_aid(Data)) := elf_sd(mod_elf(mod_aid(Data))) ||
   app_elf(app_aid(Data)) := mod_elf(mod_aid(Data)) ||
   app_privileges := app_privileges ∪ {(app_aid(Data), privileges(Data))} ||
   app_life_cycle(app_aid(Data)) := SELECTABLE ||
   IF pr_default_selected ∈ privileges(Data) THEN
     default_selected := app_aid(Data)
   END
END
```

Fig. 7. Install_For_Install_1 operation in *Process*

from where the application is to be instantiated exists, and the AID and privileges assigned to the application would not leave the card in an inconsistent state, an entry is created in the registry for the application, its associated security domain, life cycle state and privileges. This last **Install_For_Install_1** operation is implemented using only the operations in *Security_Features*, which correspond to the Security Features described in [2].

The example above may not give much insight into the dimension of the specification. Every APDU command and GP API function is specified like the the INSTALL[FOR INSTALL AND MAKE SELECTABLE] command just described. The complete specification being around eight thousand lines long is not a trivial case study.

6   Formal Proof

The B method semantics allows to mechanically generate the *Proof Obligations* (PO) to be discharged in order to guarantee that the model is mathematically consistent. The PO may come from the need to prove different kinds of properties:

Initialisation consistency. Assuming the stated properties of constant and sets, the initial state of an abstract machine must be established by the generalised substitution under its **INITIALISATION** clause;

Invariant preservation. As state transitions in the B language are specified via operations, and transitions shall not violate the invariant, each operation in an abstract machine must preserve the invariant;

Refinement correctness. The **INITIALISATION** substitution and each operation in a refinement shall fulfil the specification of their abstract versions.

With the help of the Atelier B automatic prover almost 90% of the generated PO were proved automatically, the remaining obligations were proved interactively. This gives a complete guarantee of the model consistency assuming the correctness of the tool and the underlying theory. As we have nothing but a natural-language specification to compare it with, the specification correctness cannot be verified. However, simple invariants can be proved to gain more confidence. Some interesting invariants may be specified in the *Process* machine. For example, that the ISD should be the default selected application when the card is in the OP_READY state

$$card\_life\_cycle = \text{OP\_READY} \Rightarrow default\_selected = ISD \ ,$$

or that selected applications shall not be in the INSTALLED state

$$selected \ \rhd \ app\_life\_cycle\_state^{-1} \left[\{\text{INSTALLED}\}\right] = \{\} \ .$$

In fact, trying to prove the following invariant

$$elf\_sd \in executable\_load\_files \rightarrow security\_domains$$

that ensures that every load file is associated with a security domain, uncovered an omission in the original specification of the DELETE command runtime behaviour that allows a security domain to be deleted even if it has executable load files associated.

Table 5 gives a summary of the formal proof of the specification. Due to the way the specification is constructed most of the PO arise in proving that an implementation is correct with respect to its abstract counterpart than in proving

Table 5. Proof summary

Component	Proved Interactively	Proved Automatically	Total
Interface	0	2	2
Interface_1	11	211	222
Validation	3	161	164
Validation_1	144	316	460
Process	54	841	895
Process_1	118	987	1,105
Security_Features	55	781	836
Total	385	3,299	3,684

that an Abstract Machine operation does not violate an invariant. The former involves proving that every possible behaviour allowed by the implementation is allowed by the original operation and that the result in terms of the implementation variables is the same, as well as proving that the preconditions of the operations on which the implementation relies are satisfied. The later amounts to proving that the operation does not violate the machine invariant. In contrast, in this specification proof obligations of invariant preservation tend to be more complicated than proof obligations of implementation correctness. As a result, the layered architecture of the specification helps to reduce the number of non-trivial proof obligations but increases the total number of proof obligations.

Much of the proof obligations generated in a component tend to be very similar. In many cases, the same proof script may be used to discharge several proof obligations. In this way, the number of actual interactive proofs is greatly reduced. There were no hard proofs, and no need to develop theories for the proof assistant with the exception of a few set theory lemmas.

7   Conclusion

While multi-application platforms have long been seen as the future of smart cards, the lack of commonly trusted standards for application management and their security concerns has slowed their deployment. We strongly believe that this work will help improve the confidence in GlobalPlatform specifications and accelerate their acceptance as trusted standards. The objective of providing a formal model of the GlobalPlatform specifications was successfully achieved in 7 men months, a neglectable cost considering the payback. As the work was in progress, omissions and inconsistencies were detected in the original specifications, including one that could lead to the execution of unauthorised APDU commands when the card is in the TERMINATED life cycle. Some of these issues were resolved in fluent contact with GlobalPlatform, while others still remain to be settled by the GlobalPlatform Card Specification Workgroup. The resulting exchange of opinions is an invaluable documentation that gives the rationale behind the decisions taken to resolve those issues. We expect most of these documentation to be included in the next release or amendment of the GlobalPlatform specifications.

7.1   Future Work

Test Automation. Reduced time-to-market is critical in the smart card industry and testing is a bottleneck for the deployment of new card platforms. The availability of the formal model opens the way to specification-driven test automation. This means that test cases can be generated, executed and assessed automatically using the formal specification, speeding time-to-market for new developments. Furthermore, the coverage of the generated tests may be measured against the specification using rigorous techniques. There exist actual tools that support test automation based on B specifications [16, 17] and there is at least one tool developer investigating the possibility of using our formal model to automate tests for GlobalPlatform compliance.

Formal Development. The B method supports fully formal software development. An interesting line of work is to investigate if the model could be, at least partially, refined down to executable code. Another possibility is to refine the existing model to specialise it for particular card configurations: proving the refinement correctness amounts to justifying compatibility with the specifications. The layered structure of the specification makes the model easy to extend.

Reference Implementation. Instead of refining the formal model to executable code, an alternative approach is to reuse the model to derive a reference implementation annotated in a specification language like JML, together with a justification that the implementation satisfies the specification. Such annotated implementation may be subject to model checking and static verification.

Specification Maintenance. The smart card field is highly dynamic, specifications must evolve to satisfy the market requirements and this formal model is not an exception. Future versions of GlobalPlatform specifications are already scheduled for 2006. Rather than becoming a load, both specifications may benefit from evolving simultaneously, envisaging the possibility of a future convergence.

7.2 Related Work

Formal methods had been applied to the verification of real-world smart card applications. Significant research effort has been put into the formalisation of specific smart card platform implementations. However, most of the work has been concerned with the Java Card platform (e.g. virtual machine, bytecode verifier and API). We detail some of the main achievements below.

Application Verification. Stepney et al. [18] give a specification and formal proofs of some security properties of an industrial strength electronic purse application using Z. Huisman and Cataño [19] use ESC/Java to annotate with functional specifications and statically verify the code of an electronic purse Java Card applet. The KeY tool [20] is an interactive theorem prover based on Dynamic Logic for Java Card source code annotated in OCL. Krakatoa [21] and Jack [22] are tools for the verification of JML-annotated Java Card programs, using the Coq proof assistant. Jack may also generate proof obligations for other theorem provers like PVS and Simplify.

Java Card Virtual Machine (JCVM). The VerifiCard [23] project succeeded in giving complete formalisations of the Java Card platform implementation at both bytecode and source code level. A partial formalisation of the JCVM using the B formal method is given in [9]. The Bali project [24] formalises in Isabelle/HOL a large body of the Java platform, including operational semantics for the source and bytecode languages and an abstract ByteCode Verifier (BCV); [25] provides executable Coq specifications for the JCVM as well as a BCV. [26] is a volume dedicated to the formal syntax and semantics of Java. All these works provide means to reason formally about applications written in the Java Card programming language and enable the verification of applet correctness.

Java Card API. Interface specifications for the Java Card API have been written in the JML and ESC/Java specification languages and are presented in [27, 28, 29]. [30] is a recent overview of JML tools and applications. The LOOP (Logic of Object-Oriented Programming) tool was used to verify that the actual Java Card API classes deployed in smart cards satisfy the JML interface specifications [31].

Protocols. Sabatier and Lartigue present their result on the validation of the transaction mechanism for smart cards using the B method in [11]. A semi-formal and a formal B specification of the T=1 protocol used to transfer messages between a smart card and a reader is presented in [12]. This approach complements our work, since we only deal with on-card features.

Acknowledgements

I would like to thank Gilles Barthe for his helpful comments on preliminary versions of this paper. Jean-Louis Lanet and Lilian Burdy kindly provided their expertise in the B method and valuable insights while the specification was being developed. Marc Kekicheff from GlobalPlatform promptly provided clarifications on the semi-formal specifications when needed.

References

1. Rankl, W., Effing, W.: Smart Card Handbook, second edition. John Wiley & Sons, Inc. (2000)
2. GlobalPlatform: Card Specification. Version 2.1.1. (2003)
3. GlobalPlatform. http://www.globalplatform.org.
4. Abrial, J.R.: The B Book - Assigning Programs to Meanings. Cambridge University Press (1996)
5. Dijkstra, E.W.: A Discipline of Programming. Prentice-Hall, Upper Saddle River, NJ, USA (1976)
6. Site B Grenoble. http://www-lsr.imag.fr/B/b-tools.html.
7. Behm, P., Benoit, P., Faivre, A., Meynadier, J.M.: METEOR: A successful application of B in a large project. In: Proceedings of FM'99: World Congress on Formal Methods. (1999) 369–387
8. Hoare, J., Dick, J., Neilson, D., Sorensen, I.: Applying the B technologies to CICS. In: Proceedings of FME '96: Industrial Benefit and Advances in Formal Methods. Third International Symposium of Formal Methods Europe. (1996) 74–84
9. Lanet, J.L., Requet, A.: Formal proof of smart card applets correctness. In Quisquater, J.J., Schneier, B., eds.: Third Smart Card Research and Advanced Application Conference, Louvain-la-Neuve, Belgium (1998)
10. Bert, D., Boulm, S., Potet, M.L., Requet, A., Voisin, L.: Adaptable translator of B specifications to embedded C programs. In Araki, I.K., Gnesi, S., Eds., D.M., eds.: FME 2003. Volume 2805 of Lecture Notes in Computer Science (Springer-Verlag)., Formal Methods Europe, Springer-Verlag (2003) 94–113
11. Sabatier, D., Lartigue, P.: The use of the B formal method for the design and the validation of the transaction mechanism for smart card applications. In: Proceedings of FM'99: World Congress on Formal Methods. (1999) 348–368

12. Lanet, J.L., Lartigue, P.: The use of formal methods for smartcards, a comparison between B and SDL to model the T=1 protocol. In: Proceedings of International Workshop on Comparing Systems Specification Techniques, Nantes (1998)

13. Casset, L., Burdy, L., Requet, A.: Formal development of an embedded verifier for Java Card byte code. In: DSN '02: Proceedings of the 2002 International Conference on Dependable Systems and Networks, Washington, DC, USA, IEEE Computer Society (2002) 51–58

14. Lano, K.: The B Language and Method: A guide to Practical Formal Development. Springer Verlag London Ltd. (1996)

15. GlobalPlatform: Card Security Requirements Specification. Version 1.0. (2001)

16. Manoranjan, M., Satpathy, M., Butler, M.: ProTest: An automatic test environment for B specifications. In: Proceedings of International workshop on Model Based Testing, ECS University of Southhampton (2004)

17. Ambert, F., Bouquet, F., Chemin, S., Guenaud, S., Legeard, B., Peureux, F., Vacelet, N., Utting, M.: BZ-TT: A tool-set for test generation from Z and B using constraint logic programming. In: Proc. of Formal Approaches to Testing of Software, FATES 2002. (2002) 105–120

18. Stepney, S., Cooper, D., Woodcock, J.: An electronic purse: Specification, refinement and proof. Technical Monograph PRG-126, Oxford University Computing Laboratory, Wolfson Building, Parks Road, Oxford, UK (2000)

19. Cataño, N., Huisman, M.: Formal specification and static checking of Gemplus' electronic purse using ESC/Java. In: FME '02: Proceedings of the International Symposium of Formal Methods Europe on Formal Methods - Getting IT Right, London, UK, Springer-Verlag (2002) 272–289

20. Ahrendt, W., Baar, T., Beckert, B., Bubel, R., Giese, M., Hähnle, R., Menzel, W., Mostowski, W., Roth, A., Schlager, S., Schmitt, P.H.: The KeY tool. Software and System Modeling **4** (2005) 32–54

21. Marché, C., Paulin-Mohring, C., Urbain, X.: The Krakatoa tool for certification of Java/JavaCard programs annotated in JML. J. Log. Algebr. Program. **58** (2004) 89–106

22. Burdy, L., Requet, A., Lanet, J.L.: Java applet correctness: A developer-oriented approach. In Araki, K., Gnesi, S., Mandrioli, D., eds.: FME 2003: Formal Methods: International Symposium of Formal Methods Europe. Volume 2805 of LNCS, Springer-Verlag (2003) 422–439

23. VerifiCard project. http://www.cs.ru.nl/VerifiCard.

24. Bali project. http://isabelle.in.tum.de/bali.

25. Barthe, G., Dufay, G., Jakubiec, L., Serpette, B.P., de Sousa, S.M.: A formal executable semantics of the JavaCard platform. In: ESOP '01: Proceedings of the 10th European Symposium on Programming Languages and Systems, Springer-Verlag (2001) 302–319

26. Alves-Foss, J., ed.: Formal syntax and semantics of Java. Volume 1523 of LNCS. Springer-Verlag (1999)

27. Poll, E., van den Berg, J., Jacobs, B.: Specification of the JavaCard API in JML. In Domingo-Ferrer, J., Chan, D., Watson, A., eds.: Fourth Smart Card Research and Advanced Application Conference (CARDIS'2000), Kluwer Acad. Publ. (2000) 135–154

28. Poll, E., van den Berg, J., Jacobs, B.: Formal specification of the JavaCard API in JML: the APDU class. Computer Networks **36** (2001) 407–421

29. Meijer, H., Poll, E.: Towards a full formal specification of the Java Card API. Volume 2140 of LNCS, Springer-Verlag (2001) 165+
30. Burdy, L., Cheon, Y., Cok, D., Ernst, M.D., Kiniry, J., Leavens, G.T., Leino, K.R.M., Poll, E.: An overview of JML tools and applications. STTT **7** (2005) 212–232
31. Poll, E., van den Berg, J., Jacobs, B.: Formal specification and verification of JavaCard's application identifier class. In Attali, I., Jensen, T., eds.: Proceedings of the Java Card 2000 Workshop. Volume 2041 of LNCS, Springer-Verlag (2001) 137–150

Author Index

Lecture Notes in Computer Science

For information about Vols. 1–3847

please contact your bookseller or Springer

Vol. 3896: Y. Ioannidis, M.H. Scholl, J.W. Schmidt, F. Matthes, M. Hatzopoulos, K. Boehm, A. Kemper, T. Grust, C. Boehm (Eds.), Advances in Database Technology - EDBT 2006. XIV, 1208 pages. 2006.

Vol. 3895: O. Goldreich, A.L. Rosenberg, A.L. Selman (Eds.), Theoretical Computer Science. XII, 399 pages. 2006.

Vol. 3894: W. Grass, B. Sick, K. Waldschmidt (Eds.), Architecture of Computing Systems - ARCS 2006. XII, 496 pages. 2006.

Vol. 3893: L. Atzori, D.D. Giusto, R. Leonardi, F. Pereira (Eds.), Visual Content Processing and Representation. IX, 224 pages. 2006.

Vol. 3891: J.S. Sichman, L. Antunes (Eds.), Multi-Agent-Based Simulation VI. X, 191 pages. 2006. (Sublibrary LNAI).

Vol. 3890: S.G. Thompson, R. Ghanea-Hercock (Eds.), Defence Applications of Multi-Agent Systems. XII, 141 pages. 2006. (Sublibrary LNAI).

Vol. 3889: J. Rosca, D. Erdogmus, J.C. Príncipe, S. Haykin (Eds.), Independent Component Analysis and Blind Signal Separation. XXI, 980 pages. 2006.

Vol. 3888: D. Draheim, G. Weber (Eds.), Trends in Enterprise Application Architecture. IX, 145 pages. 2006.

Vol. 3887: J.R. Correa, A. Hevia, M. Kiwi (Eds.), LATIN 2006: Theoretical Informatics. XVI, 814 pages. 2006.

Vol. 3886: E.G. Bremer, J. Hakenberg, E.-H.(S.) Han, D. Berrar, W. Dubitzky (Eds.), Knowledge Discovery in Life Science Literature. XIV, 147 pages. 2006. (Sublibrary LNBI).

Vol. 3885: V. Torra, Y. Narukawa, A. Valls, J. Domingo-Ferrer (Eds.), Modeling Decisions for Artificial Intelligence. XII, 374 pages. 2006. (Sublibrary LNAI).

Vol. 3884: B. Durand, W. Thomas (Eds.), STACS 2006. XIV, 714 pages. 2006.

Vol. 3882: M.L. Lee, K.-L. Tan, V. Wuwongse (Eds.), Database Systems for Advanced Applications. XIX, 923 pages. 2006.

Vol. 3881: S. Gibet, N. Courty, J.-F. Kamp (Eds.), Gesture in Human-Computer Interaction and Simulation. XIII, 344 pages. 2006. (Sublibrary LNAI).

Vol. 3880: A. Rashid, M. Aksit (Eds.), Transactions on Aspect-Oriented Software Development I. IX, 335 pages. 2006.

Vol. 3879: T. Erlebach, G. Persinao (Eds.), Approximation and Online Algorithms. X, 349 pages. 2006.

Vol. 3878: A. Gelbukh (Ed.), Computational Linguistics and Intelligent Text Processing. XVII, 589 pages. 2006.

Vol. 3877: M. Detyniecki, J.M. Jose, A. Nürnberger, C. J. '. van Rijsbergen (Eds.), Adaptive Multimedia Retrieval: User, Context, and Feedback. XI, 279 pages. 2006.

Vol. 3876: S. Halevi, T. Rabin (Eds.), Theory of Cryptography. XI, 617 pages. 2006.

Vol. 3875: S. Ur, E. Bin, Y. Wolfsthal (Eds.), Hardware and Software, Verification and Testing. X, 265 pages. 2006.

Vol. 3874: R. Missaoui, J. Schmidt (Eds.), Formal Concept Analysis. X, 309 pages. 2006. (Sublibrary LNAI).

Vol. 3873: L. Maicher, J. Park (Eds.), Charting the Topic Maps Research and Applications Landscape. VIII, 281 pages. 2006. (Sublibrary LNAI).

Vol. 3872: H. Bunke, A. L. Spitz (Eds.), Document Analysis Systems VII. XIII, 630 pages. 2006.

Vol. 3871: E.-G. Talbi, P. Liardet, P. Collet, E. Lutton, M. Schoenauer (Eds.), Artificial Evolution. XI, 310 pages. 2006.

Vol. 3870: S. Spaccapietra, P. Atzeni, W.W. Chu, T. Catarci, K.P. Sycara (Eds.), Journal on Data Semantics V. XIII, 237 pages. 2006.

Vol. 3869: S. Renals, S. Bengio (Eds.), Machine Learning for Multimodal Interaction. XIII, 490 pages. 2006.

Vol. 3868: K. Römer, H. Karl, F. Mattern (Eds.), Wireless Sensor Networks. XI, 342 pages. 2006.

Vol. 3866: T. Dimitrakos, F. Martinelli, P.Y.A. Ryan, S. Schneider (Eds.), Formal Aspects in Security and Trust. X, 259 pages. 2006.

Vol. 3865: W. Shen, K.-M. Chao, Z. Lin, J.-P.A. Barthès, A. James (Eds.), Computer Supported Cooperative Work in Design II. XII, 659 pages. 2006.

Vol. 3863: M. Kohlhase (Ed.), Mathematical Knowledge Management. XI, 405 pages. 2006. (Sublibrary LNAI).

Vol. 3862: R.H. Bordini, M. Dastani, J. Dix, A.E.F. Seghrouchni (Eds.), Programming Multi-Agent Systems. XIV, 267 pages. 2006. (Sublibrary LNAI).

Vol. 3861: J. Dix, S.J. Hegner (Eds.), Foundations of Information and Knowledge Systems. X, 331 pages. 2006.

Vol. 3860: D. Pointcheval (Ed.), Topics in Cryptology – CT-RSA 2006. XI, 365 pages. 2006.

Vol. 3858: A. Valdes, D. Zamboni (Eds.), Recent Advances in Intrusion Detection. X, 351 pages. 2006.

Vol. 3857: M.P.C. Fossorier, H. Imai, S. Lin, A. Poli (Eds.), Applied Algebra, Algebraic Algorithms and Error-Correcting Codes. XI, 350 pages. 2006.

Vol. 3855: E. A. Emerson, K.S. Namjoshi (Eds.), Verification, Model Checking, and Abstract Interpretation. XI, 443 pages. 2005.

Vol. 3854: I. Stavrakakis, M. Smirnov (Eds.), Autonomic Communication. XIII, 303 pages. 2006.

Vol. 3853: A.J. Ijspeert, T. Masuzawa, S. Kusumoto (Eds.), Biologically Inspired Approaches to Advanced Information Technology. XIV, 388 pages. 2006.

Vol. 3852: P.J. Narayanan, S.K. Nayar, H.-Y. Shum (Eds.), Computer Vision – ACCV 2006, Part II. XXXI, 977 pages. 2006.

Vol. 3851: P.J. Narayanan, S.K. Nayar, H.-Y. Shum (Eds.), Computer Vision – ACCV 2006, Part I. XXXI, 973 pages. 2006.

Vol. 3850: R. Freund, G. Păun, G. Rozenberg, A. Salomaa (Eds.), Membrane Computing. IX, 371 pages. 2006.

Vol. 3849: I. Bloch, A. Petrosino, A.G.B. Tettamanzi (Eds.), Fuzzy Logic and Applications. XIV, 438 pages. 2006. (Sublibrary LNAI).

Vol. 3848: J.-F. Boulicaut, L. De Raedt, H. Mannila (Eds.), Constraint-Based Mining and Inductive Databases. X, 401 pages. 2006. (Sublibrary LNAI).